WASHINGTON IRVING:

An American Study, 1802–1832

WASHINGTON IRVING:

An American Study, 1802–1832

By William L. Hedges

The Goucher College Series

The Johns Hopkins Press   Baltimore 1965

FOR JAMES B. HEDGES

PREFACE

IN 1824 a short-lived Boston periodical, the *United States Literary Gazette*, predicting that American literature would come to reflect primarily the qualities of newness, boldness, and practicality in American life, classified Washington Irving, for all his popular success, as atypical. Geoffrey Crayon seemed too "exquisite" and "elegant" for the American genius, which was destined to be "somewhat rash, enterprising, forgetful of the majesty of criticism, and regardless of artificial rules, venerable precedents, and obsolete things in general." Within a few weeks, however, the *Gazette*, as it reviewed successive installments of Irving's current work, *Tales of a Traveller*, began complaining of Crayon's "vulgarism and indelicacy"; it had found coarse jokes and an undercurrent of indecent innuendo.

Literary history has never dealt satisfactorily with the apparent contradictions in Irving. Generally, the line of least resistance has been followed: the raucous side of him has been deemphasized; he has been refined almost out of existence as a writer who significantly reflects American attitudes or feelings, and a close reading of his work has been discouraged on the ground that what is most charming and delightful in him is either unanalyzable or too elusive to be pinned down by intense scrutiny. Only in the last few years has criticism begun to take a second look.

Here and there one sees signs of a less tangential Irving. Like most good stories, "Rip Van Winkle" and "The Legend of Sleepy Hollow" have by now been mined for symbol and archetype and

begin to appear to be something more than felicitous German
borrowings. An anxious Van Winkle has been unearthed, who,
Leslie Fiedler goes so far as to say, "presides over the birth of
the American imagination." I am not fully convinced that there
is one and only one American imagination, and if there is, I am
sure it evolved and was not born. But if American literature at
its best is not always the progressive, brusque, straightforward,
practical-minded expression which the *Gazette* foresaw, if it has
something to do with mysteries, obscurities, devious approaches,
and backward glances, then Rip is someone to be reckoned with.
So too are Geoffrey Crayon and queer old Diedrich Knickerbocker. As Harry Levin has briefly suggested, there are tinges of
shadow in the allegedly lighthearted Irving that ultimately relate
him to the darker aspects of Hawthorne, Poe, and Melville.

Here, then, is an extended essay on the relevance of Irving.
It tries to define his major contributions as a writer and to work
out in detail his relation to his intellectual environment. Its
method is primarily that of literary analysis and comparison.
The purpose, however, is not to unearth neglected masterpieces or
start an Irving revival. I claim only that critical neglect of his
work perpetuates misconceptions which jeopardize our understanding of some important aspects of American literature.

The justification for not treating the last twenty-seven years of
Irving's life is that with his celebrated return to the United
States in 1832 his career was in one sense completed. The works
on which his reputation as the nation's first successful professional author primarily rests were behind him. He had made
his mark, and a new generation of writers, several with intellectual and emotional commitments that went deeper than his, was
coming on the scene. He kept on writing but not developing as
a writer.

The documentation of this work needs some explanation.
Whenever it is consistent with clarity, I have cited Irving's works
(exclusive of letters and journals) by page and volume number
in parentheses in the text. Where there is any possibility of confusion as to the particular work being cited, I include in the

parenthetical citation the abbreviation of the title. The list of abbreviations is given on page xiv and specifies particular editions. It also includes editions of Irving's letters and journals as well as biographical works frequently referred to in the notes.

In citing standard literary texts I have usually, except with Irving, given the titles or numbers of individual stories, poems, or essays, or the chapter numbers of longer works, instead of referring to the pagination of particular editions.

Given the nature of the sources and the fullness of the notes of this book, a bibliography would be less a service than an inconvenience. Beyond their relevance to my conception of Washington Irving, the materials I have used do not organize readily. My major sources are Irving's literary works and his journals, notebooks, and letters. These I have read in a broad context of British and American literature and historiography in the eighteenth and nineteenth centuries, of documents in intellectual history to which he was directly exposed or which seem relevant to his work, of contemporary comment on his works, and of special sources to which his works are in some way indebted. This is to say nothing of the numerous secondary sources to which I refer. There is no way of packaging such materials in a bibliography except to list alphabetically every work which I have cited in the notes, a procedure which would waste space, obscure the usefulness of particular sources, and duplicate bibliographical assistance already available.

The notes indicate, wherever it seems to me that it might be useful, what works a reader should consult initially if he is interested in further pursuing an issue raised in the book. I have tried, when I do not actually discuss them, to make reference to Irving's sources, or at least to major source studies. The same is true for significant critical comment on his works. To save the reader trouble in hunting for the first reference to a work, I have given adequate bibliographical data the first time it is cited in each chapter.

There are a few facts in regard to Irving scholarship that one should keep in mind. To begin with, the texts of the Author's Revised Edition of his works, issued in 1848–50 and often reprinted, in several instances significantly differ from the texts of original editions. Thus the Irving whom most readers have come to know is not necessarily the Irving of the time when a particular work was first composed. One must be prepared to make frequent comparisons. Most of his journals and notebooks and a great many of his letters have been published. They appear in numerous separate editions which vary greatly in quality; a committee of scholars is now making plans to meet the need for a uniform and complete edition of the letters and journals (see H. L. Kleinfield, "A Census of Washington Irving Manuscripts," *Bulletin of the New York Public Library*, LXVIII [Jan., 1964], 13–32). But the papers as now published provide a reasonably full picture of Irving and can be used if one proceeds with caution.

The Life and Letters of Washington Irving (4 vols.; 1863–64) consists primarily of excerpts from his journals and letters selected by his nephew, Pierre M. Irving. The indispensable guide to all basic investigation of Irving is *The Life of Washington Irving* (2 vols.; 1935), by Stanley T. Williams. Its voluminous notes and special supplementary studies of Irving's works offer a wealth of bibliographical assistance. Together with Mary Ellen Edge, Williams compiled a useful check list, *A Bibliography of the Writings of Washington Irving* (1936). *Washington Irving: Representative Selections* (1934), edited by Henry A. Pochmann, contains a good basic bibliography of works about Irving. For more recent scholarship and criticism one should begin with the bibliographical volume (III) in Robert Spiller *et al.*, *Literary History of the United States* (1948) and the supplement to that work (1959), compiled by R. M. Ludwig.

My debt to the many scholars who, following the lead of Constance Rourke and F. O. Matthiessen, have developed what probably should be called the ideology of American literature, should be obvious. I am aware, however, of the risks of distortion which one runs in the search for correspondences between the shape of American experience and the form, structure, style, and theme of a literary work, and have tried to proceed with caution. My respect for the discipline of intellectual history derives from Perry Miller, under whose tutelage I began to investigate Irving some time ago. Years of talk with John J. Enck about criticism and literary technique have also shaped my thinking.

Kenneth B. Murdock was very helpful in criticizing the doctoral dissertation which was the earliest of many versions of this study. Discussions with Thomas Walsh about Hawthorne stimulated my thinking about the significance of Geoffrey Crayon. Edward Wagenknecht's reading of an article in which I sketched in several of the major ideas of this work has saved me from several errors. David Levin's generous comments on the book over a period of years and through several drafts have helped sustain it in its trials. The reader whose standards have been the most challenging and whom I have worked the hardest to please is Elaine R. Hedges. She has exacted as much effort of herself as of me.

A research grant from Goucher College expedited the final preparation of the manuscript. The Edgar Allan Poe Society of Baltimore, at the suggestion of Brooke Peirce, kindly allowed me to try out some of my ideas in a lecture in 1962. I am grateful to the Houghton Library of Harvard University and to the Manuscript Division of the New York Public Library for making available to me their collections of Irvingiana.

Portions of this book restate and amplify conceptions of Irving's work which I briefly outlined in an essay in *Major Writers in America*, edited by Perry Miller and published by Harcourt, Brace, and World, Inc., in 1962. Earlier, expanded versions of portions of Chapters III and IX have appeared in articles in the *Journal of the History of Ideas* and *The Americas*.

Contents

ABBREVIATIONS

1. FROM *The Works of Washington Irving*, 21 VOLS. (NEW YORK, 1860–64):

   AL   *The Alhambra.*
   B   *Bracebridge Hall, or The Humorists. A Medley.*
   C   *Life and Voyages of Christopher Columbus.*
   G   *Chronicle of the Conquest of Granada.*
   SAL *Salmagundi.*
   SB   *The Sketch-Book of Geoffrey Crayon, Gent.*
   TT   *Tales of a Traveller.*

2. MISCELLANEOUS WORKS, JOURNALS, AND LETTERS OF IRVING:

   K   *Diedrich Knickerbocker's A History of New York*, ed. Stanley T. Williams and Tremaine McDowell (New York, 1927).
   JO   *Letters of Jonathan Oldstyle*, ed. Stanley T. Williams (New York, 1941).
   NP   *Notes While Preparing Sketch Book &c., 1817*, ed. Stanley T. Williams (New Haven, 1927).
   TIE *Notes and Journal of Travel in Europe, 1804–1805*, 3 vols., ed. W. P. Trent (New York, 1921).
   TS   *Tour in Scotland, 1817*, ed. Stanley T. Williams (New Haven, 1927).
   WIHB *The Letters of Washington Irving to Henry Brevoort*, 2 vols., ed. George S. Hellman (New York, 1915).

3. OTHER WORKS:

   AN   *Analectic Magazine.*
   PMI Pierre M. Irving, *The Life and Letters of Washington Irving*, 4 vols. (New York, 1863–64).
   STW Stanley T. Williams, *The Life of Washington Irving*, 2 vols. (New York, 1935).

Introduction

THE gentle and affable Washington Irving handed on to us by Thackeray[1] and the nineteenth century is a partial distortion that needs correcting before we can appreciate Irving's place in American literature. This book is, among other things, a corrective effort, although much of the time only implicitly so. In these opening pages, however, which are intended not as a systematic formulation of a thesis to be maintained but as a quick foreshadowing of the way the subject will be exhibited, I offer a summary view of Irving specifically aimed at weaknesses in the standard treatment of his work. My reliance for the time being is deliberately on a few peremptory strokes rather than on fullness of statement. I trust that more interest than annoyance will be aroused if I seem to proceed with certain assumptions that cannot be fully explored until later in the book.

The prevailing stereotype of Washington Irving stems ultimately from the overly enthusiastic reception originally given *The Sketch Book* (1819–20) in England, where readers were surprised to discover an American writing an easy, graceful prose. Certain elements in the book—its sentiment and the gentlemanliness of Geoffrey Crayon—were particularly stressed, and the memory of Goldsmith was invoked. An image of Irving as a writer emerged to which he himself in later years gradually surrendered—romantic escapist, lover of the picturesque, genial humorist. Most of his work after *The Alhambra* (1832) sustains

---

[1] "Nil Nisi Bonum," *Roundabout Papers.*

1

this image, and the final revision of his works (1848–50) stamps it more firmly on some of the earlier books.[2]

His reputation remained fairly high as long as gentility was valued, but in the twentieth century it has often proved an embarrassment. At the same time modern scholarship has tended to reinforce basic misconceptions by allowing political labels to interfere with readings of Irving. The problem is especially acute in considering the early phase of his career. As the study of American literature apart from English literature became a respected discipline in the first half of this century, Irving's interest in Europe and the European past was used as a way of distinguishing him from writers alleged to be more truly "American." Vernon L. Parrington, for instance, saw him as basically antibourgeois and anti-industrialist. Parrington did recognize the provincial element in Irving's early work and its close connection with the "frank evaluation of progress in terms of exploitation" in New York in the first decade of the nineteenth century, and he found a latent liberalism in the later Irving. But his general view was that Irving had "gently detached himself from contemporary America."[3] Subsequently another critic, Henry S. Canby, perhaps feeling that Irving might at least get

[2] The revised edition was reprinted in numerous multivolume sets in the second half of the nineteenth century. They sold well and probably increased Irving's popularity. See STW, I, 202. (For a list of abbreviations, see p. xiv.) The illustrations with which these sets, as well as individual works, were often copiously supplied reflected the mid-century sense of Irving and must have helped make reading him a conditioned response for many people. I have not seen many illustrations that do justice to his major works. A few, notably the caricatures by Felix Darley, manage to capture the grotesque comic qualities in Irving. But the process of softening and sentimentalizing, which began in the first half of the century (one finds it in some of Washington Allston's illustrations for *Knickerbocker's History of New York*), intensified with the issuance of the revised edition. Darley, who illustrated many of the volumes in a de luxe edition put out by Putnam beginning in 1848, had a deeply sentimental as well as a comic side. He and illustrators such as K. H. Schmolze, by ignoring the half-humorous tone in which Irving is apt to present extravagant action, made him out to be more melodramatic than he is. They even changed the costumes and appearances of characters in the interest of promoting an exceedingly refined and delicately romantic Irving. Stanley T. Williams and Mary Ellen Edge indicate illustrated editions of Irving's works in *A Bibliography of the Writings of Washington Irving: A Check List* (New York, 1936).

[3] Vernon L. Parrington, *Main Currents of American Thought*, II (New York, 1927), 193–206.

credit for being a good conservative instead of being damned for
not being liberal, completed his transformation into an elegant,
stylish spokesman for Federalism, which Canby defined as
"essentially an aristocratic ideal struggling to adapt itself to the
conditions of a republic."[4]

Irving's politics are a matter to be discussed in detail in
Chapter II, but I shall anticipate here to the extent of insisting
that to read the early Irving as "erudite, polished, suave"[5] is to
let both the man and the work slip beyond one's grasp. A
supercilious English reviewer of 1811, who wished that the
comic periodical *Salmagundi* (1807–8), the joint work of
Irving, his brother William, and James K. Paulding, were more
like the *Spectator*, was hardly a fair judge of the magazine's
ultimate worth. But the fact that this writer was offended by the
"want of good style" in *Salmagundi*, that was, he said, "unfortunately obvious," ought to warn us against measuring Irving by
stock notions of Federalist propriety. The reviewer complained
of "many . . . vulgarisms, or at best provincialisms" in the
American work, of the "poverty" of a typical pun, and of
classical allusions that "would shock the ears of a north-country-
schoolboy." He also found "hyperbolical ridicule" sometimes
carried to such an extreme as to frustrate the intentions of
the magazine.[6]

The first post-Revolutionary generation of American writers,
it has been said, "often considered itself 'lost' and traced its
plight to a society whose values were too confused and crude to
sustain a mature literary art."[7] While Irving was not always
self-conscious about the problem, he was hardly exempt from
it. Born into an immigrant family that was rapidly moving up
the social scale through business, law, medicine, and journalism,
he found nowhere in his youth a set of beliefs or attitudes to
which he could wholeheartedly commit himself. There is much
in him which suggests a sense of the world as ungraspable. His

[4] Henry S. Canby, *Classic Americans* (New York, 1931), pp. 77–78.
[5] *Ibid.*, p. 86.
[6] Anonymous review, *Monthly Review*, LXV (August, 1811), 419–20.
[7] Benjamin T. Spencer, *The Quest for Nationality* (Syracuse, 1957), p. 68.

work raises questions as to the applicability in the United States
of artistic criteria established in the Old World and of the relation of literature to business and politics. His cultural uneasiness
distorts his youthful writings into curious shapes. The elegant
past to which those writings refer is, at least for Irving, less a
reality than a fiction, a vestige of the periodical essay convention. It is true that he already had access to fashionable New
York society, particularly through the family of Josiah Ogden
Hoffman, the Federalist judge with whom he began to study law
in 1802. But his experience as the son of a New York hardware
dealer hardly squared with the cultivated past assumed by the
periodical tradition. And even if his fashionable contacts gave
him glimpses of what the distinguished society that had graced
colonial New York had been like, how was he, as a writer born
after 1776, to define his attitude toward a culture so firmly
rooted in the usages of the English upper classes? For most
Americans the Revolution had at least partially invalidated the
appeal to an aristocratic tradition, even in manners and taste.

Furthermore, while Timothy Dwight, the president of Yale,
may have overstated the case, he was probably essentially correct
in saying that the "general attachment to learning" in New York
was "less vigorous" than in Boston, since "commerce" had
"originally taken a more entire possession of the minds of its
inhabitants." The "prepossession" with wealth seemed to Dwight
a "blast upon all improvement of the mind: for it persuades
every one in whom it exists, that such improvement is insig-
nificant, and useless."[8] The bourgeois state of mind was hardly
conducive to the kind of Federalism often ascribed to Irving.
Yet something not far removed from that state of mind is reflected in his writing from *Letters of Jonathan Oldstyle* (1802–3)
through *Knickerbocker's History of New York* (1809). He cannot be sure that he has an identity beyond that of being one in a
scrambling democratic throng. The legacy of 1776, the Revolutionary resentment of traditional authority, finds an outlet in the
irreverence and irresponsibility of his early literary productions,
even if they take no real comfort in freedom. The old bachelors

[8] *Travels in New-England and New-York* (New Haven, 1822), III, 473.

of these works are emasculated father figures. In the midst of a longing for tradition, for images of authority, there is idol-smashing.

Irving's suavity, to whatever degree it existed, was not acquired effortlessly. The journals and letters of his youth suggest a high-spirited and not altogether self-controlled young man, bouncy and brash, yet sensitive and easily hurt, even while fearful of seeming to take himself too seriously. Youthful rough edges show through the surface of his maturity. One glimpses them in the few portraits which refrain from smoothing, slenderizing, and paling his features, curling and glossing his hair to a rich darkness, and personifying him as romantic youth. One suspects, on the strength of depictions by Vogel von Vogelstein and C. R. Leslie,[9] that he had the congenial, well-fed good looks conventionally associated with the average middle-class American. The face was round, the nose a trifle long and broad; the eyes perhaps came close to looking calculating.

Unfortunately—or was it fortunate?—he was never educated systematically. His family may have looked upon his first trip to Europe (1804–6) as a substitute for Columbia College, where two of his brothers had studied, but he had not been prepared intellectually to take full advantage of the opportunity. Though an avid reader, he taught himself by fits and starts, often reading good and bad works indiscriminately and seldom arriving at comprehensive views.[10] Socially he had fewer handicaps. Had business or the law, at which he worked off and on for more than a dozen years, involved only entertaining clients, he might have made a fortune. Even the frivolity of tea-table gossip accorded with his temperament, at least if it meant a release from office routine. Later, in moments of middle-aged pontification, he regretted the time he had wasted in "idle society" and grumbled, "Young people enter into society in America at an age that they

[9] Reproduced in Walter Reichart, *Washington Irving and Germany* (Ann Arbor, Mich., 1957), Frontispiece, and STW, I, 202.

[10] Thus Reichart (pp. 20–22) pictures him between 1817 and 1819 laboriously teaching himself German as a result of Scott's suggestion and his own belated realization that he ought to know the new German literature, and then, having decided to do *The Sketch Book*, struggling through German texts in search of "bits of lore that might furnish bone and sinew for a tale."

are cooped up in schools in Europe."[11] But this was only half the story. He never absented himself from fashionable society for very long and took a quiet satisfaction in the familiarity with prominent and cultivated people which his eventual success brought him. Yet there were always recurrent guilt feelings and the fear of wasting time.

Just as one detects in Irving's later prose certain traces of crudeness or nervous laughter, so one sees him in Europe after 1815 still awkward and uneasy at times, fearful, as one of his biographers suggests, of being embarrassed by the "exuberance" of fellow Americans,[12] though getting along capitally for the most part on an American good-naturedness. Many observers found him pleasant, genial, but at the same time quiet. John Neal put it rather rudely: "very amiable—no appearance of especial refinement—nothing remarkable—nothing uncommon about him:—precisely such a man . . . as people would continually overlook, pass by without notice, or forget, after dining with him."[13]

Irving's restless peregrination abroad between 1815 and 1832, his inability to become deeply involved in any phase of European life—these outward forms of an inner unsettledness, qualify the genteel view of him as America's first cultural attaché to Europe. His continual references to himself as an idler, drifter, and dreamer are more than perfunctory. The boisterous flippancy of his early works should not blind us to his personal vulnerability. His youthful cocksureness in print only partially masks the hesitancy that eventually came out in the character of the bachelor, Geoffrey Crayon.

The bachelor is a dominant image in Irving; he embodies, like those other recurring figures the antiquarian and the traveler, a degree of alienation from the reality which common sense takes

[11] Letter to Pierre Paris Irving, 29 March 1825, PMI, II, 334–35.
[12] Edward Wagenknecht, *Washington Irving: Moderation Displayed* (New York, 1962), p. 89. Wagenknecht has a good discussion of the various impressions Irving made on observers (pp. 88–90). An abnormal fear of speaking in public was one of his social handicaps.
[13] "American Writers, No. IV," *Blackwood's Edinburgh Magazine*, XVII (January, 1825), 60. Neal also noted "a sort of uneasy, anxious, catching respiration of the voice, when talking zealously."

for granted. Most of his pseudonyms, early and late, including the fictitious "editors" of *Salmagundi*, Diedrich Knickerbocker, Crayon, and the narrator of *A Chronicle of the Conquest of Granada* (1829), derive from his earliest mask, Jonathan Old-style, even though in some cases the type is modified almost beyond recognition. They are, at least in part, extensions of the stock character of the old bachelor in the eighteenth-century periodical essay, who began by representing social irresponsibility and eccentricity in need of correction or regularization[14] (for example, Will Honeycomb in the *Spectator*), but who in the course of the eighteenth century had gradually turned into a ridiculous or pathetic figure. The ineffectual character of a bachelor in the mid-century *Connoisseur*, for instance, simply invited practical jokes, and they were played on him, not until he really changed, but until he promised to marry in return for gentler treatment. Another, in Mackenzie's *Mirror* (1779–90), on the other hand, was finally given enough sympathy for his one great disappointment in love to justify his retirement. And in the *Looker-On* (1792) the realization emerged that one might not be adequately equipped to serve society as a husband: Simon Olivebranch came, he said, from a family whose members shriveled up and assumed the appearance of old age at twenty-five.[15]

Salmagundi made periodical bachelorhood unashamedly Quixotic. The pseudonymous editors, Launcelot Langstaff,

[14] See *Spectator*, No. 530. Sir Roger de Coverley's bachelorhood is not a matter of choice but of the failure of the widow he loves to recognize *her* obligations as a woman and take a gentleman's suit seriously (*Spectator*, Nos. 113, 118). Hymenaeus, a man of healthy instincts in the *Rambler* (Nos. 113, 115, 119, 167), has to be encouraged to keep his good humor until the right woman comes along. Instead of falling into melancholy or into romantic love in his frustration at failing to find what he is looking for, he is allowed to continue to exercise his discretion until he discovers an old maid with good common sense like his own and marries her. Some of Irving's bachelors are also descendants of the archetypal Spectator himself. The diffidence and disinterestedness of such a character may verge on antisocial withdrawal, even though he is authorized to abstain from marriage, presumably because he fulfills an obligation to society in trying to improve it. In America the "Old Bachelor" in the *Pennsylvania Magazine* (1775–76), partly the creation of Francis Hopkinson, is an interesting combination of the Honeycomb and the Mr. Spectator types of bachelor.

[15] *Mirror*, Nos. 1, 19; *Connoisseur*, No. 19; *Looker-On*, Nos. 1, 12, 15. See also Colonel Caustic in *Lounger*, No. 4.

Anthony Evergreen, and Will Wizard, claimed to be "true
knights," who, though they loved "noble dames and beauteous
damsels," wanted little more from them than the "smile of
beauty." They had acquired the necessary supply of whims,
"without which" they considered "a man to be mere beef without
mustard" (*SAL*, p. 125).[16] And they were given a library that
"would bear a comparison, in point of usefulness and eccentricity, with the motley collection of the renowned hero of La
Mancha" (pp. 399–400). Their bachelorhood was on the whole
a neurotic shrinking back from overly close contact with the
world at large.

Yet as the story of "The Little Man in Black" shows, the "editors" had a fearful awareness of what happens to the eccentric
who moves too far away from ordinary social contexts. Beginning
as a humorous view of a scholar far gone in whimsy, the tale
approaches terror when the people of his village reject him
in superstitious fear. *Salmagundi*'s antiquarian, an obvious variation of Goldsmith's "man in black," a disappointed bachelor
in the *Citizen of the World*,[17] is distinguished by being the most
withdrawn of all the eccentrics in *Salmagundi*: "He sought no
intimacy . . . nor ever talked; except sometimes to himself in an
outlandish tongue. He commonly carried a large book, covered
with sheep-skin, under his arm; appeared always to be lost in
meditation . . ." (p. 353). In the end he proves to have human
sentiments, but his life has already been ruined. And the books
that have destroyed him are the same set still to be found in the
library at Cockloft Hall, the gathering place of Langstaff and his
colleagues. Here is neither pure pathos nor comedy, but something for which *Salmagundi*'s term "gothic risibility"[18] seems
appropriate, as it does for Diedrich Knickerbocker; quite
literally another little man in black, unaccommodated with a real
present, Knickerbocker gives expression to his desire to live with

[16] For an explanation of page references included in the text, see the Preface.
[17] Letters XXVI and XXVII.
[18] The phrase describes Will Wizard, who in the latter part of *Salmagundi* takes
to deciphering "old, rusty, musty, and dusty" manuscripts and books. *SAL*, pp.
341–43.

the past by keeping his room "always covered with scraps of paper and old mouldy books" (*K*, p. 2).

Irving's imagery of estrangement, no matter how laughable initially, undoubtedly embodies motives which he felt within himself, even if he only half-understood them. The quest for literary identity, which is the story of his career, often mirrors a quest for personal identity. Irving eventually became a wistful and more or less resigned bachelor; his courtship of Matilda Hoffman and her languishing illness and death in 1809 provided him with a legend of true love and loss—all that was needed, according to some of the eighteenth-century periodicals, to make a staunch bachelor. Irving could play the part well, as when in 1820 he wrote Paulding, confessing that he had hoped that his friends would also remain unmarried, so that with him they could "form a knot of queer, rum old bachelors, at some future day to meet at the corner of Wall Street or walk the sunny side of Broadway and kill time together."[19]

Irving's love for the shy Matilda, who was only fourteen or fifteen when he began to pay her serious attention and only seventeen when she died, was obviously highly idealized. "Never did I meet," he wrote years later, "with more intuitive rectitude of mind, more native delicacy, more exquisite propriety in thought word & action than in this young creature. . . . I felt at times rebuked by her superior delicacy & purity and as if I am [sic] a coarse unworthy being in comparison."[20] Yet underneath his Pierrot-like need to idolize her innocence, there may have lurked latent hostilities. His semiofficial engagement meant that he was to try in earnest to make himself a lawyer. This was his understanding with his fiancée's father, Josiah Ogden Hoffman, the legal mentor under whom he had trained for several years. Irving, who had already passed the bar examination, later vividly described the conflict which was now thrust upon him:

> I set to work with zeal to study anew, and I considered myself bound in honour not to make further advances with [Matilda] until I should feel satisfied with my proficiency in the Law—It was all in

[19] PMI, I, 457.
[20] "Manuscript Fragment," in STW, II, 256.

vain. I had an insuperable repugnance to the study—my mind
would not take hold of it; or rather by long despondency had become
for the time incapable of dry application. I was in a wretched state
of doubt and self distrust. I tried to finish the work [*Knickerbocker*]
which I was secretly writing, hoping it would give me reputation and
gain me some public appointment.[21]

Matilda's death, no matter how deeply it grieved him, at least
freed him from certain frustrating entanglements. Small wonder
that in *Knickerbocker* lawyers come to be associated with the
denial of freedom. Satirical attacks on lawyers and the law
had been a part of the humorous tradition within which Irving
was accustomed to working, but the vehemence of the abuse in
Knickerbocker suggests a dissatisfaction with the career to which
his engagement to Matilda had committed him. Law is seen, for
instance, to work hand in hand with religion, cloaking robbery
and murder with pretentious rhetoric; according to the anachro-
nistic Knickerbocker, Spanish missionaries who forced the Indians to give up "a little pitiful tract of this dirty sublunary
planet in exchange for a glorious inheritance in the kingdom of
Heaven" had "Blackstone, and all the learned expounders of the
law" to sustain them (pp. 61–62). By the time of the first revision of the book in 1812, Irving's feelings on the subject had
apparently intensified. The "noble independence" in men, he
then wrote,

revolts at this intolerable tyranny of law, and the perpetual inter-
ference of officious morality, which are ever besetting his path with
finger-posts and directions to "keep to the right, as the law directs;"
and like a spirited urchin, he turns directly contrary, and gallops
through mud and mire, over hedges and ditches, merely to show
that he is a lad of spirit, and out of his leading-strings.[22]

It has been suggested recently that what Irving took to be his
love for Matilda served only as a mask for a stronger but not
fully avowed emotion, a filial or fraternal affection for her stepmother, Maria Fenno Hoffman, a woman not very much older

[21] *Ibid.*, II, 257.
[22] *A History of New York . . . by Diedrich Knickerbocker* (New York, 1812), I,
119. The 1809 edition contains a conscience-stricken assertion that what is said
about lawyers does not apply to the many worthy members of the profession in
New York City (*K*, p. 215). But it is so exaggerated as to appear in part ironic.

than himself. His real motive in wooing Matilda, according to this view, was his unconscious desire, now that he was growing too old to be nurtured by his own family, to establish himself in the security of a foster family, with Judge and Mrs. Hoffman as substitute father and mother.[23]

One may not want to accept this theory, but it is difficult to deny that bachelorhood was a role for which Irving was fitted by personality and temperament, although he worked himself into it only with considerable stress and recurrent misgivings. Certainly the sheltering which he received from the females in his own family as a child and young man, his guaranteed refuge against paternal severity, was hardly calculated to make a grown man of him in a hurry. Until well along in adult life he showed little taste for assuming the kind of responsibilities that marriage would have entailed; in his later works the frequent pattern of the impulsive son driven to rebellion against a stern father indicates a preoccupation with the problem of assuming manhood.

The Matilda figure lives on in his fiction primarily as an ideal, while at the same time the mothers of youthful sons are also often glorified. Simplification, however, will not serve in these matters. Irving may generally have "desexualized women and delibidinized love and passion,"[24] but we must still account for a certain bawdy strain in his work. An interplay of desire, fear, and guilt, as we shall see, characterizes his treatment of love, sexuality, and marriage. It is not a coincidence that he kept returning to themes and images of sterility and fertility. Certain ominously wizened figures in his later fiction suggest that he was not unmindful that he ran the risk of losing himself, like Knickerbocker and the man in black, in antiquarian futility.[25]

"The great charm of English scenery . . . ," Irving wrote in *The Sketch Book*, "is the moral feeling that seems to pervade it.

[23] Marcel Heiman, "Rip Van Winkle: A Psychoanalytic Note on the Story and its Author," *The American Imago*, XVI (Spring, 1959), 18–26.

[24] *Ibid.*, p. 23.

[25] Heiman sees Knickerbocker as partly Irving's father, partly Irving himself (pp. 14–16).

It is associated in the mind with ideas of order, of quiet, of sober well-established principles, of hoary usage and reverend custom. Every thing seems to be the growth of ages of regular and peaceful existence" (p. 87). Such pronouncements ring slightly false. The effort to find "ideas of order," to smooth things over, is never quite convincing when it comes from one who as a young man lampooned the law and took positive delight in demolishing smugness and exposing the fatuous feeling for order that underlies a cliché. One is still tempted to regret, with the elder Richard H. Dana, that in *The Sketch Book* Irving abandoned the unrestrained Knickerbocker style, with its "words and phrases, which were strong, distinct and definite, for a genteel sort of language."[26] The pompous and sentimental tendencies, however, represent only one side of the man; the youthful flair for self-ridicule kept intruding.

What he apparently faced after *Knickerbocker* was the prospect of turning into the family errand boy unless he found a regular way of making his living. In 1811 and 1812 he was acting from time to time as the Irvings' representative in Washington, a job that gave him opportunity to dance attendance at Dolly Madison's levées. For two years he did literary hackwork as editor of the *Analectic Magazine*, published in Philadelphia, and he volunteered for a brief tour of military duty during the War of 1812. He was not able to devote himself extensively to his own writing again until 1817, when the idea of *The Sketch Book* began to form in his mind. Meanwhile, in 1815, for want of anything better to do, he drifted to Liverpool, England, and before long was working overtime to help his brother Peter salvage one of the Irving enterprises. They failed, Peter fell ill, and *The Sketch Book* seems to have been an almost desperate effort to overcome the depression, mental and financial, which followed.

Some of the loathing that he expressed for business probably ought to be charged to an exuberant prose style. "By all the martyrs of Grubstreet," he once wrote while working in his

[26] Unsigned review of *The Sketch Book, North American Review*, IX (September, 1819), 348.

brothers' store, "I'd sooner live in a garret . . . than follow so sordid, dusty, soul killing way of life; though certain it would make me as rich as . . . John Jacob Astor himself."[27] Yet to some it appears that by 1835 he was in effect working for Astor, writing a history of the great merchant's early fur-trading ventures in the Pacific Northwest.[28] Irving never stopped being partially commercial; he never as a writer raised himself to a devoted singleness of artistic purpose.[29] And he came to look back on the composition of *The Sketch Book* as an almost heroic achievement, undertaken to raise the family name above the humiliation of financial failure.

Nevertheless, there is some sense of dedication in his reference to himself in 1819 as "a poor devil of an author"[30] and in his statement of purpose to his brother William: "I certainly think that no hope of gain . . . would tempt me again into the cares and sordid concerns of traffic. . . . I look forward to a life of loneliness and of parsimonious and almost painful economy."[31] When *The Sketch Book* appeared, he was thirty-six years old. He had been trying for the ten years since *Knickerbocker* to find a career for himself. *The Sketch Book* was a gamble for literary success taken by a man who felt that in the ordinary concerns of this world he had been something of a failure.

[27] Letter to Henry Brevoort, 15 May 1811, *Letters of Henry Brevoort to Washington Irving*, ed. George S. Hellman (New York, 1916), II, 185–86. The large correspondence between Irving and Brevoort is full of indictments of business, the morals of businessmen and lawyers, and the manners and taste of commercial families; neither, however, could altogether escape involvement in, and nearly constant anxiety over, the cycles of boom and panic. By 1843, after a series of financial losses to "our cheating . . . corporations," Brevoort decided that the country was "degenerate & corrupt to the very core." *Brevoort to Irving*, II, 132–33.

[28] Astor suggested Irving's doing *Astoria* (1836) and supplied him with the basic historical materials for it, but, argues Wagenknecht (p. 84), Irving was scrupulous about not taking money from Astor. Whether Irving served Astor as apologist in the book remains debatable.

[29] He was capable of urging a business career on others as an honorable calling with the same energy with which he shunned it himself; see for instance, letter to P. P. Irving, 7 December 1824, PMI, II, 218–22. Once he began writing for a living, he quite frankly aimed to please the public, and was willing within limits, to alter his style or mood to suit their taste. See "L'Envoy" in *SB*; *WIHB*, II, 106; PMI, I, 430–31.

[30] Letter to Brevoort, 9 September 1819, *WIHB*, II, 117.

[31] 23 December 1817, PMI, I, 393.

Beyond a certain point, authorship in the United States in
the early nineteenth century constituted something of a repudia-
tion of the middle-class values of practicality and industry. To
be sure, there was among the business community of New York
a certain tolerance for, and benevolent interest in, culture, and
the Irvings were willing to encourage their youngest son's literary
effusions and even to assist him to make something of his talent.
Still, it seems clear that they did not plan to support him in
gentlemanly leisure indefinitely. Irving probably exaggerated,
but not greatly, when, before he won fame with *The Sketch Book,*
he wrote: "Unqualified for business, in a nation where every one
is busy; devoted to literature, where literary leisure is con-
founded with idleness; the man of letters is almost an insulated
being, with few to understand, less [sic] to value, and scarcely
any to encourage his pursuits."[32]

The romantic extreme toward which this dilemma helped drive
several major American writers was a more or less defiant isolation. Irving had more luck to begin with than Poe, Thoreau,
Melville, or Emily Dickinson. The humor that he fell heir to
in the Knickerbocker period was based on assumptions so vaguely
defined that, up to a certain point, it could be used to criticize
with impunity the very class that patronized it. In the next stage
of his career, however, he attempted to balance appeals to a
popular audience against a desire to sustain artistic integrity or
at least stylistic excellence, a feat which he failed to accomplish
more than once (and not always because he truckled to his audience). Only later (after 1832) did he achieve relative composure by his willingness to capitalize on his reputation and to
repeat tested formulas.

In the meantime, doubts about the legitimacy of the writer's
calling were hardly to be allayed by an awareness of the difficulty
of creating techniques appropriate to the newness of American
experience. Ultimately, the problem was how to perceive significant form in the experience itself. In the absence of the kind

[32] Review of *The Works of Robert Treat Paine, AN,* I, 252. Spencer (p. 68)
speaks of the "salient fact in post-revolutionary America" that "the man of letters
was neither honored nor respected by the majority of his compatriots."

of social hierarchy assumed as the norm by English literature, the "important questions," as one scholar puts it, "of where authority was and whence it came were not yet fully answered." The author thus "confronted experience in bulk, experience badly in need of synthesis—social, economic, and political, as well as artistic."[33] The synthesis was not to come until the period now known as the American Renaissance, beginning in the 1830's. The transition to this period must be a central concern in any detailed examination of Irving's career, and that transition was toward a full-fledged romantic subjectivism. Emerson was to make his own mark and that of American literature as well when in 1836, at the beginning of *Nature,* he dared reduce *his* universe to a naked self confronting in all the rest of creation simply a negative, "NOT ME."

Scholars have carefully observed Irving's gradual appropriation of romantic devices and absorption of romantic influences. We know that he sometimes utilized sentimental plots with gothic trappings, that meeting Walter Scott in 1817 intensified his interest in folklore, that reading Mrs. Radcliffe years earlier had alerted him to Italian bandits. The net effect of the work done so far, however, is to give the impression of a romantic façade slapped section by section onto a fundamentally neoclassical frame. Actually, his early orientation toward the eighteenth century was of a wholly unsettled kind, and the romantic awarenesses that he gradually developed came in large part as the natural consequence of the tensions, personal, intellectual, and literary, in which he was immersed.

He finally lifted himself out of the negativism of his early phase by what we can now see as the comparatively simple and probably inevitable expedient of parlaying his own uncertainty into something positive. This was a romantic strategy, and it enabled him to develop as a writer. But it did not mean that his waverings had ceased or that the tensions had essentially changed. He remained diffident about insisting on his own individuality or exploiting himself except in a somewhat self-

[33] Terence Martin, "Social Institutions in the Early American Novel," *American Quarterly,* IX (Spring, 1957), 73.

deprecatory way. In the United States both experience and the democratic dogma tended to jar one free from the customary identities of class and creed, but individual identity did not come automatically. Self-reliance was a conditioned, not a natural, reflex. Both an asset and a disability, Irving's original penchant for whimsy, his feeling for the "farce of life" (*SAL*, p. 18), was something he never fully lived down.

I

The Provincial Quest for Style

AT nineteen Irving was calling himself "Jonathan Oldstyle" —not exactly the signature to a declaration of independence. In the folklore of the period "Jonathan" signified the unsophisticated, if not uncouth, American, jealous of the freedom he had recently won from John Bull. The irony of yoking him to an "Oldstyle" points to the precariousness in Irving's situation as a writer. Unwilling or unable in the nine epistolary essays that he published in his brother Peter's New York *Morning Chronicle* to present his comment on local manners, especially in the theater, in his own voice, he is nonetheless not entirely comfortable speaking as Oldstyle. The dilemma is that of a provincial writer pretending to urbanity. The reader—and perhaps the writer—cannot be sure whether the mimicry expresses respect or mockery, is an effort to see through adult eyes or to prolong and accentuate youth.

He describes himself as an "uninterested spectator" of current events (*JO*, p. xvii), but the character in the periodical essay tradition with whom he strives to identify himself, having held himself aloof since the time of Addison, seems largely exhausted. After the *Spectator* the British essayist had often pretended to be, if not an elderly gentleman, at least the close associate of one or more aging bachelors well versed in old fashions and customs. Senex had come to America under numerous pseudonyms, such as the *Pennsylvania Magazine's* "Old Bachelor" (1775–76)[1] and (the immediate precursor of Oldstyle) Joseph Dennie's "Oliver Oldschool" in the *Port Folio* (1801), helping

[1] See Introduction, p. 7, n. 14.

17

to round out a century during which the periodical writer tried, though with increasing irony as time went on, to sustain the character of a person wise enough to lecture readers on their shortcomings without fear of reprisal.

Now the assurance with which Oldstyle's prototype in the *Spectator* had once located himself in relation to an observed "world" was harder to maintain. The tone of Augustan London had been able to support the authority of a character who lived "rather as a Spectator of mankind, than as one of the species," who speculated on life "without ever meddling" in it.[2] But such a figure was less at home in the United States in 1800. True, the epistolary essay had been the dominant literary form in eighteenth-century America. It had effectively served a society in which busy men needed a single vehicle for conveying information or instruction and releasing creative energy. As long as conscious loyalty to British culture dominated American thinking, there was no reason for the writer who could manage an urbane style to conceal it. Nevertheless, in appealing to a provincial audience, American essayists had often helped to vulgarize the tradition, broadening the humor and substituting a more familiar manner—sometimes brusquely slapdash and colloquial—for the earlier moderation and gentility. Extremes of irony and burlesque, which blurred intention and point of view, often reflected the essayist's uncertainty as to how an American audience should be approached.[3] The intrusiveness earlier made explicit in Benjamin Franklin's choice of a pseudonym, the "Busy-Body," had become, at least stylistically, a part of the American periodical character, taking more of the starch out of a reserve that had begun to wilt even in England; the ordinary citizen or the almost illiterate hayseed was beginning to emerge as a mask or mouthpiece more appropriate than the gentleman for comment on American manners. Such pseudonymous characters, for instance, as Franklin's Poor Richard,

[2] Addison and Steele, *Spectator*, No. 1.

[3] The native traditions behind Irving's early work have been carefully examined by Robert S. Osborne in "A Study of Washington Irving's Development as a Man of Letters to 1825" (unpublished Ph.D. dissertation, University of North Carolina, 1947), pp. 8–9, 19–20, 32–73.

Philip Freneau's Robert Slender (a weaver), and St. John de Crèvecoeur's American farmer had already anticipated the high authority that Jack Downing, Huck Finn, and other vernacular spokesmen were to achieve in the nineteenth century.[4]

Born in the year in which the Revolutionary War officially ended and named for the "father" of the newly united States, Irving belonged to the first generation of writers to think of themselves from childhood on as American citizens, not British subjects. But circumstances gave him a small reputation, as the author of *Oldstyle*, before he had time to ponder the role of the writer in a new nation. Provided with an outlet in print, he accepted as a matter of course the obvious journalistic convention of the pseudonymous letter to the editor. And in assuming the mask of Oldstyle he committed himself, but only in theory, to an auctorial character which the eighteenth century had established as standard. Irony, however, strips most of the dignity from the old-fashioned spectator in the opening sentence: "If the observations of an odd old fellow are not wholly superfluous, I would thank you to shove them into a spare corner of your paper" (p. xvii). Irving thus begins his career in part playing, in part struggling, with an outmoded form.

In the first of his *Letters* Oldstyle does not sound his age; his voice, although the language is thoroughly literate, remains com-

[4] Walter Blair calls attention to the gradual replacement of the gentlemanly by the vernacular voice. *Native American Humor* (San Francisco, 1960), pp. 24–25. Kenneth Lynn, concerned specifically with Southwestern humor, discusses at length the problem of the literate author's relation to his rustic character. *Mark Twain and Southwestern Humor* (Boston, 1959), chaps. i–vi *passim*. Settling into that character was not easy for the writer who, even if he was not partly patrician in background or aspiration, was apt to possess a good deal more sophistication than the bumpkin he pretended to be. Crèvecoeur, the French aristocrat, might theorize on the necessity for a plain American prose, but he did not always sound as rustic as he should have. And Freneau, who saw the need of emphasizing his weaver's political naïveté, did not fully solve the problem: Slender had to be not only unsophisticated enough to be ludicrously amusing on occasion but also intelligent enough to be taken seriously as the voice of sound common sense, once a good Republican paper like William Duane's *Aurora* had given him the facts and liberated him from Federalist propaganda. See "Letters on Various Interesting and Important Subjects" and "Uncollected Letters by Robert Slender," in *The Prose of Philip Freneau*, ed. Philip M. Marsh (New Brunswick, N.J., 1955). These letters originally appeared in the *Aurora* (Philadelphia) between 1798 and 1801.

paratively youthful. Irving deliberately undermines the connotations of a few elegant clichés, such as "bewitching languor"
and "all the airy lightness of a sylph," with the brusqueness of
statements like "the fashionable belle resembled a walking
bottle" (*JO*, pp. XVII–III). He seems to be speaking in something
close to a natural voice, balancing a mildly explosive directness
against a studied but not particularly formal grace, alert always
to possibilities for pleasure or amusement in rhythm, harmony,
and dissonance. He remembers that he is Oldstyle only to the
extent of laughing at him:

> Heavens! how changed are the manners since I was young!—then,
> how delightful to contemplate a ball-room: . . . nothing more com-
> mon than to see half a dozen gentlemen knock their heads together
> in striving who should first recover a lady's fan or snuff-box that
> had fallen. (p. XIX)

True, the first letter chides the younger generation for its slovenly
manners, but through his pseudonym Irving makes fun of traditional customs—old styles as well as new.

In Letter II,[5] as the old gentleman reminisces about the
elaborate gallantries of courtship and marriage in his youth,
one wonders momentarily whether the feeling for old times is
not genuine. This would accord with the popular conception of
Irving as a lover of the antique. But if there is a part of him
that is prone to identify with Oldstyle and to sentimentalize over
an allegedly happier past, he is willing to mock it. The old
man's style soars into excessive gentility and once or twice
reaches a maudlin summit:

> It is with the greatest pain that I see those customs dying away,
> which served to awaken the hospitality and friendship of my
> ancient comrades—that strewed with flowers the path to the altar,
> and shed a ray of sunshine on the commencement of the matrimonial
> union. (p. 8)

---

[5] The 1824 edition of *Jonathan Oldstyle* omitted the first letter of the original
series in the *Morning Chronicle*. The remaining letters were renumbered, I–VIII.
They appear this way in the 1941 edition, which is a facsimile reprint of the 1824
edition with the original first letter inserted as part of the front matter. What I call
Letter II, or the eighth letter, is thus in *JO* Letter I or Letter VII, respectively, etc.

Letter II on the whole reads as though Irving, having adopted a stock literary character as his pseudonym, is beginning in earnest to exploit the comic possibilities of lampooning him.

Only later, when Oldstyle starts reporting on the theater—the main concern of Letters III through VIII—does his creator come close to sympathizing with him. And even when this happens, a brusque, short-tempered, not-quite-gentlemanly outspokenness is apt to scratch through the polish of Oldstyle's manner. This is the touch of the abrasive Jonathan. Irving is unsparing in his criticism of everything in the theater from the mural in the dome to the footwear of the actors. He strongly hints at drunkenness on stage, points out errors in the playbills, and complains about poorly constructed plays, miscasting, and inept acting and costuming. He concludes Letter VI by recommending "To the whole house, inside and out, a total reformation" (p. 33). But his censure of the theater does not come as the direct expression of a consistently characterized narrator. Oldstyle can be at one moment a blunt youth, then a silly old fool, and soon afterwards a sharp ironist.

Writing in New York at the beginning of the nineteenth century meant writing for an audience bent on viewing itself as sophisticated. The literary clubs to which some of Irving's brothers belonged—the Calliopean Society and the Belles Lettres Club—and by which his own talents were probably stimulated, were one of the evidences of developing interest in literature and the arts in New York. The opening in 1798 of the Park Theater, the haunt of Jonathan Oldstyle, was another, and the enthusiasm with which Irving's early works were received was the best proof of all. But the city presented in *Oldstyle* and *Salmagundi* hardly lives up to the image of seaboard urban elegance that historians sometimes stress in their depictions of eighteenth-century America. Irving's early works expose a culture that is in many ways barren and primitive. The situation is neatly epitomized in a revelation by *Salmagundi* in 1807: "Custom-house partly used as a lodging-house for the pictures belonging to the Academy of Arts—couldn't afford the statues house-room,

most of them in the cellar of the City Hall—poor place for the
gods and goddesses—after Olympus" (p. 240). To be sure, the
plight of the Academy of Arts might have been worse. The
customhouse had been designed originally as the executive
mansion for the first President of the United States during New
York's tenure as national capital. And the city hall, though built
in 1699 and soon to give way to a more famous successor, had
been remodeled with "monumentality and simplicity" by Pierre
Charles L'Enfant in 1788–89 so as to accommodate the national
Congress for a few months after Washington's inauguration.[6]
Only a year or two before the *Salmagundi* comment, however, the
Academy's collection had been housed in a riding school which
was about to be torn down.[7] As the magazine observed, while
lauding the Academy members for their worthy efforts, "it is a
pity . . . they began at the wrong end—maxim—If you want a
bird and a cage, always buy the cage first" (p. 240).[8]

Undoubtedly Irving's evenings at the Park Theater were not
as riotous as he made them out to be in conformity with the conventions of journalistic satire. Still, the *Oldstyle* letters had
substantial basis in fact. Completion of the Park had given the
city a playhouse rivaling those in Boston and Philadelphia,
which in turn compared favorably in "elegance" and "convenience" with the better British theaters. But American dependence
on British actors and secondhand British costumes and scenery
makes the comment of one visitor to the theater in Philadelphia,
"I should have thought I had still been in England," a dubious
compliment. Indeed it was something like provincial British

---

[6] John A. Kouwenhoven, *The Columbia Historical Portrait of New York* (New
York, 1953), pp. 54, 83–85.

[7] Winifred E. Howe, *A History of the Metropolitan Museum of Art* (New York,
1913), [I], 7–18.

[8] It appears that there had been trouble even at the wrong end—an insufficiency of
funds for procuring the plaster casts of famous pieces of sculpture which most early
American museums were forced to rely on almost exclusively. In Paris in 1805
Irving had met the painter John Vanderlyn, who had been "sent out . . . by the
Academy to collect casts &c." and who was "extremely in want of money. . . . He
has written repeatedly to the Academy, but has received no answer." Letter to
Peter Irving, 15 July 1805, PMI, I, 148.

theater that American companies at their best were offering in 1800.[9]

"When the visitor went to the Park Theater," says a modern historian, he discovered one of the "advantages of the American wage-earner. The pit was full of workingmen who, in England, would not be able to buy a pint of porter. . . ."[10] As Isaac Weld had noted,[11] however, the privileges of American liberty actually went a good deal further: workingmen might even drink their porter in the theater, "precisely as if they were in a tavern." Thus the democraticalness of American audiences proved a mixed blessing. Jonathan Oldstyle, who says that the audience imitated "the whistles and yells of every kind of animal" (p. 18), was hardly surprised that the man next to him was "more diverted with the queer grimaces and contortions of countenance exhibited by the musicians, than their melody." What Oldstyle "heard of the music," he "liked very well; . . . but it was often overpowered by the gentry in the gallery, who vociferated loudly for *Moll in the Wad, Tally ho the Grinders,* and several other *airs* more suited to their tastes" (p. 23). Patrons also threw fruit. Hit on the head by a "rotten pippin," Oldstyle was about to shake his cane at the gallery, but a "decent looking man" nearby explained that protest was useless: "They are only *amusing themselves* a little at our expense, said he; sit down quietly and bend your back to it" (p. 19).

The relation of Irving's early work to the community in which he lived can best be appreciated at this point by a brief look ahead at the extent to which *Salmagundi* ridicules early American avidity for culture. The society presented in its pages does not exactly ape foreign manners, but it shows itself hypersensitive to a need for propriety and up-to-the-minute fashions, as it abandons itself to English and French milliners and French

[9] Henry Wansey, "An Excursion to the United States of North America in the Summer of 1796," in Allan Nevins, ed., *American Social History as Recorded by British Travellers* (New York, 1931), pp. 9–10. See also Isaac Weld, *Travels through the States of North America* (London, 1800), I, 24.

[10] Nevins, p. 15. He is speaking of Henry B. Fearon's visit to the United States in 1817.

[11] *Travels through the States,* I, 24.

dancing masters. In the absence of real refinement, money is
the key to culture: "society" is aggressively parvenu. "The lady
of a southern planter," noticed at Ballston, a spa near Saratoga
Springs, "will lay out the whole annual produce of a rice planta-
tion in silver and gold muslins, and new liveries; carry a hogs-
head of tobacco on her head, and trail a bale of sea-island cotton
at her heels. . . ." Meanwhile a Boston merchant's wife is tying
on her bonnet "with a quintal of codfish" (p. 319). Richard H.
Dana observed in 1819 that *Salmagundi*'s paper on Ballston
"must have been a true and faithful account of the birth and life
of half the stylish families in New York, as it is of every other
city." That the magazine "survived it," he said, "is a prodigy."[12]

Paulding and the Irvings see contemporary culture as largely
a matter of show, not of taste. In a rival magazine pretentious
pedantry passes for dramatic criticism. Businessmen and politicians manipulate the social scene in order to promote their own
advancement. The dominant impression is of furious energy ex-
pended in activity that is largely of no consequence. At banquets
politicians incapable of good government try to make themselves
immortal by the quantities of food they consume and the rhetoric
they exhale. The magazine presents a society, indeed a nation, of
"LITTLE GREAT MEN," not amounting to much but nearly
frantic in aspiration. Yet the authors are quite willing to be loud
and vulgar themselves in print in order to attract attention.
Obviously they are both attracted to, and repulsed by, the vitality
and vulgarity of republican institutions and the social climbing
and moneygrubbing that citizens of New York engaged in.

Another comment by Dana, who was discussing Irving for that
organ of staid Boston, the *North American Review,* helps clarify
Salmagundi's situation:

> It was fortunate . . . that the work made its first appearance in New
> York—"where the people—heaven help them—are the most irregu-
> lar, crazy-headed, quicksilver, eccentric, whim-whamsical set of
> mortals that ever were jumbled together." Had it first shown its face
> in any other part of the country, how soon would it have been looked

[12] *N. A. Review,* IX, 343.

out of countenance . . . by your "honest, fair worthy, square, . . .
upright, kind of people!"

New York being a city of large and sudden growth, with people
from all parts of the country, and many foreigners, individuals, there
do not feel every chance sarcasm or light ridicule of some foible
in the rank or set they belong to, as a personal attack, as is the case
in smaller cities, where sets must be small, too, or as in older cities,
where they are more distinctly marked. Neither have they enough
of clanship in the different classes into which society will always be
in some degree divided, to allow any lady or gentleman authority to
dictate what a man shall be taken into favor for, and for what he
shall be put down.[13]

Paulding and the Irvings apparently had no class or clan with
which to ally themselves unequivocally and no assurance that as
a clique they possessed the necessary judgment, taste, or authority to dictate to the town.

Launcelot Langstaff may, in an essay "On Greatness," invoke
the gentlemanly concepts of honor and honesty in order to indict
Timothy Dabble, the typical young American struggling up the
ladder of popular favor toward success in politics, but Langstaff
himself admits that "to stand up solely for the broad interests"
of the nation as a whole is "in this country" to be "like a body in
a *vacuum* between two planets," remaining "forever . . . motionless" (p. 313). This is in effect all that "the editors" can do.
Even Langstaff's savage attack on Dabble and unprincipled party
politics is undercut in advance by a note from his colleague
Anthony Evergreen explaining that the "essay was written . . .
in one of the paroxysms" of a "splenetic complaint" (p. 308).

Langstaff and his friends have no positive commitment, even
if on occasion one or another of them is allowed to speak out in
a loud, clear voice. Through them Paulding and the Irvings have
from the beginning made parody of the periodical essay tradition
explicit. Like "all true and able editors," Langstaff, Evergreen,
and Wizard in the first number put forth the claim of being
"infallible." Their "intention," they say, is "simply to instruct
the young, reform the old, correct the town, and castigate the age;
this is an arduous task, and therefore we undertake it with con-

---

[13] *Ibid.*, pp. 334–35.

fidence." While professing "the customary diffidence" of their
"brethren of the quill," they promise to interfere "in all matters
either of a public or private nature." Yet they will not "puzzle
[their] heads to give an account" of themselves. The publisher
explains that the magazine "will be printed on hot-pressed vellum
paper, as that is held in highest estimation for buckling up young
ladies' hair" (pp. 13–15).

Making fun of self-styled authorities and arbiters of taste is
an essential part of Irving's early humor. The praises of folly
bestowed by *Salmagundi,* as we shall see in the next chapter,
often ironically convey the displeasure of Paulding and the
Irvings. But they are also a sign of the incompetence of Langstaff, Evergreen, and Wizard. No sure sense of authority is established in the magazine. By contrast, Oldstyle's pretensions to
taste may seem more solidly based; at least in the letters on the
theater the facetious approval of bad taste and ineptness are apt
to be read as *his* irony (as well as Irving's). But what happens
to Oldstyle in the theater serves the same larger purpose. After
being subjected for several evenings to the coarse manners of the
audience and the wretched performances of the players, he is
personally humiliated by an actor on stage who resents Oldstyle's
published criticism. The old man leaps to his feet, ready to
return the abuse or stalk out; persuaded to sit down, he is again
provoked shortly afterward by a crude satirical characterization
of an old maid, which does drive him away. It turns out that he
has a maiden sister, whom he takes the opportunity to describe
pathetically.

In the end, he renounces criticism altogether. True, he goes
down rather gallantly, having borne discomfort and ill will in
the name of culture. There is a nice irony in his pretending to
have been convinced by philistinism that there is no role for the
critic in society. The reader is more sure than ever of the need
for criticism. Yet Irving himself is unable to offer it clearly
and simply through an appeal to well-established tradition. To
do so might smack of aristocratic affectation, and he is uncom-
fortably aware of living in a rampantly commercial republican
society.

Andrew Quoz, one of the minor characters, a belligerent and, in his own way, a highly articulate philistine, argues that critics are "the very pests of society," since

> they rob the actor of his reputation—the public of their amusement; they open the eyes of their readers to a full perception of the faults of our performers, they reduce our feelings to a state of miserable refinement, and destroy entirely all the enjoyments in which our coarser sensations delighted. (p. 37)

In the world of *Oldstyle* intellectual and artistic standards seem to be denied a place: everyone is as free as everyone else, and all *"have paid their dollar,"* so that they "have a right to entertain themselves as well as they can" (p. 35). Nor is it the patrons of the gallery alone who thrive on bad taste. People of means and position, who ought to know something about the theater, seem interested only in gossip and fashions.

If the issue could be clearly drawn between republican vulgarity and aristocratic taste, Irving's job would be relatively easy. But he shows awareness of a potential cultural value in republicanism by lending Oldstyle moral support in the figure of "an honest countryman" (p. 17) befriended during a performance. This rustic, though not a bumptious *young* Yankee, clearly derives from the playgoing Jonathan of Royall Tyler's *The Contrast.* His literal-minded responses directly recall the earlier character's mistaking boxes in the theater for "little cabins, just like father's corn-cribs," and his amazement that those staging the play "lifted up a great green cloth, and let us look right into the next neighbor's house."[14] The pairing of Oldstyle and the countryman suggests the curious nature of Irving's commitment to culture: a bourgeois longing for aristocratic cultivation, tempered by a sense of the discrepancy between such a longing and the basic value in the simplicity which ought to be a part of republicanism. Too much of an urbanite to try fully to identify himself with his countryman, he uses him as a comic character much in the fashion that was to become typical of "native American" humor, laughing at his ignorance and lack of sophistication while at the same time making fun of

[14] *The Contrast,* Act III, scene 1.

fashionable urban affectations through his innocent misunderstanding of them.

> By the way [says Oldstyle], my honest friend was much puzzled about the curtain itself. He wanted to know why that *carpet* was hung up in the theatre? I assured him it was no carpet, but a very fine curtain. And what, pray, may be the meaning of that gold head, with the nose cut off, that I see in front of it? The meaning—why, really, I can't tell exactly—though my cousin, Jack Stylish, says there is a great deal of meaning in it. But surely you like the *design* of the curtain? The design,—why really I can see no design about it, unless it is to be brought down about our ears by the weight of those gold heads, and that heavy *cornice* with which it is garnished. I now began to be uneasy for the credit of our curtain, and was afraid he would perceive the mistake of the painter, in putting a *harp* in the middle of the curtain, and calling it a mirror;[15] but his attention was *happily* called away by the *candle-grease* from the chandelier, over the centre of the pit, dropping on his clothes. This he loudly complained of, and declared his coat was *bran-new*. (pp. 24–25)

Republican simplicity may be simple-minded some of the time, but its honesty embarrasses Oldstyle, with his fondness for decorative elegance. And, curiously, his own feigned innocence gives him a resemblance to the countryman: "The Queen was followed by a pretty gentleman, who, from his winking and grinning, I took to be a court fool; I soon found out my mistake. He was a courtier 'high in trust,' and either a general, colonel, or something of martial dignity" (p. 12). After he has fraternized with his new acquaintance for a while, Oldstyle even seems to begin looking with the countryman's eyes: "What can be more pretty than the paintings in the front of the boxes, those little masters and misses sucking their thumbs, and making mouths at the audience?" (p. 31)

There ought to be a voice between that of Oldstyle and the countryman, one more suited to Irving, a plain, direct voice, affecting neither ornateness nor vulgarity. Indeed, a somewhat different environment might have induced him to give greater prominence to those qualities of vigor and directness which are

---

[15] "The curtain of blue mohair, fringed in gold, contained in the center a lyre and the motto: 'To hold the Mirror up to Nature.'" Oral S. Coad, *William Dunlap* (New York, 1917), p. 65.

often a part of his style, even though they may be toned down. In the backwoods, for instance, writing in his notebook, he could manage by a simplicity of imagery and diction to render experience starkly.[16] But the social climate of New York was not conducive to the growth of a closemouthed and workmanlike prose. A certain parvenuism in American literature reveals itself at the turn of the nineteenth century in the prevalent taste for gaudy styles staggering under a "gorgeous load of ornaments."[17] When he later depicted the American muse as a pawnbroker's widow, Irving could hardly have been unaware that he had invoked her services himself.[18]

His early correspondence with friends and family, for instance, reveals the new society as it awkwardly puts on a grand manner and rejects a style more obviously reflective of qualities which we, in looking back, consider essential to the period. In their quotations, classical allusions, elaborate metaphors, stately cadence, and poetic diction, these correspondents echo the epistolary flourishes of the great age of English letter writing in the preceding century. Though Irving and others in his circle sometimes shouldered this style with unabashed seriousness (in a sense they had to, since they refused a more natural one), they could not always refrain from laughing, or at least smiling, at themselves for it. Thus Henry Brevoort, in a letter to Irving in 1811 (the manner had been initiated much earlier), in order to avoid sentimentality as he voices his homesickness, resorts to a humor of overblown rhetoric: "How shall I eke out this whining epistle? The exchequer of my imagination is exhausted, and the wayward spirit will not advance a line without halting." Further on in the letter he tries to give vent to his feelings directly, dis-

[16] See, for instance, his *Journal, 1803*, ed. Stanley T. Williams (New York, 1934), pp. 34–35.

[17] William Wirt, quoted in Spencer, p. 54. Or see [Richard Alsop, Theodore Dwight, *et al.*], "The Echo," Preface, and No. 1, in *The Echo, with Other Poems* (n.p., 1807).

[18] See his review of E. C. Holland's *Odes, Naval Songs, and Other Occasional Poems*, AN, III, 248. Dana, though an admirer of Irving's early style, found its faults "violent and obvious"—a "multiplying of epithets, which, making no new impression, weaken from diffusion," "the employment of certain worn out veterans in the cause of wit," and the "forcing" of "wit as if from duty." *N. A. Review*, IX, 338, 348.

daining "to apologize for this dolour." But the literary diction—
"dolour" instead of "sadness"—still stifles direct expression.
The flamboyance of the style that he and his friends insist on
using will not permit the direct expression of any but earth-
shaking emotions. As Brevoort continues, he becomes ridiculous:
"I have often thought that if such a reptile as myself, has the
power of forming sympathies, so indissoluble towards particular
persons & places, how irresistable must be the longings of the
exile whose consequence and talents, made him the idol of that
society which he once adorned!"[19]

Used ironically, however, as when Oldstyle pretends to admire an inept or overly ornate decoration, or when used in
tandem with blunt informality, this style becomes a useful instrument for exposing the smallness and pretentiousness of a
youthful culture. At the beginning of the nineteenth century
the attempts of the fledgling literature of the United States to
develop a soaring style tend to become tiresome, and it is with
some relief that one turns to the relentless ridicule that distinguishes what was to be known as the "Knickerbocker" manner
in the literature of New York. Cultural and intellectual bewilder-
ment began operating early to produce the peculiar quality of
Irving's early work, its all-encompassing, self-mocking irony,
constantly verging on nonsense. In *Oldstyle* he traps himself and
his reader by failing to keep a consistency of character and by
mixing irony and direct statement indiscriminately. In itself
this is bad writing, but Irving seems already to be capitalizing
on his mistakes and feeling his way toward a comic style that
deliberately, and successfully, exploits abrupt shifts of tone and
betrayals of character. By the time Oldstyle takes his leave, he
is anticipating the greatest achievement of Irving's early period,
the development, in Diedrich Knickerbocker, of a consistently
inconsistent character as the only logical vehicle for projecting
the author's blurred image of the world.

When one concentrates on the major purpose of Oldstyle's
comments on the theater, one can discern Irving's dissatisfaction

[19] 14 July 1811, *Brevoort to Irving*, I, 38–40.

through almost everything that his pseudonym says. But if one
is momentarily distracted by a recollection of how Oldstyle has
been belittled, it is easy to slip in the middle of one of his
passages of mock-admiration and take him, not for a fairly
urbane ironist, but for an addlepate. And the spurious arguments
of the philistine Quoz in favor of everything that Irving presumably opposes only complicate the problem. We assume Quoz
to be serious—which makes him an insane vulgarian. Then we
pick up Oldstyle again, and, instead of making the adjustment
we should to allow for the irony of his approval of incompetence and bad taste, we blunder and start taking him seriously.
Bouncing back and forth from one character to another, one is
struck by odd impressions. If Quoz helps make Oldstyle look
silly, Oldstyle makes Quoz seem at times almost reasonable:

> To be plain, my friend, an actor has a right, whenever he thinks his
> author not sufficiently explicit, to assist him by his own *wit* and
> *abilities;* and if by these means the character should become quite
> different from what was originally intended, and in fact belong more
> to the *actor* than the *author,* the actor deserves high credit for his
> ingenuity. And even though his additions are *quaint* and fulsome,
> yet his *intention* is highly praiseworthy, and deserves ample encour-
> agement. (pp. 55–56)

Quoz may ludicrously exaggerate the actor's rights, as elsewhere
he does the playwright's need to rely on stereotypes and established conventions. But he manages to suggest how complicated
a thing is just criticism. Given the general interplay of sense
and nonsense, one has to be on guard not to be lured, at least
momentarily, into sympathizing with his assertion that "judgment, and taste, and feeling" are "ridiculous principles" (p. 57).
If no one knows what they mean, they are, for all practical purposes, ridiculous. And Oldstyle, in spite of his good intentions,
has no head for definitions.

In Addisonian terms Irving would now seem to "qualify . . .
for Bedlam" for "not considering that humour should always
lie under the check of reason," for ignoring the specific warnings
which the *Spectator* had issued against "False Humour," that
"monstrous infant," related through "Frenzy" and "Laughter"

to "Nonsense," and ultimately to "Falsehood." Since he is "entirely void of reason," the *Spectator* had maintained, this infant "will bite the hand that feeds him." A writer dominated by False Humour accordingly "pursues no point either of morality or instruction, but is ludicrous only for the sake of being so."[20]

It is fortunate that Irving, having started on the road to nonsense, does not turn back. In the end he reduces Oldstyle to utter absurdity. Thus the hilarious ninth letter serves as a rousing finale to a divertimento whose central theme has become, perhaps inadvertently, growing confusion. Here the comedy of manners almost breaks up into slapstick. Most of the characters who have been introduced in the series—Oldstyle, his sister, his cousin Jack Stylish, and Quoz—argue the merits of a recent New York law denying political privileges to anyone convicted of dueling. While everyone favors the ancient custom and opposes the law, Oldstyle, fond and foolish once more, at first only laments the passing of old ways when "nothing could equal the tenderness and attention with which a wounded antagonist was treated; his adversary, after wiping his sword, kindly supported him in his arms . . . and inquired, 'how he felt himself now?' " (p. 63) Meanwhile, the younger and more active men offer countermeasures. Quoz advises circumventing the law by having antagonists draw lots to determine which is to win the right to drop a "purely accidental" brick on the head of the other. Stylish insists on a new law requiring offending and offended parties to fight to the death in public after taking out a "regular license from what might be called the *Blood and Thunder Office*" (p. 66).

Then at the last minute Oldstyle snaps out of his hopeless sentimentality and becomes Washington Irving making a sarcastic comment on the psychology and sociology of dueling. His earlier nostalgia for the decorum of old-fashioned affairs of honor notwithstanding, Oldstyle now endorses Stylish's idea:

Our young men fight, ninety-nine times out of a hundred, through *fear* of being branded with the epithet of *coward*; and since they fight to please the world, the world, being thus interested in their

[20] *Spectator*, No. 35.

encounters, should be permitted to attend and judge in person of their conduct. (p. 67)

The reversal is so sudden and so complete that it amounts to a complete denial of Oldstyle's character. Yet this may be his deepest significance. Unable to play the spectator in a world that doesn't seem to run reasonably, Oldstyle finally becomes a proto-Knickerbocker, a Bedlamite in whose poor cracked skull stupidity and nonsense rattle against what occasionally sounds like wisdom and insight.

If the surface manner of the periodical essay was particularly unsuited to the boisterousness of life in the United States at the beginning of the nineteenth century, the intellectual assumptions behind the tradition were being questioned everywhere as well. Those assumptions were in large part, of course, identical with the ones underlying neoclassicism as a whole. The early development of American literature coincides with the final breakdown of a set of ideas that had dominated European and American thought for several generations. Irving's work to a considerable extent embodies the realization that eighteenth-century Reason, though it may have helped to provide the United States with desirable political institutions, not only had not made man any wiser than he was to begin with or perfected him in moral virtue, but had actually rendered much more difficult the satisfaction of his longing for a positive belief in something beyond his fleeting presence in the physical world.

The elder William Irving, a Presbyterian deacon, had hoped that at least one of his sons would go into the church, but in an age when revolution and republicanism were still activating ideas, the ministry was a less attractive calling than it had once been. John Irving did study theology briefly but gave it up under the pressure of his brothers' badgering. Washington, immunized intellectually at an early age against most aspects of religion, rejected church affiliation as an adult until long after his literary reputation was won.

The disassociation was in part a rebellion against the religious discipline imposed upon the household by his father, "a sedate,

conscientious, God-fearing man, with much of the strictness of
the old Scotch Covenanter in his composition,"[21] and against
what Irving called the "hypocrisy, cant, and worldliness imposed
upon mankind under the external forms of religions."[22] Still he
was to retain a lingering interest in religion, his attitudes toward
it being partly involved with his feelings toward his parents. He
was attracted early, perhaps because of its greater emphasis on
form and ritual, to the Episcopal church, in which his mother,
an "ardent and impulsive" woman, had been raised before sub-
mitting somewhat reluctantly after marriage to her husband's
"more rigid" faith.[23] As he matured, he often reflected on the
difficulty of sustaining a simple belief in a skeptical age.

It is hardly surprising that Irving, who grew up in a household
dominated by the deaconly reserve of his father, and was used
to having his paths smoothed for him by seven brothers and sisters, matured into a not very robust young man. A respiratory
ailment and the need for a change of climate and a respite from
work and study were the ostensible reasons for his twenty-one-
month trek through France, Italy, Switzerland, the Low Countries, and England, which began in 1804. But his indifferent
health would seem to have been partly temperamental. He was
to return from his trip, if anything, even more incapacitated, at
least as far as getting on with a career was concerned.

His *Notes and Journal of Travel in Europe, 1804–05* often
reveal little more than the delight of a young man on an extended
vacation, but the trip as a whole is best viewed as part of an early
American quest for style. It is here that one sees most clearly
Irving's encounter with ideas and attitudes that were standard
equipment for the cultivated man of his day. If the family did
not expect a direct return on their investment in Washington's
health in the form of a young man of the world who would represent them in business, they did expect him to get their money's
worth in "culture." Thus his brother William protested against

[21] PMI, I, 23.
[22] Letter to Emily Foster, 23 August 1825, in Stanley T. Williams, "Washington
Irving's Religion," *Yale Review*, XV (January, 1926), 415–16.
[23] PMI, I, 24–26.

the haphazard character of Washington's tour, which idled a long time in an unimportant city like Genoa and made extensive explorations of Sicily, only, as William's irony puts it, to discover "that all that is worth a stranger's curiosity in Naples and in Rome, may be completely viewed . . . between the 7th March . . . and the 4th April." Irving missed seeing Florence and Venice altogether, much to the disgust of William, who chided the younger brother on his willingness to sacrifice everything for the sake of "good company" on the road.[24] Yet, equipped with guidebooks that were models of elegant prose and with notebooks in which he could record his observations, Irving pursued his travels much of the time in a frame of mind well calculated to "profit," at least in some sense, from the experience. He worked at his prose style, studied landscape and architecture with a painter's eye, toured galleries and museums, attended the theater, mixed in polite society, meditated on religious, philosophical, and political questions, and even amused himself with rudimentary scientific experiments—he made observations of volcanic phenomena when he climbed Vesuvius and helped to ascertain the acoustical properties of the cave at Syracuse known as the Ear of Dionysius.

Yet, lacking the assurance and sophistication of the young English gentleman in the eighteenth century on the Grand Tour, he did not play the dilettante particularly well. His immediate reactions to what he saw were larded over with recollections of, or references to, books he had read or paintings he had seen. Often, his comments echo one or another of the eighteenth-century guidebooks he used. The practice of verifying in actual experience the observations of art or literature had become the standard procedure for eighteenth-century travelers. The concept of the Grand Tour testifies to the general acceptance of the idea of traveling as higher education. Dr. John Moore, one of the travel writers whom Irving consulted, voiced the prevailing view perfectly in saying that nothing could repay one for the discomforts of foreign travel except the "sight of places cele-

[24] William Irving to Washington Irving, 8 July 1805, PMI, I, 139–40.

brated by favorite authors" or "the thought of treading the same
ground . . . with persons who lived there fifteen hundred or two
thousand years ago."[25] Irving was quite willing to pay homage
to the past, especially since he was, as Geoffrey Crayon would
later say, "a man from a young country," to whom "history was,
in a manner, anticipation" and "all old things . . . new" (*B*,
p. 14). Yet in trying to understand and assimilate classical
views of Italy and Sicily, he was often aware that he could not
see famous sights as they had once been seen.

Cruising southward from Genoa along the Italian coast, he
used Patrick Brydone's *A Tour through Sicily and Malta* as a
guide in following the landmarks, and behind Brydone stood
Homer and Vergil. Thus Irving kept watch on deck half-expect-
ing a glimpse of Neptune, Amphitrite, and the Nereids, and
trying to realize in the caves and volcanoes of the Lipari Islands
properties associated with Aeolus, Vulcan, and the Cyclops. But
the "days of romance are over," he had already complained.
"The Gods are tired of us heavy mortals and no longer admit us
to their intimacy. In these dull *matter of fact* days our only
consolation is to wander about their once frequented haunts and
endeavor to make up by imagination the want of reality" (*TIE*,
II, 20).

Such remarks are part of a melancholy uneasiness which
colors *Travel in Europe*. A castle on a hill might suggest
Spenser's "gallant knight that 'ever was ydrad,'" but Irving's
dawning interest in the Middle Ages was not strong enough for
him to overlook "misery indigence & ignorance on every side";
"beggary," he said, "stares the traveller in the face." If Italy
on occasion seemed "a perfect Canaan," there was nonetheless
starvation "in the midst of it," peasants laboring "with a heavy
brow" able to "snatch" only a "scanty subsistance [sic]" from
the soil (III, 24–25). Irving responded, in spite of his Protestant
origins and his formal disassociation from religion, to appeals,
"chiefly against the imagination," in Catholic architecture,
music, and ritual (II, 10–11). Yet the "solemn farce" of a

[25] *A View of Society and Manners in Italy* (London, 1783), II, 98.

Cardinal, "swelling with vanity and pride," enacting Christ in an Easter week ceremony, infuriated him (III, 68–69).

Since he thought of himself as liberated from the stultifying effects of religious ritual and tradition, he was obliged in his notebooks to bear down heavily on Catholic "superstition." He saw the lower classes in Italy "gradually returning to a state of brutality," a fate which he blamed on "the baneful effects of despotic governments—of priest craft & superstition, of personal oppression and slavery of thought" (III, 24–25). At times, it is true, his comic fancy was aroused, as when he noted that the "disciples must have been an uncommon bony set of fellows," since he had "seen no less than five thigh bones of St. John the Baptist[,] three arms of St. Stephen and four jaw bones of St. Peter."[26] But too often he allowed himself to become exercised in a thoroughly sophomoric way over the abuses of a "priest craft" which he saw conniving at the acceptance of patent fictions as virtual dogma. Where Brydone had been able to accept legends of Catholic saints as folklore, and almost admire the imagination that had constructed them,[27] Irving leaned toward literal-mindedness, although, ironically enough, behind his quickness to condemn one notices his avidity to collect and record legends: the folklorist impulse was already awakening in him.

In his eagerness to deprecate superstition, he was keeping faith with the tradition of the Englishman in Italy in the eighteenth century, a tradition that went back as far as Addison's *Remarks on Several Parts of Italy* (1705) and his verse *Letter from Italy* (1701). It was customary to hold medieval tyranny and gothic superstition responsible for the present sad plight of Italy. With this historical development the Englishman seemed to believe that he had little connection, and he was in effect free for the most part to disregard the present and the medieval past and to concentrate on an appreciation of the remains of classical antiquity, which he felt was closely related in spirit to the

[26] And if the fragments of the cross were "collected together they might form a tolerably stought [sic] ship of the line" (*TIE*, II, 93–95).

[27] Patrick Brydone, *A Tour through Sicily and Malta* (London, 1776), I, 154–57, 162–63, 178–85.

modern tradition of English freedom. It was as though England
were more the heir of Rome than Italy was. But Irving did not
find it so easy to disregard the present. Conscious of his own
heritage of political freedom, he tried to use the old formulas.
But to quote Addison's invocation, "Oh liberty thou goddess
heavenly bright" (III, 25), did not reconcile him to the indigence of the Italian peasantry and the lack of liberal political
institutions in Napoleonic Italy. Or, if he dutifully lamented
(III, 30), in the words of Pope's "Epistle to Mr. Addison,"
"Rome her own sad sepulchre appears," the melancholy per-
sisted, whereas for Pope and Addison the unpleasant apparition
of the Italian present had been transcended in an awareness
of the grandeur of the classical past.

Attitudes toward the past were changing. Between Pope and
Irving nearly a century of looking at ruins had intervened—a
century in which marbles, inscriptions, and other evidences of
antiquity were shipped to British museums, artificial ruins were
created in English gardens, and Gibbon's *Decline and Fall* was
written. The eighteenth-century dilettante's amused reflection on
the wreckage of previous civilizations had helped to produce the
romantic return to the past, which was also an awareness of the
present as a product of history. Revolutionary doctrine had been
propagated on the basis of the observations of writers like
Jefferson, Paine, and Crèvecoeur, who insisted that most of
European civilization had fallen under the influence of corrupt
anciens régimes: this was a seemingly logical corollary of the
classical conclusions of travelers to Greece and Rome. And a
traveler to Egypt and Syria, Constantin de Volney, had wandered among the ruins of Palmyra and discovered, he claimed,
a clear connection between the downfall of civilizations and the
need for an egalitarian politics.[28] Certainly, without the prospect
of some sort of brake on the cycle of the rise and fall of empires,
it was becoming difficult to avoid the primitivist conclusion that
civilization was a mistake, a series of unfulfilled possibilities.

[28] His *Ruins, or Meditations on the Revolutions of Empires* was translated by
Jefferson and Joel Barlow (Paris, 1802).

One might begin to wonder what assurance there was that the British empire was more permanent than Rome or that English liberty was indeed an absolute value, worth, for example, what it seemed to cost in character. Reaching England at last after months of traveling in countries where human rights existed only on the sufferance of arbitrary governments that were often in league with a corrupt clergy, Irving was disappointed and troubled, as he was to be intermittently for years, by the coldness and reserve he discovered in the English people.[29] Here again his response was probably conditioned by reading and hearsay,[30] but he seems to have felt strongly enough to need to summon up reassurance, and he did so, apparently out of his experience as a lawyer's apprentice. "In England," he was finally able to say, as though he had read just far enough in Blackstone to learn about freedom within the law, "I feel a man—in France I was a cypher" (III, 171).

Skeptical of the categories of the Enlightenment but not altogether liberated from them, Irving had little to fall back on intellectually save a certain ability which he had mentioned in his description of Mons, on the road from Paris to Brussels:

> This is a large town the walls of which are in a very ruinous condition. As I am not however a great connoisseur in fortifications and do not contemplate them with the eye of an Engineer, an old ruind [sic] wall with crumbling towers pleases my eye more than when in the strength and regularity of perfect repair. I look with an eye to the *picturesque*. (III, 132)

Here spoke the Irving who, when he was in Rome in the company of Washington Allston, had momentarily considered turning artist, the amateur draftsman who was to be a lifelong friend to painters and who would rise to fame on the strength of a

[29] He found himself a "wary person," with a heart "closed up," "standing . . . guard for fear of insult." If he had to ask directions, "I first examine the phizognomy [sic] of my neighbor" and then "make an enquiry with caution." "In no other country," he concluded, "have I felt any thing like this." *TIE*, III, 170.

[30] Goldsmith, one of Irving's favorite authors, had much earlier connected English pride and reserve with the English love of liberty (*Citizen of the World*, Letter IV). And the British were beginning to find a similar connection in the United States. See Nevins, ed., *American Social History*, pp. 6–7; Weld, *Travels through the States*, I, 21–22.

"sketch" book.[31] In general, seeing picturesquely meant seeing pictures in actuality, looking for the balance and proportion of art in life. More specifically it meant seeing Italian landscapes through the eyes of Mrs. Radcliffe and Patrick Brydone, who, in turn, had seen them through the eyes of Lorrain, Poussin, and Rosa. Irving had Ann Radcliffe's *The Italian* with him,[32] and in Rome he found a "superb gallery" of the great school of landscape painters themselves (II, 66–67). Inevitably, his own descriptions of Italian scenes struggled for picturesque effects, sometimes verging on the sublime.[33]

The picturesque was an acquired taste. For all his fondness for picturesque views, Irving sensed distortions in them, fearing that they were not quite real.[34] In Italy he felt that he often had to look at things through "a romantic medium that gives an illusive tinge to every object" (II, 20–21). The word "romantic," appearing this early in his work, carries connotations of excitement mixed with a slight sense of guilt, anticipating the apologetic nature of the romanticism to which he eventually subscribed. He was bothered by what potential readers of his descriptions of Italian sunsets might think. Was he recording his responses "intelligibly"? Did the term "poetic charm," which he was tempted to use, mean anything? Would his romantic rhapsodies only bore his readers? For he knew that sunsets produce an "illusive veil" and lend to landscape a "loveliness of coloring— not absolutely its own" (II, 59–60).

[31] Besides Allston, Irving was to know John Vanderlyn, Gilbert Stuart Newton, C. H. Leslie, and David Wilkie. On his relation to art and artists see STW, I, 63–65, 164–65, 184, and *passim*.

[32] STW, I, 52, n. 33.

[33] George S. Hellman discusses the resemblance between Irving's descriptions and Mrs. Radcliffe's in *Washington Irving Esquire* (New York, 1925), pp. 28–29. On connections between landscape painting and early literary interests in scenery, see Christopher Hussey, *The Picturesque: Studies in a Point of View* (London, 1927), pp. 10–12, 231, 233; Robert A. Aubin, *Topographical Poetry in XVIII-Century England* (New York, 1936), pp. 72–73 and *passim*.

[34] Van Wyck Brooks believed that Irving "had been predisposed" by "the Gothic mood," just becoming stylish, "to see in Italy during this early visit the scenes that appeared later in his writings," especially in *Tales of a Traveller—The Dream of Arcadia* (New York, 1958), pp. 23–25. This, I think, is an overstatement of the extent of Irving's romanticism in 1805, although there is no doubt that it was a gothicized Italy that he remembered when he came to write *Tales of a Traveller*.

Eventually, however, in spite of his reservations, his eye for the picturesque was to serve him fairly well. There might be something arbitrary about applying the Claude-glass to a landscape, but it forced one to discover a unity, to compose scenes within a frame. Already his descriptive writing, which used his own situation as a spectator overlooking a vista for the point of reference, was taking on symmetry and balance. Here was the beginning of the Irvingesque sketch.

> Beautiful features of the valley—chest nuts—Wall nuts &c—the Ticino winding thro it—rich pasturages coverd [sic] with flowers. Mountains bristle with trees—green about the bottom brown higher up—Mountains vast—Torrents—charnel houses—peasants working at the road—honest people—picturesque convents among the mountain[s]—Goats on the precipices. . . . (III, 80)

Irving may at this time have had little formal knowledge of associationism through Hartley or Alison, but he at least knew Moore's concept of the Grand Tour as a continual treading where the saints had trod. The picturesque started with "objects . . . that reminded a person of pictures he had seen,"[35] and it was apt to develop into a general attitude of subdued amazement at the ironies of existence, if not a melancholy cultivation of contradictions. Contrast and comparison had turned Patrick Brydone philosophical as he viewed the scene about the Bay of Naples, which had "formed our greatest landscape-painters."

> You see an amazing mixture of the antient and modern; some rising to fame, and some sinking to ruin. Palaces reared over the tops of other palaces, and antient magnificence trampled under foot—by modern folly.—Mountains and islands, that were celebrated for their fertility, changed into barren wastes, and barren wastes into fertile fields and rich vineyards. Mountains sunk into plains, and plains swelled into mountains.

---

[35] This is Hussey's explanation (p. 15) of the theory of the picturesque set forth by Archibald Alison in *Essays on the Nature and Principles of Taste* (1790). For further explanation of the picturesque and its relation to the "sublime" see Hussey, pp. 9, 14, 18–50, 107; Elizabeth M. Manwaring, *Italian Landscape in Eighteenth Century England* (New York, 1925), pp. 167–200; Walter Hipple, *The Beautiful, The Sublime, and the Picturesque in Eighteenth-Century British Aesthetic Theory* (Carbondale, Ill., 1957), *passim*.

At first he had shrugged off the scene as a mere product of the
"most capricious mood" of "Nature." But when he looked over
at Vesuvius and began to associate freely, projecting his thoughts
into the future, he saw in panorama "a variety of beautiful towns
and villages, round the base of the mountain, thoughtless of the
impending ruin that daily threatens them." Now Brydone began
to find in the scene an emblem of a considerably larger stretch of
the imagination. It was, he explained, volcanic fire itself which
was responsible for the fertility of the Neapolitan soil.

> It is strange you will say, that Nature should make use of the same
> agent to create as to destroy; and that what has only been looked
> upon as the consumer of countries, is in fact the very power that
> produces them. Indeed, this part of our earth seems already to have
> undergone the sentence pronounced upon the whole of it; but like
> the phoenix, has risen again from its own ashes, in much greater
> beauty and splendour. . . .[36]

The sentimentality of the gothic revival and of the vogue for
ruins was essentially a luxurious awareness of the inevitable
involvement of present and past in one great process of decay.
Seeing picturesquely only intensified this awareness, focusing on
mouldering reminders of past achievement, and made it natural
for Irving to find scenes like the following "most melancholy
yet pleasing":

> Hills covered with the picturesque but mournful Italian pine-groves
> of cypress—among which were seen in partial glimpses the temples
> & statues that decorated the gardens of different villas—they re-
> minded me of the simple yet elegant fanes of antient Rome—and
> resembled faint efforts to imitate her glories. (III, 50–52)

Irving's picturesque feeling for ruins came close to being a
concept, the one intellectual frame he had to put around his
picture of the world. His sense of inevitable decay was to be his
substitute for a theory of history or a philosophy. As he stood
between the conflicting claims of past and present, it suited his

---

[36] Brydone, I, 19–24. Brydone had helped start a new vogue for traveling in
Sicily, off the "beaten track" (I, 1) of the Grand Tour; he was an amateur scientist
as well as a prose stylist whose descriptions of Italian scenery probably influenced
Ann Radcliffe. See Roderick Marshall, *Italy in English Literature, 1755–1815* (New
York, 1934), p. 108.

needs, though it gave no permanent satisfaction. It explained everything and nothing—explained everything by reducing it to nothing. Its annoying aspect, for an American, was that it made one picture ruins in the path of progress. But this was, as we shall see in a later chapter, an American writer's cramp that did not wear off easily. When Irving a few years later packed eleven pages of a commonplace book with extracts from the *Consolations* of Boethius, he was doing more than preparing to mock the cult of sensibility in *Knickerbocker*. The old story of the transience of human existence, the vanity of earthly endeavor, the corruptibility of virtue, the "mutability" of fortune, and the consequent "anxiety" attendant upon prosperity was one that never ceased to move him.[37]

[37] Irving, "Notes taken while preparing Knickerbocker, 1807–8," manuscript in Houghton Library, Harvard University.

II

Logocracy in America

THE four years following Irving's return from Europe in
March, 1806, offer abundant evidence of the "impossible
flow of spirits that often went beyond my strength" that he later
said characterized his youth.[1] A variety of endeavors, business,
social, and literary, made this the most active era of his life—
even if some of his socializing appeared to be little more than
cultivated idling. Though "a very heedless student," he finished
his training with Judge Hoffman, took the bar examination in
November, 1806, and passed, "more through courtesy than
desert, for I scarcely answered a single question correctly; but
the examiners were prepossessed in my favour."[2] He then began
a partnership at law with his brother John.

Lack of success here partly explains the amplitude of his
social and literary life. Not that official working hours were
spent only in waiting for clients. He sometimes traveled as a business agent for members of the family, to Montreal, for instance,
to look after a land speculation for one of his brothers. He
served as a minor aide on Aaron Burr's legal staff in Richmond
during the trial for treason. Law and business connections drew
him occasionally into politicking. But there was still extra time
for fraternizing with his brothers and several other young business and professional men about town (including Brevoort and
Paulding) who had begun to call themselves the "Lads of Kil-
kenny" and had got into the habit of gathering at a summerhouse
in suburban New Jersey donated to the group by Gouverneur

[1] "Manuscript Fragment," STW, II, 255.
[2] *Ibid.*, p. 256.

44

Kemble. There was time also to plan *Salmagundi* with brother William, Paulding, and the publisher David Longworth. Irving's part in the success of *Salmagundi* would seem in itself to represent the better part of a year's work.

There is some poetic justice in the close juxtaposition of his first trip abroad and the final successful establishment in the United States in *Salmagundi* of a separate periodical publication—not simply an epistolary essay series in a newspaper or magazine—more or less in the tradition of the *Spectator* papers. Having consorted with European aristocracy and gentry, Irving was quite willing, at least up to a certain point, to lord it in print over what passed locally for fashionable society. Yet, like *Oldstyle*, *Salmagundi* has more than a single cutting edge.

There was a precedent in some of the British descendants of the *Spectator* for making fun of the didactic intention behind the periodical essay.[3] But *Salmagundi* pushes the tendency of self-mockery to the point of explicitly defying its readers to make sense of the contents. On the one hand, it holds out the most specific offers: "parents shall be taught how to govern children, girls how to get husbands, and old maids to do without them" (p. 23). But with the other hand, it, in effect, slaps the reader in the face:

> We *care* not what the public think of us, and we suspect before we reach the tenth number they will not *know* what to think of us. In two words, we write for no other earthly purpose but to please ourselves—and this we shall be sure of doing, for we are all three of us determined beforehand to be pleased with what we write. (pp. 17–18)

Literary historians and anthologists still refuse to acknowledge the pervasiveness of parody in *Salmagundi*. Its resemblances to British periodicals—the device, for instance, of the fictitious editors who form a club and talk about their imaginary friends and relatives—are a temptation to see Paulding and the Irvings largely in the shadow of Addison and Steele and their successors. But one must not overlook the fact that the very format of the magazine was designed to remind readers of its ancestry. The

---

[3] See in particular Edward Moore's *World* (1753–56), No. 1.

intention was partly parody and partly to make clear from the beginning the spirit in which *Salmagundi* was conceived. Each number carried the subtitle "The Whim-Whams and Opinions of Launcelot Langstaff, Esq., and Others," and the first number promised to give a bit of everything, including " 'the life and amours of mine Uncle John' " (p. 15). These are surely allusions to (not plagiarisms from) *Life and Opinions of Tristram Shandy* and from a work only recently published and very much in the tradition of Sterne, Isaac D'Israeli's *Flim-Flams! or, The Life and Errors of My Uncle, and the Amours of My Aunt.*[4] But the most obvious indication of the intention of *Salmagundi* occurs in the nonsense inscription that the authors printed on the cover of each issue. It begins, "In hoc est hoax," and is signed "Psalmanazar."[5]

Some of Irving's contemporaries missed the tone. Joseph Dennie, for instance, even while taking notice of the ludicrousness of the rubric on the cover, was able to assert that *Salmagundi*'s "design," like that of the *Spectator*, was "to mend the morals, correct the manners, and improve the taste of the age."[6] The British *Monthly Review* in 1811 caught "the general habits of burlesque, observable throughout these volumes," only to complain about them and lament the dearth of "moral reflections and instructive lessons" after the fashion of the British essayists. Addison's "classical taste," the *Monthly* suggested, "if it had

[4] London, 1805.

[5] The name of an early eighteenth-century Frenchman who masqueraded as a Korean. *Salmagundi*'s first critic, Thomas Green Fessenden, in 1807 attacked it as derivative, charging that Launcelot Langstaff was "a vile daub of a caricature of 'Isaac Bickerstaff,' " that "Will Honeycomb sat for 'Anthony Evergreen,' " and that "Will Wizard's original may be found in the British classics." Ironically, Fessenden himself was writing in the *Weekly Inspector* under the name of Dr. Caustic, obviously derived from a colonel of the same name in Mackenzie's *Lounger* (1785–87). See *SAL*, pp. 67–70, 84–95, and notes. Fessenden took "Whim-Whams" as a steal. See *SAL*, pp. 69, 86, and notes. And later John Neal helped mislead readers by picking up the same charges and dismissing *Salmagundi* as little more than a parcel of clever plagiarisms. Osborne's dissertation, "Irving's Development" (University of North Carolina, 1947), stresses the element of parody in *Salmagundi* (p. 116).

[6] *Port Folio*, New Series, III (March, 1807), 178.

been made an object of imitation by the authors . . . would have prevented many of the errors into which they have fallen."[7]

Parody of the tradition was not the sole, or perhaps even the primary, motive behind *Salmagundi*. But criticism of the age was not offered with the hope that it would be socially usable. Before they were finished the authors managed to make the periodical essay look like the product of a pathetically naïve assumption that mankind can be made to listen to reason and thereby improved.

> I expected [says one of the pseudoeditors] long ere this to have seen a complete reformation in manners and morals, achieved by our united efforts. . . . Much does it grieve me to confess, that after all our lectures, precepts, and excellent admonitions, the people of New York are nearly as much given to backsliding and ill-nature as ever; they are just as much abandoned to dancing, and tea-drinking; and as to scandal. . . . (pp. 267–68)

The magazine hardly exaggerates when it makes the half-regretful declaration that it belongs to an "odd, singular, and indescribable age—which is neither the age of gold, silver, iron, brass, chivalry or *pills*." In such an age, "a grave writer" using "the heavy artillery of moral reasoning" would be "laughed at for his pains." Thus his only recourse is to "a little well-applied ridicule" (p. 271).

Salmagundi on the whole lacks the warm glow of the instinct for companionship which in *Tristram Shandy* binds human beings together and compensates for the variable humors which make man incapable of understanding himself or his kind intellectually. As Langstaff's venting his spleen on Dabble suggests, Paulding and the Irvings have obligations to Swift as well as to Sterne. Indeed, the following passage implores the reader to see one:

> To be concise: our great men are those who are most expert at crawling on all fours, and have the happiest faculty of dragging and winding themselves along in the dirt. This may seem a paradox to many of my readers, who, with great good nature be it hinted, are

---

[7] LXV, 418–23. "The Style of [Johnson] we certainly would not *as yet* recommend to the study of American writers: since nothing but a correctly classical taste can ensure a judicious imitation of Johnson. . . ."

too stupid to look beyond the mere surface of our invaluable writings; and often pass over the knowing allusions, and poignant meaning, that is slily couching beneath. It is for the benefit of such helpless ignorants, who have no other creed but the opinion of the mob, that I shall trace, as far as it is possible to follow him in his progress from insignificance—the rise, progress, and completion of a LITTLE GREAT MAN.[8] (pp. 309–10)

The worthies "expert at crawling on all fours" obviously derive from the floor-licking sycophants in Book III of *Gulliver's Travels,* as, a little earlier, a French courtier "who can most dexterously flourish his heels above his head" is a descendant of the Lilliputian ministerial gymnasts. Langstaff goes on to make "the candidate for greatness" a virtual Yahoo: like maggots "hatched from the dirt," he "labors" in it, "collecting . . . tribute from the dregs and offals of society." And the literary reverberation is made even stronger by the image of purity and dignity used in contrast to the Yahoo-like great man: "The horse, in his native state, is wild, swift, impetuous, full of majesty, and of a most generous spirit" (pp. 309–11).

But there are no Houyhnhnms in New York. *Salmagundi* can make no sustained appeal to reason, common sense, or moderation.

Dabble was . . . very loud in his professions of integrity, incorruptibility, and disinterestedness; words which, from being filtered and refined through newspapers and election handbills have lost their original signification; and in the political dictionary are synonymous with empty pockets, itching palms, and interested ambition. (p. 313)

It is the fate of Langstaff and his colleagues to be writers in an age notorious for its extravagant verbiage. Peter Porcupine

[8] A comparison of Goldsmith's essay on "little great men" (*Citizen of the World,* Letter LXXIV) and "On Greatness" is a measure of the stridency of *Salmagundi.* Evidence indicates that there was collaboration, at least between Paulding and Washington Irving, on most of the prose pieces—what one wrote initially the other usually revised. Opinions differ as to the primary responsibility for specific items. No one, however, denies that Irving had a large share in the more splenetic sections. See PMI, I, 163–220, *passim*; STW, II, 271–73; William R. Langfeld and Philip C. Blackburn, *Washington Irving, A Bibliography* (New York, 1933), p. 10; Amos L. Herold, *James Kirke Paulding* (New York, 1926), pp. 34–35; Osborne, pp. 124–63, *passim.*

(William Cobbett) on the French Revolution in 1798 is a good example of the supercharged hyperbole which, spewed out in lip service to republican dogma, continually beclouded basic issues:

> When Ami mounted the walls of the Bastille, I had figured to myself the shades of patriots long departed, the Bruti and Sidneys, and all the spirits of the illustrious dead, hovering in the air over the battlements, and smiling upon the children of liberty in France, and my soul, in imagination, flew to join them. Alas! it was no such heavenly vision! The demons of perdition rode in the air! The towers of the Bastille fell before the incantations of the enemy of man! The shades of the brave and free did not tune their harps to the immortal song of liberty! The spirits of the abyss discordantly howled the dirge of the human race.[9]

Inflated rhetoric was only one of the faults of contemporary political journalism. Hugh Henry Brackenridge in *Modern Chivalry* was forced to resort to strong and coarse irony in attacking Cobbett's *Porcupine Gazette* as a vehicle of politically inspired billingsgate and personal abuse. And *Porcupine* was essentially no different from many other newspapers. This was tacitly admitted by Brackenridge, who complained of the countless "volumes of scurrility" being inked by an "abominably gross" American press.[10] Thus *Salmagundi*, in revulsion against various abuses of language, labels contemporary newspaper editors "SLANG-WHANGERS" and redefines the United States as a "LOGOCRACY," or government of words.[11] Yet to a degree this vituperation is itself a surrender to the forces working to debase language.

---

[9] William Cobbett, *Porcupine's Works* (London, 1801), VIII, 24–25.

[10] *Modern Chivalry* (1804), Part II, chap. iv.

[11] The following passage from *Knickerbocker*, not included in the final revised edition (cf. Irving, *Works*, I [New York, 1863], 339) in the wake of Irving's own diplomatic tour of duty as United States Minister to Spain, is a further example of his impatience with political clichés:

. . . I cannot possibly pronounce, what was the tenor of governor Stuyvesant's speech. Whether he with maiden coyness hinted to his hearers that "there was a speck of war in the horison;"—that it would be necessary to resort to the "unprofitable trial of which could do each other the most harm," or any other delicate construction of language, whereby the odious subject of war, is handled so fastidiously and modestly by modern statesmen; as a gentleman volunteer handles his filthy salt-petre weapons with gloves, lest he should soil his dainty fingers. (*K*, pp. 313–14)

The confusion, however, went beyond politics. An essay which demonstrates "style" to be little more than a word, something proclaimed by a person temporarily in a position to make his or her voice heard, illustrates the quagmire of relativity in which the magazine is stuck. "Style . . . consists in certain fashions, or certain eccentricities, or certain manners of certain people, in certain situations, and possessed of a certain share of fashion or importance" (p. 161). After all, Dabble's efforts to win favor are analogous to the social exhibitionism at the Ballston Spa. The interest of everyone—authors included—in being in fashion, in style, creates a universe of odd bedfellows. *Salmagundi* thus tends to become a verbal stew, as though the "editors" were determined to prove that they live in a logocracy simply by taking pleasure in the sounds of their own words. Seized in one section, for instance, "with a violent fit of the *pun mania*" (p. 203), and generally entranced with the onomatopoetic possibilities in bizarre canting names, they seem to be saying that words can be delightful to play with but that one must be careful when one attempts to make them mean something.[12]

Inevitably in the general scramble—"salmagundi" means hash—points of view are radically shifted. In an essay such as "On Greatness" the pseudoeditor speaks on the whole directly as a critic, as a superior who passes judgment. But the delight that Anthony Evergreen finds in a "New York Assembly" remains largely ironic, and one is not sure to whom to attribute the irony,

---

[12] "I cannot speak two sentences but that I see a pun gathering in the faces of my hearers," Irving wrote from Philadelphia. "I absolutely shudder with horror—think what miseries I suffer—me to whom a pun is an abomination. . . ." Letter to Mary Fairlie, 17 March 1807, PMI, I, 180–81. *Salmagundi* made the same complaint about Philadelphia and then proceeded to entertain its readers with Philadelphia puns (p. 203). The pun was a part of the Knickerbocker manner. Passages like the following (*Letters from Washington Irving to Mrs. William Renwick, and to her Son, James Renwick* [privately printed, n.p., n.d.; copy in New York Public Library], pp. 10–11) are not uncommon in Irving's correspondence:

. . . in the midst of my musings I stumbled over some thing, which on getting up & rubbing my eyes I found to be a little presbyterian church, where a young apostle by the name of Gunn (an old acquaintance of mine) kept up a constant firing upon the world, the flesh & the devil. I was seized with a great curiosity to see how Master Gunn, who I had not known since he was as big as a pocket pistol, discharged his duties. . . .

to Evergreen or the authors. While his glowing descriptions of ladies' gowns and French dances satirize the vulgarity of the gathering, some of the vulgarity rubs off on Evergreen. And Will Wizard on at least one occasion is vulgarized from head to toe, throwing Evergreen into "absolute dismay." Calling on him before a ball, Evergreen discovers that his friend's hair is "frizzled out at the ears"; his wig ends in a "long plaited club," which swings "gracefully from shoulder to shoulder, describing a pleasing semicircle of powder and pomatum." He has a "claret-colored" coat with "gilt buttons," "white casimere small-clothes," "sky-blue silk stockings," a waistcoat of "China silk" decorated with "roses and tulips," and a "silver-sprigged Dickey." At the ball he takes "his stand in the middle of the floor, playing with his great steel watch-chain; and looking around . . . with the air of a man 'who has seen d----d finer things in his time.'" Finally, to Evergreen's horror, Wizard takes out "his villainous old japanned tobacco-box, ornamented with a bottle, a pipe, and a scurvy motto, and help[s] himself to a quid in face of all the company" (pp. 107–9).

Wizard is introduced in the first number as a person who "has improved his taste by a long residence abroad," a characterization which presumably buttresses *Salmagundi*'s "authority" in speaking out on matters of style. Foreign travel has served him as a substitute for "an education," not at Columbia College, but "at Oxford or Cambridge, or even at Edinburgh or Aberdeen." But as a world traveler, he is more closely associated through overt description with the Orient than with Europe. And the association ironically denies him most of the authority he ought to have: "He has improved his taste . . . at Canton, Calcutta, and the gay and polished court of Hayti" (p. 21). The snobbery implicit here becomes the basis for satirical attacks on New York taste: Will Wizard in one notable passage favorably compares a local fop, Billy Dimple, to Tucky Squash, "the mirror of fashion, the adoration of all the sable fair ones of Hayti." Tucky was a beau in whose perfumed presence the "yellow beauties blushed blue, and the black ones blushed as red as they could, with pleasure" (p. 110). The magazine and its audience were not sophisticated in their racial attitudes. Yet making Haiti, Canton, and Calcutta seats of fashion and culture was also a way of ridiculing appeals to foreign standards. On certain occasions Will Wizard criticizes American styles knowingly, but often he appears merely eccentric, a returned traveler bent on judging Americans by partially inapplicable criteria.

Thus it is hardly surprising to find Wizard usually associated with cockneys. In particular, he is said to have been for a while the "great crony" of one Tom Straddle, who, intriguingly in view of the Irving family business, was a dashing young Englishman "just arrived in an importation of hardware, fresh from the city of Birmingham." In the "manufactories of gimlets, penknives, and pepperboxes" in Birmingham, Straddle had been "a young man of considerable standing," who "sometimes had the honor to hand his master's daughter into a tim-whisky"; he

> had been splashed half-a-dozen times by the carriages of nobility, and had once the superlative felicity of being kicked out of doors by the footman of a noble duke; he could, therefore, talk of nobility and despise the untitled plebeians of America. In short, Straddle was one of those dapper, bustling, florid, round, self-important "*gemmen*" who bounce upon us half beau half button-maker; undertake to give us the true polish of the *bon ton*, and endeavor to inspire us with a proper and dignified contempt of our native country. (pp. 229–31)

Straddle is so extreme that even Wizard apparently has to disown him. Yet how curiously his career parodies Irving's own.

First and last, *Salmagundi* manifests a great deal of interest in travelers and traveling. Much of the concern, complementing the anticockneyism, consists of resentment at the pompous ignorance and flagrant misrepresentations of American life in the works of foreign travelers. "America has had its share of these buzzards," says Langstaff, thanking them ironically for "the variety of particulars" about his native country which would never have been "discovered without their assistance" (p. 71). Their eagerness to find fault is lampooned in passages such as the following one from an item called "Memorandum for a Tour": "negro driver could not write his own name—languishing state of literature in this country; philosophical inquiry . . . why the Americans are so much inferior to the nobility of Cheapside and Shore-ditch, and why they do not eat plum-pudding on Sundays —superfine reflections about anything." The object of this satire, as *Salmagundi*'s note makes clear, is the kind of indictment which "Anacreon" (as the magazine called him) Moore had penned in plaintive verse, lamenting the absence in the United States of a literature commensurate with some of its scenery: nature's Muse, the poet had said, "whispers round," but "the words . . . in the air" are "unheard" and frozen, "Without one breath of soul, divinely strong, / One ray of mind, to thaw them into song" (p. 80).[13]

But often *Salmagundi*'s satire is directed as much at "travel-mongers" in general. Moreover, in the very act of satirizing foreign travelers for trying to read European meanings into America, the magazine is not above exposing the barrenness of certain native scenes and institutions. A remark such as the following on Princeton, "N. B. Students got drunk as usual" (p. 79), reflects on American education as much as on foreign observers.[14] To Isaac Weld, one of the travelers specifically cited in *Salma-*

[13] The lines are from Thomas Moore's "To the Honourable W. R. Spencer," in *Poems Relating to America.* Having come to the United States in the expectation of finding "the elysian Atlantis," Moore had abruptly concluded that freedom here had deteriorated into what was little better than mob rule. In the "dawn of life," he wrote, the nation's "sickly breath / Burns with the taint of empires near their death." The conception of America as an already ruined civilization was one that *Knickerbocker* was soon to entertain, but only half-seriously. It was the unequivocalness of Moore's attitude that was calculated to arouse *Salmagundi*'s ire. Only once in his journey, he claimed, had he found escape from "the Gallic dross" corrupting America. That was among the "sacred few" of Joseph Dennie's circle, whom he had encountered "by Delaware's green banks." Only there in the "enlightened zeal" of the kind of Federalism which, as Henry Adams said (*History of the United States* [New York, 1891], I, 122; IX, 198–99), was committed to judging America by British standards, had Moore discovered a single "stamp of human kind." *Poems Relating to America*, Preface, "To the Lord Viscount Forbes," "To the Honourable W. R. Spencer."

[14] On the whole, *Salmagundi*, stressing the drunkenness and practical joking (a recent fire at the college is interpreted as a student prank at the expense of the professors), bears out the view of Isaac Weld that Princeton was not academically strong. With its library consisting chiefly of old books of theology, it appeared to Weld no better than other institutions of higher education he had seen in America. And like them, "it better deserves the title of a grammar school than a college." *Travels through the States* (London, 1800), I, 259.

gundi's notes (pp. 74, 76), the journey from Philadelphia to New York had been dreary monotony. He complained of the sameness of both the American people, except in the cities, and the landscape. His comment on Brunswick, New Jersey, typifies his responses: the town contained "about two hundred houses"; there was "nothing very deserving of attention in it, excepting it be the very neat and commodious wooden bridge that has been thrown across the Raritan River."[15] Jeremy Cockloft, *Salmagundi*'s patented traveler, makes the journey in the opposite direction, and even if his jottings in part ridicule the traveler who would expect anything more out of the trip, they nonetheless sustain the same impression of flatness: "country finely diversified with sheep and hay-stacks." A typical passage begins by satirizing pedantic traveling—"Bridgetown . . . according to Linkum Fidelius, from *bridge,* a contrivance to get dry shod over a river or brook"—only to turn into a stark comment on the hinterland beyond New York: "and *town,* an appelation given in America to the accidental assemblage of a church, a tavern, and a blacksmith's shop" (pp. 76–79). *Salmagundi* aimed at an urban audience.

The extent to which the foreign view or the foreign standard applied in the United States was a question that *Salmagundi* found it impossible either to answer or to avoid. It was most flagrantly raised in the series of letters to the "editors" from a foreign traveler par excellence, Mustapha Rub-a-Dub Keli Khan, a Tripolitan, prisoner of the United States in the Barbary War, who was on parole in New York. A descendant of Goldsmith's "Citizen of the World," Mustapha presents a point of view which is so alien to the society he is observing that his reports on the most ordinary occurrences in New York make them out to be largely nonsensical. As with so many other devices in *Salmagundi,* Mustapha is used partly to parody a hackneyed convention. In this case it is the Oriental traveler, a throwback to Montesquieu and eighteenth-century *chinoiserie,* who comments with sage irony on western manners. Yet obviously Mustapha also gives

[15] Weld, I, 260.

voice to many of the authors' own attitudes. It is he, for instance, who supplies the term "logocracy."

In all the moil and contradiction it was inevitable that *Salmagundi* would finally make even the New Yorker an alien in New York. This development occurs in Jeremy Cockloft's notes for a tour of the city, which are also in part a parody. Here the object of the satire is a stuffy contemporary guidebook.[16] "The Stranger at Home" shows Cockloft overwhelmed by the task of trying to understand his native city, especially by looking at it in a broad perspective. It works up to a veritable "salmagundi" of abstract ideas and specific feelings, of conflicting attitudes toward past and present, toward Europe and the United States. Instead of finding a larger significance for New York, Cockloft succeeds only in belittling the rest of the world:

> Dey street—ancient Dutch name of it, signifying murderers' valley, formerly the site of a great peach orchard; my grandmother's history of the famous Peach war—arose from an Indian stealing peaches out of this orchard; good cause as need be for a war; just as good as the balance of power. Anecdote of war between two Italian states about a bucket; introduce some capital new truisms about the folly of mankind, the ambition of kings, potentates, and princes; particularly Alexander, Caesar, Charles the XIIth, Napoleon, little King Pepin, and the great Charlemagne.—Conclude with an exhortation to the present race of sovereigns to keep the king's peace, and abstain from all those deadly quarrels which produce battle, murder, and sudden death:—mem.—ran my nose against a lamp-post—conclude in great dudgeon. (p. 245)

While climbing Mt. Aetna and indulging in what Cockloft would have called "superfine reflections"—comparing the seething crater and the placid slope of the volcano to hell and paradise —Patrick Brydone had not run into a lamppost, but he did sprain an ankle, whereupon with worldly composure he made the ultimate and routine concession: "how vain are all our reasonings!"[17] By contrast, Cockloft's "great dudgeon," refusing as it does to admit that an irrational world does not make final sense, further exemplifies the provincial dilemma.

[16] Dr. Samuel Mitchill's *The Picture of New York* (New York, 1807). See *SAL*, p. 237.
[17] *A Tour through Sicily and Malta* (London, 1776), I, 217–18.

   To accept *Salmagundi* with all its contradictions is to respond
to the cultural frustration which it represents and which is its
abiding significance. Disregarding the interplay of burlesque
and self-mockery, the usual reader has sought a more genteel
Irving than *Salmagundi* will validly yield. The tradition is an
old one, and a good example of an American need for prettying
up the face of native culture. Dana was already at work in
1819,[18] reading the magazine in the light of *The Sketch Book*
(which was to become a standard distraction), although the latter
work was still only partly published. He found the style relatively proper and admired in *Salmagundi* the grace, charm, wit,
gentle good-naturedness, and touching pathos mixed with humor
—precisely the qualities which stood out for him in *The Sketch
Book*. Perceptive as he sometimes is, Dana gives only a partial
response or several loosely related, and to a degree contradictory,
partial responses. He praises Irving for never overdrawing his
characters, for never pushing their eccentricities beyond "prob-
ability"; in the next breath he revels in the exaggerated and
somewhat "forced" humor of "Style, at Ballston." And he becomes sentimental over the story of "The Little Man in Black,"
finding the death of that outcast antiquarian "sublime" in spite
of his "turning out to be the last descendant of the renowned
Linkum Fidelius," another of *Salmagundi*'s burlesques of the
eighteenth-century stereotype of the wise Oriental. Linkum is
the personification of extreme pedantry; he is repeatedly lauded
for such achievements as writing famous but unheard-of books.
To the British reviewer of 1811 the name "Linkum Fidelius" is
a "miserable latinization of a piece of English buffoonery."[19] But
Dana sees the connection between Linkum and the little man in
black as a way of leaving the reader in "a most humorous
sadness."
   Similarly, Dana appreciates the "wit, drollery, oddity" of
Will Wizard without seeing that his "ludicrous uncouthness"
virtually turns *Salmagundi* into a fiction about a set of pseudo-
sophisticates who attempt to make themselves custodians of

---

[18] *N. A. Review*, IX, 334–45.
[19] *Monthly Review*, LXV, 419–20.

fashion in a raw society. Fun poked at Wizard is, for Dana, only a part of the general "good feeling," that tag phrase for Irving's humor which developed out of nineteenth-century America's need for a culture of comfort and consolation. His later work finally did degenerate into the mere "good feeling" that his public demanded. But Dana can assert the generally "perfect" good-naturedness of Irving's early work only in the teeth of a persistent recognition that in Boston, or anywhere else but New York, the satire of *Salmagundi* would not have been tolerated. He even winces in print for the parvenu New Yorkers who must read about themselves in *Salmagundi:*

> For their own sakes, to be sure, they would say nothing about style or the Giblets,[20] or if they did, with a forced smile and awkward compliment. But then it is so convenient, when one meets with any thing that comes home to him and makes him uneasy, to say, "why, this is very well," and then turn to a part he cares nothing about, be highly offended, and end with declaring, that "such things will never do."[21]

Dana's mixed reaction to *Salmagundi* is typical of the confusions one encounters generally in discussions of Irving's early work, and because in our own day the misunderstanding is so closely related to the question of Irving's political allegiances, these need to be discussed. As was suggested in the Introduction, Irving's conservatism was of a not very stable variety. One can begin by referring to the foremost authority on Irving, Stanley T. Williams, whose biography contains material that seriously qualifies, if indeed it does not render altogether untenable, Canby's conception of Irving as an elegant Federalist. Williams stressed, for instance, Irving's lifelong interest in political preferment: "he was no tyro in the art of progress through favor." And the fascination that, as Williams showed, financial investment and speculation had for Irving gives some bourgeois shading to Canby's portrait of the aristocrat. But on this matter one cannot follow Williams very far without running into inconsistencies reminiscent of Dana's. Far from rejecting the Parrington-Canby view of Irving, he specifically endorsed it; unable to for-

[20] A family who have "worked themselves into notice." *SAL*, p. 165.
[21] *N. A. Review*, IX, 339, 343.

give him for not being a liberal, he denigrated him as a romantic escapist and hero-worshiper, dazzled by celebrities and high style and utterly incapable of understanding the dynamics of politics.[22]

It is true, of course, that Irving makes fun of Tom Paine and of Tom Jefferson's red hair and red smallclothes. He uses the philosopher-president's "projects" and speculative ingenuity as obvious targets for satire in the well-established tradition of antirationalism which extends back through Book III of *Gulliver's Travels*. But one must remember how willing Irving was to satirize vested interests—in the feeble and foolish characters, for example, who, as we have seen, personify adherence to time-worn traditions. He poked fun at the Dutch aristocracy of New York in *Knickerbocker* in the same way that he helped demolish the pretensions of the city's polite society in *Salmagundi*.

And if his humor sometimes reduces American politics to the activity of querulous mobs, it does so no more than that of so good a Republican as Hugh Brackenridge. *Salmagundi* is often anti-Republican in feeling, but in working to a frenzy against political factionalism it refuses much of the time to see essential differences between Federalists and Republicans. When it ful-minates against demagoguery, it realizes that both parties grub for votes among the rabble. Critical as he was of Irving's con-servatism, even Williams admitted that in collaborating with two Republicans, his brother and Paulding, Irving, though tech-nically a Federalist, "laughed heartily at the arrogant illusions of his own party."[23]

Though he was in and out of politics all his life, Irving's political connections were, variously, Republican, Federalist, Democratic, and Whig. His commitment at a particular moment was not always strong enough to keep his bent for self-satire in check. Furthermore, in his daily life one discerns not a genteel diffidence but a sometimes hectic involvement in politics. The

[22] STW, I, 93–96, 403. Earlier, however, Williams participated in a more appre-ciative response to Irving's allegedly aristocratic stance. See below, n. 36.

[23] STW, I, 95. For a similar comment on *Knickerbocker*, see the Introduction by Williams and Tremaine McDowell to *K*, p. lxxii.

Morning Chronicle, Peter Irving's paper, had been a blatant mouthpiece for Burrite Republicanism at the time of *Oldstyle.* Then in 1804, already branded "Dr. Squintum" and "Citizen Pestle and Mortar" by rival journalists,[24] Peter had taken on the editorship of the more notorious *Corrector,* also a Burrite organ, to which Washington, eager for publication, was prevailed upon to make anonymous contributions. "The severest sarcasm . . . came from [Washington's] pen," his nephew later explained: " 'They would tell me what to write . . . and then I'd dash away.' "[25] Nor was he above "dabbling" in politics at the ward level himself. Only a short time before "On Greatness" he had electioneered for the Federalists; apparently, like Timothy Dabble, he helped to bring "more negroes to the polls" and probably knew "where votes could be bought for beer."[26]

In New York in 1807 it was not always easy to tell a Federalist from a Republican. On both sides politics was a matter of somewhat tainted alliances, of factions dominated by powerful families struggling for economic advantage at the polls and in the legislative councils. In New York, said Henry Adams, "society, in spite of its aristocratic mixture, was democratic by instinct; and in abandoning its alliance with New England in order to . . . elect Jefferson . . . it pledged itself to principles of no kind. . . . The political partnership between the New York Republicans and the Virginians was from the first a business firm. . . ."[27] Aaron Burr's failure in his bid for the presidency in 1800 cost him control of patronage in New York, and in spite of his great personal popularity for helping to engineer the Republican victory, he found it politically expedient to ally himself with the opposition. In 1804 he ran for governor in New York as a Federalist, splitting the party, whose leaders after 1800, "sulking in defeat," had not kept "firm in doctrine."[28]

[24] Samuel H. Wandell and Meade Minnegerode, *Aaron Burr* (New York, 1927), I, 240. Peter Irving was originally a medical doctor.
[25] Pierre M. Irving, quoted in STW, I, 35.
[26] *SAL,* p. 315; cf. Irving to Mary Fairlie, 2 May 1807, in PMI, I, 187–88.
[27] *History,* I, 112–14.
[28] Dixon Ryan Fox, *The Decline of the Aristocracy in the Politics of New York* (New York, 1919), p. 61.

Irving had friends and relatives in almost every faction. If
he wrote in 1804 for Peter's *Corrector*, which supported Burr as
a Federalist, a short time after the election, on hearing of Hamilton's death in the duel with Burr, he professed himself "a
partisan" of the former.[29] His law clerkship under the Federalist
Hoffman was undoubtedly a factor in his politics. He had
switched to Judge Hoffman's office in 1802, when Brockholst
Livingston, the Republican with whom he had been reading, was
appointed to the Supreme Court of New York. Soon after passing the bar examination in 1806 he was writing Hoffman, asking
for a " 'crumb from the table' " of patronage:

> I learn with pleasure, that the council of appointment are decidedly
> Lewisite. As there will, doubtless, be a liberal dispensation of loaves
> and fishes on the occasion, I would humbly put up my feeble voice
> in the general application. Will you be kind enough to speak a
> "word in season" for me.[30]

Who were the Lewisites? Three years after his election as a Republican with the help of Hamilton, Governor Morgan Lewis,
a member of the Livingston clan, was still on good terms with
those Federalists who "were convinced that their policy of
opportunism must be continued." In the meantime he had been
read out of the Republican Party by the Clinton faction. The
followers of the Livingstons were now called "Lewisites" or
"Quids."[31]

The situation was Lilliputian or worse. At least this was the
way Irving was to see it in the *History of New York*, where, in
the course of talking about politics in seventeenth-century New
Netherlands, he found pretexts for alluding to his own time. Even
when toned down in a revised edition, this section of the book
brings out the pettiness of New York politics as it playfully attributes "the rise of parties" in the New Netherlands to a "fatal
schism in tobacco pipes" during Governor Kieft's tenure. A
"kind of aristocracy" (of "burghers who had made their fortunes
and could afford to be lazy") comprised the *"Long Pipes."* The

---

[29] Letter to William Irving, December 1804, PMI, I, 91.
[30] 2 February 1807, PMI, I, 174–75.
[31] Fox, pp. 69–72.

"plebeian" party were the *"Short Pipes."* And between them arose a third party of *"Quids"* formed by "the descendants of Robert Chewit." But the original edition of 1809 speaks scathingly of the spirit of factionalism which in almost every age for insufficient reasons divides men into violently opposing parties like Swift's Big-Endians and Little-Endians. Irving specifically mentions the Jacobin and anti-Jacobin, Federalist and anti-Federalist parties and then goes on to characterize "a certain mongrel party called *Quid*; which seems to have been engendered between the two last mentioned parties, as a mule is produced between an horse and an ass—and like a mule it seems incapable of procreation, fit only for humble drudgery . . . and to be cudgelled for its pains."[32] In 1809 Irving's designations for the original parties in New Netherlands were not Long and Short Pipes but *"Square head"* and *"Platter breech,"* that is, those deficient in "pericranium" and those deficient in sound *"bottom,"* or the brainless and the gutless. Knickerbocker defies "all the politicians of this great city to shew me where any two parties of the present day, have split upon more important and fundamental points" (*K*, p. 224).

Disappointment at the frenzy of partisan politics in the United States, far from being a monopoly of arch-Federalists like Joseph Dennie or Timothy Dwight and the other Hartford Wits, was fairly widespread among American intellectuals. Freedom from Great Britain and a guarantee of republican institutions had only whetted the national appetite for politics. The new Constitution, whatever its virtues, was not a foolproof system for insuring gov-

[32] *K*, p. 223, and *Knickerbocker's History of New York* (New York, 1863), p. 242. The Quids, as presented in the final revised edition, have been interpreted—apparently under the influence of the stereotype of the Federalist Irving—as "the mob who follow blindly" one party after another. *Washington Irving: Representative Selections*, ed. Henry A. Pochmann (New York, 1934), p. 382. Neither history nor the original edition, however, supports the interpretation. Irving in his own time may have come close to being a Quid. P. K. McCarter argues that Irving probably voted for Lewis in the election of 1807 because there was no Federalist candidate for governor. "The Literary, Political, and Social Theories of Washington Irving" (unpublished Ph.D. dissertation, University of Wisconsin, 1939), pp. 283–85. What is possibly relevant to the satire also, though of less immediate significance to Irving, the followers of John Randolph after his break with Jefferson (1806) were likewise called Quids.

ernment by disinterested officials elected for their ability and
training rather than for their identification with a particular interest group or political objective. The unhappy realization that
politicking was inevitable and was going to be intense even in the
United States was as much a factor in Brackenridge's *Modern
Chivalry* and Cooper's *The Pioneers* as in *Salmagundi* or *Knickerbocker*.

The high Federalist was apt to equate politicking with law-
lessness or subversion, but to Irving the illusion or pretense that
any political activity was a product of purely disinterested
patriotism was a prime object of ridicule. He would not have
been taken in by the claim of the Hartford Wits, who are perhaps
a fair example of aristocratic Federalism, that they themselves
were above partisanship or, as it was derisively termed, factionalism. Much as he fretted about the vehemence of party
conflicts, he could have seen only a greater evil in the Wits' ideal
of good citizenship as being, for most men, quiescence—resignation of the control of government to the wealthy, the wellborn,
and the highly educated. The Wits presented themselves and
their adherents in all earnestness as the only upholders of religion and morality, law and order. But Irving never put on the
cloak of sanctity. He was not, as we have seen, one who always
identified liberty with law. And one can only see him as im-
patient of any demand that automatic deference be paid to
authority.

The spectacle of a philosopher-president confronting political
actuality and trying to square practice with theory is perfectly
consistent with the basic irony of *Salmagundi* and *Knickerbocker*,
which swamps common sense in whim and illusion. Henry Adams
long ago pointed out, however, that the satire against Jefferson
in the guise of Governor Kieft in *Knickerbocker* is far less severe
than the standard Federalist attack on the Republicans.[33]   A
vicious invective was the practice of political satirists such as
those at Hartford, who were capable of assaulting real individuals with more savagery than that with which *Salmagundi* had

[33] IX, 210–11. See also Williams and McDowell, Introduction to *K.*, p. lxxii.

castigated Timothy Dabble.[34] But although Irving indicted such Republican policies as economizing in government—the maintenance of what *Salmagundi* called a mere *"river fleet . . .* to protect the hay-vessels" (p. 77)—he vilified neither Jefferson nor the party. He refrained from attacks on the personal integrity of political opponents.

Henry Adams' label for Irving is "Burrite," which, if technically incorrect in 1809, may be more indicative of Irving's actual political stance than "Federalist." As Williams pointed out, Irving had none of the "fear, experienced by orthodox and even by liberal men in New York, of a nation without a puissant, central government, a rudderless ship, piloted by French radicalism and mobocracy. He did not share the 'Hartford Wits' ' terror of Jacobinism."[35]

Irving's Federalism seems more a matter of economics than of class. Williams condemned him for failing to understand Jefferson's "determination that Americans should really obtain the rewards of the Revolution," and indeed for failing to foresee in 1807 the downfall of Federalism and the ultimate triumph of Jacksonian democracy.[36] Yet it was precisely in 1806 and 1807 that the acts and policies of the Jefferson administration began to give most annoyance to certain political elements in New York and to provide a substantial reason for working hopefully for the Federalist cause. Though it was actually in effect only in November and December, the Non-Importation Act of April, 1806, during much of that year threatened to cut off the supply from

[34] Lemuel Hopkins of Hartford in 1795 attacked Brockholst Livingston, an opponent of the Jay Treaty, as one who would "cheat, or break" or use "every trick of knavery" to advance a political measure calculated to profit him financially. He characterized the whole Livingston clan as "sunk" in "filth" and "enslav'd" by "vice and infamy." Their followers, Hopkins claimed, were chiefly Irish pickpockets and hen-roost robbers. See [Hopkins], *The Democriatad* (Philadelphia, 1795), pp. 12–13. This poem is No. 18 of "The Echo" (chiefly the work of Richard Alsop and Theodore Dwight), though the lines on the Livingstons are omitted in *The Echo, with Other Poems* (n.p., 1807).

[35] STW, I, 93.

[36] *Ibid.* See, however, Williams and McDowell's earlier sympathetic presentation of Irving's response to the Jeffersonian period. Introduction to *K*, pp. lxx–lxxi. They see him as "aristocratic by nature" and disgusted with the "cheap machinery of American politics."

England of the sort of goods in which the Irving family business traded. Throughout most of 1807, during the trial for treason, Jefferson hounded Aaron Burr in spite of scanty evidence against him, spurring on government attorneys and capitalizing at every opportunity on the publicity value of the case. And at the end of the year he ordered the embargo, which "so stiffened the resistance of the business interests that the Federalist party in New York, as elsewhere, shook off its lethargy of hopelessness."[37] In the temporary resurgence that followed, it sought to broaden its base and to compete with Tammany for the votes of laborers and small freeholders.

Although Irving declared himself "opposed . . . in political principles" to Burr,[38] he sympathized with him at Richmond, and his sense that Burr was being exploited for political advantage may well have had something to do with the vehemence of *Salmagundi*'s opposition to the Republicans. On the whole, however, the anti-Jeffersonianism of *Salmagundi* and *Knickerbocker* seems a protest against the policy of neutrality, which extended, except for brief interludes, back to Washington's administration, against the Republican willingness to sacrifice American commerce and preserve the peace (or "fight" by proclamation, as Irving's satire has it), rather than to build a strong navy to protect American shipping and neutral rights on the high seas. *Knickerbocker* is a product of a time when, with the harbor "full of shipping . . . the masts stood gaunt and bare of sails. . . . Of all the carts that had rattled through the streets, scarcely one in ten was now offered for employment. . . ."[39]

---

[37] Fox, p. 88.

[38] Letter to Maria Fenno Hoffman, 1807, PMI, I, 191.

[39] Fox, p. 102. Edwin A. Greenlaw makes this point very effectively in "Washington Irving's Comedy of Politics," *Texas Review*, I (April, 1916), 291–306. For further discussions of the political satire in *Knickerbocker* see Tremaine McDowell, "General James Wilkinson in the Knickerbocker *History of New York*," *Modern Language Notes*, XLI (June, 1926), 353–59.

III

The Fiction of History

THE key to Irving's achievement in the *History of New York* is the ingenious device of Diedrich Knickerbocker, who manages to sound at once like Sterne's first person narrators, and Fielding's cultivated omniscience going berserk in mazes of irony. Knickerbocker is totally eccentric and solitary, even more "extravagant" (in the root sense) than Tristram Shandy, Yorick, or the bachelors in *Salmagundi*. He is, from the Addisonian point of view, a candidate for Bedlam, though quite harmless and capable of serious insight and reflection in the midst of his grossest misunderstandings. At one moment he is guilty of utterances so absurd that we must conclude that they express exactly the opposite of Irving's view; at the next, he is ready with opinions that simply cannot be taken ironically. As one reviewer put it, somewhat too solemnly but with general accuracy, Irving "contrived, with singular skill and effect, to intermingle, with his burlesque narrative, the most profound reflections . . . and to speak out, from behind his mask, not a few . . . harsh and unpalatable truths. . . ."[1] Knickerbocker moves back and forth in time at will, contradicts himself within a page, and loses himself in diatribes that are completely off the subject, all of which allows Irving to shift tone abruptly and to wax ludicrous and serious almost simultaneously without seeming to violate the character of his narrator. The strategy of using a spokesman as zany as Knickerbocker justifies a conglomerate technique and saves Irving from embarrassment over his borrowings from satirists as far back as Rabelais and Cervantes.

---

[1] *Edinburgh Magazine and Literary Miscellany*, VII (December, 1820), 544.

More self-conscious than Jeremy Cockloft, Knickerbocker calls himself "a stranger and a weary pilgrim" in his "native land" (*K*, p. 106).[2] His obsession with ruins turns him into a kind of tourist with an eye for the picturesque. He laments, for instance, that the lack of reliable historians leaves to "the rubbish of years" so many of the "feeble memorials" of the empires of the Old World. But of course there is irony in his eagerness to save the early history of New York from "entering into the widespread, insatiable maw of oblivion," for he proves that he is not the impartial, objective historian he often claims to be; his exaggerated fears about losing the past expose at the very beginning his tendency to overestimate his own importance. He wishes that as a "modern historian" he were not "doomed irrevocably to . . . dull matter of fact." If only he were a poet, entitled to "wander amid . . . mouldering arches and broken columns, and indulge the visionary flights of his fancy" (pp. 11–13).

Knickerbocker is fond of talking about the "classic days of our forefathers" (p. 148). But the era of Dutch supremacy in New York was not "classic." Knickerbocker's need to think it so primarily reflects his dissatisfaction with the present, which he considers an "age of skepticism," a "degenerate age" (pp. 42, 106). Private resentment animates such remarks: Knickerbocker belongs to a nationality that has been politically disinherited in New York. Finding in the present nothing in which to believe, he has given his life to creating a largely mythical past. But, though his inability to refrain from epic, lyric, and elegiac eloquence vitiates his narrative as history, it is precisely what sustains Irving's fiction.

Knickerbocker is often aware of his shortcomings; he openly acknowledges that he is a "sentimental" historian (p. 105). He uses the past as an escape from time and change. Thus even

[2] My discussion of *Knickerbocker* depends for the most part on two editions of the book, primarily on the original of 1809 and to a lesser degree on the final "Author's Revised Edition" of 1848. The former, in the 1927 reprint, is cited as *K* or simply by page number in parenthetical references in the text. Quotations from, or allusions to, the latter, in the 1863 reprint, the first volume in the standard edition of Irving's *Works* (21 vols.; New York: Putnam, 1860–64), are documented only in notes.

before making the adjustments which the ironic narrative renders essential in calculating Irving's own view, one notices an ambivalence in the attitude of the *History of New York* toward its subject. Knickerbocker may long for an heroic past filled with daring explorers and bold warriors, but his vision of eternal bliss is Communipaw, "a small village, pleasantly situated among rural scenery" on the New Jersey shore across the Hudson from New York. Communipaw, even more than Sleepy Hollow, is a village that history has left behind. "As to the honest dutch [sic] burghers . . . , like wise men . . . they never look beyond their pipes, nor trouble their heads about any affairs out of their immediate neighborhood; so that they live in profound and enviable ignorance of all the troubles, anxieties, and revolutions of this distracted planet" (pp. 83–85). Knickerbocker believes, on the whole, that New Amsterdam itself was esentially like Communipaw from its founding through the Golden Age of Wouter Van Twiller, a drowsy town where Dutchmen smoked their pipes, ate heartily, and lived harmoniously with one another because they had not had the misfortune to develop complicated social and political institutions. By contrast, bewildering entanglements of legal and governmental procedures are particularly indicted, not only in the reign of William the Testy, which followed the Golden Age, but also in the post-Revolutionary present. Knickerbocker compares the Dutch of early New Amsterdam with the classical Locrians, who had so few laws and courts "that we scarce hear anything of them throughout the whole Grecian history———for it is well known that none but your unlucky quarrelsome, rantipole nations make any noise in the world" (p. 212).

Knickerbocker longs for greatness but seems afraid of the responsibilities that greatness entails. He would have a civilized society but shrinks from the conflicts through which decent institutions are established and maintained. As he reveals the compulsion of some of his characters to monumentalize themselves for eternity, on occasion the impotence behind his conscious longing for greatness almost turns to rage. Whether he applauds or secretly abhors what he describes we cannot always be sure: his

almost frantic tone at times might imply either. But in the end
Irving's caricature is apt to suggest affinities between whimsy
and monomania, as in the case of one General Von Poffenburgh:
his "martial spirit waxing hot within him," this Dutch commander

> would prudently sally forth into the fields, and lugging out his trusty
> sabre, . . . lay about him most lustily, decapitating cabbages by pla-
> toons—hewing down whole phalanxes of sunflowers, which he termed
> gigantic Swedes; and if peradventure, he espied a colony of honest
> big bellied pumpkins quietly basking themselves in the sun, "ah
> caitiff Yankees," would he roar, "have I caught ye at last!"——so
> saying, with one sweep of his sword, he would cleave the unhappy
> vegetables from their chins to their waistbands. . . .

When he finally returned, with his "choler" to some degree
"allayed," it was "with a full conviction that he was a very
miracle of military prowess" (p. 292).

Knickerbocker thus sometimes shows a deep antipathy to history, and the interinvolvement of his attraction to, and fear of,
memorable historical achievement is a central irony of the book.
He boasts that he aims to produce a "foundation" work, which,
when other scholars add a "noble superstructure" to it, will in-
sure a history of New York as grand as *"Gibbon's Rome,* or
Hume and Smollet's [sic] *England"* (p. 13), but he frequently
shows that he is fearful lest the heroic surfaces of history prove
mere masks concealing a basic destructiveness in human nature.
We are told, for instance, that Peter Stuyvesant "wanted only a
few empires to desolate to have been immortalized as a hero!"
(p. 452). In the light of such an observation, wishing history on
a new nation is invoking on it the curse of human vanity.
Knickerbocker too seems to have been reading Boethius, if indeed he has not been browsing in one of Irving's commonplace
books and improving his sense of man as a vain oddity dominated
by the prevailing superstition of a given time and place, prone
initially to foolish whimsy, and in the end, to self-destruction.[3]

[3] See "Notes taken while preparing Knickerbocker, 1807–8," a manuscript in the
Houghton Library, Harvard University. Philosophy, history, and what we would
call anthropology are the main concerns of this notebook. In addition to Boethius,
Irving was reading extensively in Plutarch, and he was using Aristotle's *Metaphysics,* or a commentary on it, to work up a basic knowledge of the Greek philos-

Knickerbocker retains his good humor only at the expense of ignoring, for all his desire to be logical, his ultimate inconsistencies. Always insisting that he is "a plain matter of fact historian" (p. 18), one whose painstaking researches mean laboring "in a little kind of Herculaneum . . . raking up the limbs and fragments of disjointed facts" (p. 156), he nonetheless does not scruple, in the absence of known facts, to rely on myths and fables. If not true, they are at least "convenient" (pp. 90–91). And his "logic" shies away from no proof, no matter how questionable the assumptions or how strained the argument. He bases the validity of European claims to Indian territories—and we cannot be sure the irony is his—on the "RIGHT BY GUN-POWDER" and the "RIGHT BY EXTERMINATION" (p. 62). He demonstrates the "necessity and importance" of his first two chapters, which in one sense are "no part of my history," by analogies to "the building of the theatre" and "the formation of the globe," which were first necessary to "the existence of the cupola, as a cupola" and "the existence of this island [Manhattan], as an island" (p. 34).

At times he takes a positive pride in the scantiness of his material. At the climax of a furious battle, in which "not a single carcass" is left to his "disposal," he does what he can with "kicks and cuffs, and bruises—black eyes, and bloody noses, and such like ignoble wounds." The fury is largely a matter of words. "Body o'me," he exclaims, being an historian "is hot work" (pp. 365–67). As though he were a legitimate son of commonsense anti-intellectualism, he deprecates the "chaff of hypothesis," dismisses "scientific jargon" as "mystic fogs," and tries to reduce philosophy to something like a "balloon" which "smoke and

---

ophers. He was also collecting observations (sometimes anecdotes or aphorisms) on such topics as honor, vice, law, love, and loquacity from a number of sources (first- or secondhand)—Thucydides, Herodotus, Menander, Theophrastus, Demosthenes, Pliny, Diodorus Siculus, Aulus Gellius, Bacon, Robert Burton, and Beccaria. Peculiar differences in manners and customs from one time or place to another are what particularly attract him. Substantial extracts, for instance, from Lord Kames's *Sketches on the History of Man* typify his interest in the variability of human behavior and belief, his awareness that what appears outrageously eccentric to an outside observer may be normality within a given society. His reading in Hume's *Natural History of Religion* must also have supplemented this point of view.

vapours" from a "heated imagination" have inflated" (pp. 10, 19, 32). But he carries common sense itself to a ridiculous extreme when he refuses "to examine the annals of the times" that he is treating "further than exactly a page in advance" of his own narrative because, he wants the reader to understand, he is "not engaged in a work of imagination, but a faithful and veritable history." And no one, least of all Knickerbocker, is surprised when, before he finishes the passage, he invokes one of the primary criteria of "a work of imagination," claiming that his approach to history actually increases the suspense: "I have just conducted him into the very teeth of peril——nor can I tell, any more than my reader, what will be the issue of this horrid din of arms . . ." (p. 344).

Again we can find in Addison the neat formulation of an eighteenth-century concept parodied by Irving. In discussing "the art . . . of the historian" in "On the Pleasures of the Imagination," Addison had insisted not only that armies be drawn up and battles fought "in proper expressions," but that the historian "lead us step by step" into the action, so that "we may be kept in a pleasing suspense, and have time given us to raise our expectations." But Addison had not been particularly embarrassed when in the course of emphasizing the artificial element in history—composition—he sensed that he was ignoring its "veracity."[4] Similarly, we find one of the more intelligent characters in Jane Austen announcing cavalierly, "I am fond of history, and am very well contented to take the false with the true." Because (so this commonsense argument goes) one can rely on the sources the historians use about as much as on anything that does not happen "under one's own observation," there is no need to quibble over "little embellishments."[5] Hume had seen clearly that history is, as one interpreter puts it, no more than "a system of reasonable beliefs based on testimony."[6] To Tristram Shandy, who read history as neither pure fact nor fiction, the difficulties

[4] *Spectator*, No. 420.

[5] *Northanger Abbey*, chap. xiv. Knickerbocker, however, was, at least occasionally, far too scrupulous to put made-up speeches into the mouths of historical figures. *K*, pp. 313–14.

[6] R. G. Collingwood, *The Idea of History* (Oxford, 1946), p. 74.

of reconciling contrary accounts and traditions, weaving in anecdotes and stories, making out inscriptions, and making up pane-
gyrics had seemed to preclude anything but an accumulation of
curiosities and digressions—like *Tristram Shandy* itself.[7] Burke
had proclaimed a forthright preference for solid prejudice over
flimsy speculation.[8] It is against such composure that the anxiety
of *Knickerbocker* in regard to history should be measured.

On the whole, the eighteenth-century attitude toward history
is summed up in the slogan, "history is philosophy teaching by
examples," an attitude which *Knickerbocker* does its best to
undermine. The concept of historiography implicit in the slogan
had received its most brilliant exposition in Bolingbroke's *Letters
on the Study and Uses of History* (1752). In his assertion, "history, true or false, speaks to our passions always," he refused to
apologize for entertaining the possibility of untruth: he treated
history as less fact than artifact.[9] Irving had copied into another
notebook containing "Notes for Knickerbocker, 1807–8" a passage in which Bolingbroke observed that in the "school of example," that is, the world, experience is the less important of the
two "masters"; the second master, history, teaches us more.[10]
For, as the *Letters on History* explain, when one looks historically
at what appear to be mere "events," they begin to fall into definite combinations and shapes. As the imagination of the historian contrives significant relations among facts assumed to be
more or less known, it imposes a useful order on the past, enabling man to employ momentary advantages with greater efficiency and in general to "improve" the human situation. In

[7] *The Life and Opinions of Tristram Shandy, Gentleman,* chap. xiv.

[8] See Daniel J. Boorstin, *The Mysterious Science of the Law* (Cambridge, Mass.,
1941), pp. 25–26.

[9] Henry St. John, Viscount Bolingbroke, *The Works* (London, 1754), II, 265.
The comparison suggested here between Irving and Bolingbroke is developed further
in my article "Knickerbocker, Bolingbroke, and the Fiction of History," *Journal
of the History of Ideas,* XX (June–September, 1959), 317–28. For a discussion of
Bolingbroke's view of history and his relation to eighteenth-century historiography,
see Dorothy A. Koch, "English Theories Concerning the Nature and Uses of
History, 1735–91" (unpublished Ph.D. dissertation, Yale University, 1946).

[10] "Memorandum Book of Washington Irving of Sunnyside," manuscript in the
New York Public Library. See *The Seligman Collection of Irvingiana* (New York,
1926). Cf. Bolingbroke, II, 268.

Bolingbroke's view, "history" proves to be a refinement of the
common sense of experience; using the past "renders a man
better, and wiser, for himself, for his family, for the little
community of his own country, and for the greater community
of the world."[11]

Bolingbroke and his more sophisticated contemporaries could
take for granted the ultimate impossibility of making a clear distinction between history and fiction without being tempted into
"universal Pyrrhonism."[12] Knickerbocker's situation, however,
was more akin to that of Charles Brockden Brown, who attempted
the desperate maneuver of formulating a theory of "fictitious history" and equating novelist and historian as purveyors of truth
through allegory. Whatever satisfaction the concept gave him,
clearly it had been necessitated by his acute consciousness of
"the uncertainty of history." "Actions and motives," Brown
said, "cannot be truly described. We can only make approaches
to the truth. The more attentively we observe mankind, and study
ourselves, the greater will this uncertainty appear, and the farther shall we find ourselves from truth."[13]

The *History of New York* consistently ridicules the possibility
of acquiring certain or reliable knowledge. The irony makes
"wise philosopher," in the guise of Governor Kieft (or Thomas
Jefferson), a synonym for "ignoramus." Scholarship is presented as a combination of pedantry, jargon-mongering, prejudice, and sheer superstition. The beginning of the book is a burlesque, which arrives at the founding of New York only after
speculations on cosmogony, the origin of the American Indian,
and the possibility of a pre-Columbian discovery of the New
World. It spoofs, as the heading of Book I (p. 15) indicates, "all
introductions to American histories," for being "very learned,

[11] Bolingbroke, II, 334.
[12] *Ibid.*, II, 329.
[13] "Walstein's School of History," *The Rhapsodist and Other Uncollected Writings*, ed. Harry R. Warfel (New York, 1943), pp. 147–54. As a periodical essayist,
he encountered a similar difficulty. "For my part," he wrote in *The Rhapsodist*
(p. 1), "were I to comply with the uniform example of my predecessors, I should,
I frankly confess, be under the necessity of somewhat disguising the truth." But
"I speak seriously, when I affirm that no situation whatsoever, will justify a man in
uttering falsehood."

sagacious, and nothing to the point."[14] If one doubts the appli-
cability of such satire, extravagant though it is, to scholarship in
Irving's own era, one need only look at such respected works as
Jedediah Morse's *American Universal Geography* (1793) and
Jonathan Carver's *Travels through the Interior Parts of North
America* (1778). True, these writers did not stand in such awe of
Noah's talents as a shipbuilder and navigator as did the Jesuit
Pierre François de Charlevoix in his *Histoire et description gén-
érale de la Nouvelle France* (1744), for which *Knickerbocker*
mocks him (p. 38). But they were still inhibited by their accept-
ance of the Bible as literal history. They took seriously the ques-
tion of whether the transplantation to America of the Indians,
assumed to be descendants of Adam, was post- or antediluvian.
So did those precocious Princetonians, Brackenridge and Philip
Freneau, in their commencement poem, *The Rising Glory of
America* (1772).[15]

Knickerbocker describes his own labors as "up early and to
bed late, poring over worm-eaten, obsolete, good-for-nothing
books, and cultivating the acquaintance of a thousand learned
authors, both ancient and modern, who, to tell the honest truth,
are the stupidest companions in the world . . ." (p. 42). Bluntness of this sort was calculated to disturb classically oriented
readers, one of whom, though generally enthusiastic about
Knickerbocker, lamented that Irving was "sacrificing the authority of criticism to what . . . may be, sarcastically denominated
the truth of history."[16] In later editions Irving saw fit to tone
down or eliminate altogether certain passages—the one just
cited, for instance, and the following, which satirically reduces
"book making" to an activity as empty and "stultifying" as book
learning and which simultaneously, in spite of a disclaimer by
Knickerbocker, ingeniously describes the *History* itself:

[14] Irving omitted this passage in revising.

[15] See, however, what was for the time the liberated approach of Lord Kames in
Bk. II, Sketch XII, of his *Sketches on the History of Man* (1774), a work that
Irving was reading a year or so before *Knickerbocker*. See above, n. 3.

[16] *Edinburgh Magazine*, VII, 544. The notion that *Knickerbocker* is in any sense
authentic history has been exploded by Osborne in his dissertation, "Irving's Development" (University of North Carolina, 1947), pp. 179–98, *passim*.

... if every writer were obliged to tell merely what he knew, there would soon be an end of great books, and Tom Thumb's folio would be considered as a gigantic production—A man might then carry his library in his pocket, and the whole race of book makers, book printers, book binders and book sellers might starve together; but by being entitled to tell every thing he thinks, and every thing he does not think—to talk about everything he knows, or does not know—to conjecture, to doubt, to argue with himself, to laugh with and laugh at his reader, (the latter of which we writers do nine times out of ten—in our sleeves) to indulge in hypotheses, to deal in dashes – – and stars * * * * and a thousand other innocent indulgencies—all these I say, do marvelously concur to fill the pages of books, the pockets of booksellers, and the hungry stomachs of authors—do contribute to the amusement and edification of the reader, and redound to the glory, the encrease and the profit of the craft! (p. 177)

In enumerating four classes of intellectual quacks satirized by Irving, the *Edinburgh Magazine and Literary Miscellany* observed that *Knickerbocker* lets loose

a general tirade against the whole tribe of historians, chroniclers, and expounders of past events, whom he not only taxes with interminable prolix posings . . . and with masses of learned nonsense . . . but, when they do come to facts, with distorting and disguising them to suit some sinister and dishonourable purpose, dwelling on things of no importance, and huddling up those of real moment, so that no mortal can distinguish the truth; exaggerating, apologising, defending, softening, extenuating, not according to individual merit or demerit, but as the impulse of faction, or the love of the marvellous, may happen to decide.[17]

[17] VII, 545. Osborne (pp. 171–78) discounts Irving's share in the anti-intellectual satire on the somewhat conjectural grounds that Book I of *Knickerbocker* was largely done by Peter Irving, who was originally to have collaborated with Washington on the whole book but who left for Europe before the job advanced very far. Osborne argues that Washington was more prone to satirize persons than to parody learned books. The satire against Jefferson as a philosopher, however, which comes in Book IV, would seem pretty close to satire against ideas. And nothing indicates that Washington did not sympathize and even collaborate with Peter in his alleged predilection. In the satire against historians in particular, many passages coming after Book I can be cited, including one late in Book III (*K*, pp. 166–67) that closely parallels sections of the passage just cited from the *Edinburgh Magazine*. And his commonplace books indicate that Washington, like Peter, had enough background in "learned, sagacious" works to know when to be amused by them. The notebook in the New York Public Library ("Notes for Knickerbocker, 1807–8") contains extracts from Bolingbroke, Cicero, Thucydides, Herodotus, Livy, Confucius, Bacon, Erasmus Darwin. And see above, n. 3.

The reviewer, who was uneasy about the attack, felt that the author had indulged himself "very improperly." But *Knickerbocker* is mired in inconsistencies which the Age of Reason had scarcely deigned to notice and from which only the radical epistemology of romanticism was to offer relief. " 'What is history,' " Emerson would eventually ask, quoting Napoleon, " 'but a fable agreed upon?' ": "poetry and annals are alike"; no one "cares what the fact was" when it has been transformed into "an immortal sign." Emerson's strategy in "History" is to exploit the subjectivity which Bolingbroke had acknowledged as the original impulse behind the historical process and to go on to convert an understanding of the past into an aspect of self-reliance or self-discovery. In a passage which suggests the one Irving excerpted from Bolingbroke, Emerson says: "The world exists for the education of each man. There is no age or state of society or mode of action in history to which there is not somewhat corresponding in his life." But whereas Bolingbroke had quickly moved beyond the "little community" of the self to a sense of history as an intellectual mainstay in the world at large, Emerson rejoices in the illumination: "All history becomes subjective; in other words, there is properly no history, only biography."[18]

Knickerbocker, finding no such joy, simply transforms himself into a sort of monstrous projection of Bolingbroke's student of history who uses the past as a basis for regulating the world he lives in. "The world—the world is nothing without the historian!" exclaims Knickerbocker in a passage that parodies metaphysical idealism. He affirms "that cities, empires, plots, conspiracies, havock and desolation, are ordained by providence only as food for the historian" (p. 12). After Bolingbroke has pictured history, in an image borrowed from Tacitus, as "a tribunal," where great men are "tried, and condemned or acquitted, after their deaths,"[19] Knickerbocker, as though giddy with the idea, speaks of himself and his colleagues as "the public almoners of fame, dealing out her favors according to our judg-

[18] Ralph Waldo Emerson, "History," *Essays, Second Series.*
[19] II, 278.

ment or caprice." His inability to tell judgment from caprice simply typifies his never knowing where to draw the line: "we are the benefactors of kings——we are the guardians of truth—we are the scourgers of guilt—we are the instructors of the world—we are—in short, what are we not!" (p. 369). Elsewhere, however, he writes, "I have too high an opinion of the understanding of my fellow-citizens, to think of yielding them instruction, and I covet too much their good will, to forfeit it by giving them good advice" (p. 455). And in still another mood he shudders "to think what direful commotions, what heart rending calamities we historians occasion in the world." He weeps at the idea. "Why," he asks, "are kings desolating empires and depopulating whole countries?" Why do "great men, of all ages and countries . . . inflict so many miseries upon mankind and on themselves?" Simply the desire for fame: "and what is immortal fame?—why, half a page of dirty paper!" (pp. 369–70).

Trying desperately to inflate his narrative and turn history into epic, Knickerbocker only betrays himself by consciously or unconsciously revealing to the reader his actual sense of the meagerness of the present he inhabits and the past he has inherited. The praises he intends to sing keep turning in his mouth to ridicule or loathing. His tribute to "that divine endowment of reason, which distinguishes us from the animals, our inferiors," becomes disgust for the human race: "Man alone, blessed with the inventive mind, goes on from discovery to discovery—enlarges and multiplies his powers of destruction; arrogates the tremendous weapons of deity itself, and tasks creation to assist him in murdering his brother worm!" (p. 256).

Such reminders of Swift are frequent. Irving is adept at the kind of irony that insists on the absolute righteousness of patently vicious behavior, as in the following caricature of the Salem witchcraft crisis, in which, incidentally, one is inclined to see Knickerbocker, a good Dutch Puritan-hater, as himself a conscious ironist:

> Finding, therefore, that neither exhortation, sound reason, nor friendly entreaty had any avail on these hardened offenders, they resorted to the more urgent arguments of torture; and having thus

absolutely wrung the truth from their stubborn lips—they condemned them to undergo the roasting due unto the heinous crimes
they had confessed. Some even carried their perverseness so far as
to expire under the torture, protesting their innocence to the last;
but these were looked upon as thoroughly and absolutely possessed
by the devil, and the pious bye-standers only lamented that they had
not lived a little longer, to have perished in the flames. (p. 284)[20]

Their common concern with pettiness, their rampant exposure
of minutiae and trivia in human affairs, is what basically relates
the *History of New York* to *Gulliver's Travels*. But the mercurial
manner of Irving's historian, in sharp contrast to the deadpan
style of Swift's mask, epitomizes the vast differences that separate them. Thus, for instance, after explaining that the original
European settlers exterminated large numbers of American Indians in the name of improving them, Knickerbocker imagines
the inhabitants of the moon treating the "civilized" peoples of
the world in the same way:

. . . let us suppose that the aerial visitants . . . possessed of vastly
superior knowledge to ourselves; that is to say, possessed of superior
knowledge in the art of extermination—riding on Hypogriffs, defended with impenetrable armour—armed with concentrated sun-
beams, and provided with vast engines, to hurl enormous moon
stones; in short, let us suppose them, if our vanity will permit the
supposition, as superior to us . . . as the Europeans were to the
Indians. . . . All this is very possible; it is only our self-sufficiency
that makes us think otherwise; and I warrant the poor savages,
before they had any knowledge of the white men, . . . were as
perfectly convinced that they themselves were the wisest, the most
virtuous, powerful, and perfect of created beings, as are, at this
present moment, the lordly inhabitants of old England, the volatile
populace of France, or even the self-satisfied citizens of this most
enlightened republick. (pp. 64–65)

The satire here is consistent with the narrator's character; it
covers targets like a spray gun, showing little inclination to
linger over and extend individual tropes and conceits after the
fashion of Swift. The argument of the passage from *Knicker-*

[20] There is more hyperbole in this passage than may be apparent at first sight.
No witches were burned in New England. The Salem delusion of 1692 resulted in
19 hangings and the pressing to death of one of the accused who refused to plead
to the charge.

bocker ironically almost turns back on itself when the "superior knowledge" of the inhabitants of the moon proves to be a greater efficiency in "extermination." Knickerbocker points directly to the fault in question, "vanity," in a tone which largely condemns it, while the full argument being developed (which extends beyond the passage quoted) ironically justifies the vanity of Christians in liquidating pagans. The nations who compose the third element in the equation are belittled by the style, which makes them in effect, "men in the moon" or, as they are actually called later, "lunatics," at the same time that the argument elevates them far above so-called civilized societies. Finally, the passage offers a reminder of a comparable set of vain pretensions exhibited by contemporary nations, one of which is the United States.

As in Swift, the total effect of the *Knickerbocker History* is to emphasize the relativity of judgment to point of view and to suggest that a position can always be found from which even the greatest achievements will appear small. But Irving gets his effect through what becomes an unending deluge of explicit or implied comparisons and contrasts—of moderns to ancients, Americans to Europeans, New Yorkers to Yankees, northerners to southerners, British colonists to United States citizens, Catholics to Protestants, the "occult sciences" of witchcraft to the "hocus pocus of trade" (pp. 284–85), Wilhelm Kieft to Thomas Jefferson, the persecution of Quakers by Puritans to the pillorying of rival factions by partisan politicians or journalists, and the Dutch settlers eating oysters in New Amsterdam to aldermen banqueting in New York. On controversial issues such a parade of conflicting opinions is given, ranging from extravagant quackery to abysmal superstition, that the most authoritative-seeming view becomes suspect as merely another instance of whimsy. Knickerbocker's inability to discriminate lumps things together and makes everything eventually look alike. Whereas Swift's assiduity in ferreting out meanness in men substantiates a clearly defined scale of values ranging, if not from Lilliputians to Gullivers to Brobdingnagians, then from Yahoos to humans to Houyhnhnms, *Knickerbocker*, like *Salmagundi*, seems deliberately to blur and confuse; it detaches the links in the great chain of being from one another and throws them into a single heap.[21]

A modified good humor prevails at the end of the book, but only as part of a pronounced tension, the other pull of which is in the direction of ridicule and mordant sarcasm. For all the buffoonery, Irving does not let the reader forget the Hobbesian view, to which Knickerbocker specifically refers, "that war was the original state of man" (K, p. 254). At times one almost senses an underlying assumption that life is "solitary, poor, nasty, brutish, and short."[22] One might argue that the book assumes the value of "common sense" as a reliable guide in the conduct of human affairs. Knickerbocker, for instance, inclines to the commonly accepted view that Columbus was the discoverer of America, and he enthusiastically supports Peter Stuyvesant, many of whose decisions are based on what could be called common sense, that is, an avoidance of extreme measures except in emergencies, a preference for immediate practical action over abstract speculation, for tried remedies over quack notions. But the hold of common sense on human affairs, granted its desirability, is made to seem, like Stuyvesant's tenure in New York,

[21] An anonymous English critic of Irving, pointing out the wide range of *Knickerbocker*, how it "touches and *tickles* the political maxims, institutions, and manners" of various regions and nations, commented that Irving lacks "the terseness and concentration" of his obvious model, Swift, and that he "plies us with a diffuseness and repetition of jokes." *Monthly Review*, XCIV (January, 1821), 74.

[22] *The Leviathan*, chap. xiii. Most of his life Irving was subject to moments or moods of depression when the "dark side of human nature" might seem so dominant that he would begin "to have painful doubts of my fellow man." Letter to Sarah Storrow, 18 May 1844, PMI, III, 343. In "A Tour on the Prairies" in *The Crayon Miscellany*, in observing that on the frontier his "ravenous and sanguinary propensities" increased daily, he wrote that "man is naturally an animal of prey; and, however changed by civilization, will readily relapse into his instinct for destruction" (chap. xv). The West that Irving discovered on his trip to the Oklahoma frontier in 1832 and in the research he did for *Astoria* and *The Adventures of Captain Bonneville* had a decidedly Hobbesian quality to it. It is doubtless true, as has been alleged, that he distorted the West in looking for romantic and picturesque elements in it—see, for instance, John F. McDermott (ed.), *The Western Journals of Washington Irving* (Norman, Okla., 1944), pp. 40–62. But he did not simply pretty it up. *Captain Bonneville* (1837), in particular, gives a grim view of the West as an extension of the wildness of its scenery. Trickery, treachery, warfare, and reckless slaughter are the rule here, and while one occasionally encounters admirable individuals, no race or nationality, American, French, Mexican, or Indian, is exempt from the brutalizing influence of the wilderness that makes human beings behave like grizzly bears, buffaloes, crows, beavers, or wolves.

precarious. By the time that all of the other theories of the discovery of America have been aired, the claim of Columbus
begins to seem doubtful. Knickerbocker may be merely capricious in fixing on 1492, for although his choice recognizes the
subsequent importance of the voyage of Columbus, at the same
time he throws up his hands in the face of conflicting evidence
in regard to the historical question with which he began, that is,
were there pre-Columbian discoveries of America? The triumph
of common sense, in the rare cases where it occurs in the book,
is made to seem the sheerest accident. Swift had condescended
to point out human follies to the reader, on the basic assumption
that man is at least capable of reason, but Irving seems to wonder
how man has managed to do as well as he has.

In his "Apology" to the 1848 edition, having, as he said, lived
on into the era of "Knickerbocker insurance companies; Knickerbocker steamboats; . . . Knickerbocker bread; and Knickerbocker ice," Irving insisted that his "main object" in writing the
book had been

> to embody the traditions of our city in an amusing form; to illustrate
> its local humors, customs, and peculiarities; to clothe home scenes
> and places and familiar names with those imaginative and whimsical
> associations so seldom met with in our new country, but which live
> like charms and spells about the cities of the old world, binding the
> heart of the native inhabitant to his home.[23]

But Irving only arrived at this conception several years after the
original publication. The *History* in its early form is much
closer in spirit to *Salmagundi*. Like Jeremy Cockloft, for instance, Knickerbocker is frustrated by his inability to dignify
his home town.[24] And Irving tends chiefly to take comic advan-

[23] *Knickerbocker* (1863), pp. 13–14.
[24] Irving wrote in 1848 that Peter and he had wanted to parody at greater length
the same guidebook which had prompted some of the mockery in "The Stranger at
Home," Mitchill's *The Picture of New York*. They planned to "begin with an
historical sketch; to be followed by notices of the customs, manners, and institutions of the city" (*Knickerbocker* [1863], p. 11). What must have made Mitchill
a tempting target was the humorlessness of his largely technical and statistical
Picture of "the commercial metropolis of North America," which began with the
geographical situation of the city, turned geological in "Size and Configuration,"
and moved on through numerous categories without giving a sense of what dis-

tage of the comparative *lack* of myth and legend in the United States, where "great men and great families of doubtful origin" cannot claim descent from gods and heroes and where no "tender virgin, who was accidentally and unaccountably enriched with a bantling, would save her character . . . by ascribing the phenomenon to a swan, a shower of gold, or a river god" (pp. 89–90). Often the legendary embellishments in the book belong to later editions, yet, regardless of when they appear, a mock-heroic facetiousness is almost sure to undercut them. In implied comparisons, for instance, between the early New Yorkers and the Pilgrims, the former are exposed as frantically enfeebled copies of the latter. And the most famous of the legendary inventions, Oloffe's dream of a great city arising on Manhattan, no matter how much it seems a joyful response to the fertile prospect of the American landscape, reflects the ambition, not of an epic hero, but of a fat Dutch land-speculator napping after dinner.[25]

If the instinctive reaction of many writers to national independence was to try to build a literature and a culture by flaunting Yankee Doodle and Brother Jonathan, hailing Columbia, presenting the British as a race of fops, and turning the hero of the sentimental novel into an American officer in the Revolution, *Knickerbocker* remembered that Americans were a nation of farmers and tradesmen with an eye to the main chance, that whether New Englanders, New Yorkers, or southerners, they had come to this country to improve themselves economically, that they practiced sharply, exploited Negroes and Indians, and that they cared as much for cockfights and cocktails, horse racing and oyster eating, bundling and political backbiting as for lofty-

---

tinguished New York from any other town with boundaries, city officials, business firms, and "Public Walks" (see pp. i, vi, 153, and *passim*). Harry M. Lydenberg, arguing that Mitchill's work is factual, not pedantic, and pointing out that Irving in 1848 was somewhat hazy in his recollection of it, discounts the importance of *The Picture of New York* as an inspiration for *Knickerbocker*. "Irving's *Knickerbocker* and Some of Its Sources," *Bulletin of the New York Public Library*, LVI (November, December, 1952), 549–52, 596–98. But Irving certainly remembered Mitchill's general procedure. Furthermore, *Salmagundi* (p. 237) had specifically chided Mitchill for the disjointed structure of his work.

[25] The dream was added in the 1812 edition (see *K*, pp. 462–72), although already in 1809 Oloffe Van Kortlandt was the Ulysses of New Amsterdam (*K*, p. 104).

sounding political and religious ideals. Commenting on the early period in American history, James Russell Lowell later said that "the details . . . were essentially dry and unpoetic" because to the viewer in the nineteenth century who really looked, everything was "near, authentic, and petty"; the view lacked a "mist of distance to soften outlines." Lowell observed that in *Knickerbocker* "Irving instinctively divined and admirably illustrated . . . the humorous element which lies in this poverty of stage properties, which makes the actors and the deeds they were concerned in seem ludicrously small when contrasted with the semimythic grandeur in which we have clothed them. . . ."[26]

Thus the *History* makes little more than passing reference to the Revolution, the culminating event in the standard, consciously patriotic formulations of American history such as Joel Barlow's attempt at a national epic, which appeared in its final form, *The Columbiad,* just two years before *Knickerbocker.* Barlow's poem treats America as a land destined from the beginning for freedom, and the discoverer of that land as a forerunner of the Enlightenment, that is, of the spirit which produced American independence. Far from dying a defeated man, Columbus is permitted on his deathbed the epic hero's conventional vision of the future—the sort of thing parodied in Oloffe's dream —extending beyond the Revolution to vignettes of American industry, science, and civilization flourishing under the care of a bountiful freedom.

"Honest Diedrich Knickerbocker," however, whom the *Edinburgh Magazine* considered "worth a whole Congress of Joel Barlows,"[27] though he frequently alludes to time present and is perfectly aware of the fact of American independence, fails to make self-government the heritage of inspired origins. The beauty of the American scene, although it is lyrically described, excites the usually "phlegmatic Dutchmen" largely as a promise of abundance sufficient to justify continued indolence. Henry Hudson is rendered as a stereotyped, stiff, duty-bound, inarticulate Englishman, who, when aroused by the unexpected loveliness

[26] "New England Two Centuries Ago," *Among My Books.*
[27] VII, 544.

of the land, becomes simply foolish and ineffectual: "He is said
to have . . . uttered these remarkable words, while he pointed
towards this paradise of the new world—'see! there!'—and
thereupon, as was always his way when he was uncommonly
pleased, he did puff out such clouds of dense tobacco smoke,
that in one minute the vessel was out of sight of land . . ." (pp.
75–76).

As it is seen in *Knickerbocker*, there is no dedication, no sense
of mission or heroic adventure in the Dutch colonization of New
Netherlands, nothing to compare with the Renaissance Englishman's desire for glory and sense of national destiny to which
John Smith had appealed in advertising for settlers to the New
World. Irving discovers a crasser motivation among the Dutch.
He is well acquainted, through works like Cotton Mather's
Magnalia, with the orthodox conception of New England history
as an escape from bondage, and is careful to play up the contrast
between the bluntly practical, commercial, and material incen-
tives behind the founding of New York and the Puritan zeal for
Zion in the wilderness. Thus the "Goede Vrouw," the ship on
which the colonists sail from Amsterdam for the New World, is
seen as a fat Dutch woman, "full in the bows, with a pair of
enormous cat-heads, a copper bottom, and withal a most prodigious poop!" Unlike more famous departures in American history—the "Mayflower" or the "Pinta," "Nina," and "Santa
Maria"—this one carries no prospect of hardship, no fear of
unknown dangers, no flight from persecution, no threat of
mutiny. Religious inspiration amounts to no more than the shipbuilder's having erected as a figurehead "a goodly image of
St. Nicholas" in "a huge pair of Flemish trunk hose." "Thus
gallantly furnished, the staunch ship floated sideways, like a
majestic goose, out of the harbour . . . and all the bells, that were
not otherwise engaged, rung a triple bob-major on the joyful
occasion" (pp. 80–81). The uneventful voyage out is scarcely
mentioned; presumably it could be described in the same way in
which Knickerbocker has already presented the crossing of
Hudson's "Half Moon": "they eat [sic] hugely, drank profusely,
and slept immeasurably, and being under the especial guidance

of providence, the ship was safely conducted to the coast of America" (p. 73).

But it is by no means New York alone which is denied a glorious past. New England pretensions are exposed as partly deceitful. If Knickerbocker finds the origins of self-government in his state in the factionalism of the "meddlesome" burghers during the tenure of William the Testy (p. 248), he also points out how the freedom of conscience which the Puritans fled England to obtain in America became merely the freedom to believe what the Puritans professed. Learning from their Anglican tormentors, the Puritans themselves persecuted Quakers. In the end Knickerbocker sees little difference between New York and New England in regard to fundamental questions. The freedom of speech implied, as Knickerbocker understands, in "liberty of conscience" seems everywhere to degenerate into malicious tongue-wagging (p. 155). "Have we not within but a few years," he asks his contemporaries, comparing them to the Puritans,

> released ourselves from the shackles of a government, which cruelly denied us the privilege of governing ourselves, and using in full latitude, that invaluable member, the tongue? and are we not at this very moment striving our best to tyrannise over the opinions, tie up the tongues, or ruin the fortunes of one another? What are our great political societies, but mere political inquisitions—our pot-house committees, but little tribunals of denunciation—our news-papers but mere whipping-posts and pillories, where unfortunate individuals are pelted with rotten eggs—and our council of appoint-ment——but a grand *auto da fe,* where culprits are annually sacri-ficed for their political heresies? (p. 158)

Instead of real freedom, then, America has produced factionalism and conformity. Of course, to attribute such a view to Irving without serious qualifications would be to ignore the ironic exaggeration in *Knickerbocker.* There is no antirepublican animus in the satire of the abuses of republican institutions. The *History* undoubtedly embraces republicanism as a going concern, for all its weaknesses. Irving certainly could not have failed to find at least equally laughable any alternative to the prevailing system in the United States.

If in the end the book becomes a mock-heroic with a hero, the effect depends on an elaborate indirection and irony within irony that leaves Knickerbocker's excessive veneration for Peter Stuyvesant as a part of that historian's huge incompetence. The ending builds on the sound proportions of the whole. The monumental sweep through world history in Book I sets up the utter insignificance of the settlement of New Amsterdam in Book II. The third book presents a golden age, the serenity of which consists in its obscurity. At last in Book IV the trouble starts, though on anything but an epic scale. Thus through somewhat more than half the "history" the sense of emptiness swells almost unchecked. But with the introduction of Peter Stuyvesant in Book V a subtle movement in the opposite direction commences. One cannot at first put any stock in Knickerbocker's enthusiasm for the governor, yet in the course of the last three books Stuyvesant's energy, courage, and honesty, which are committed to the community as a whole rather than to a particular party or section, begin to command a certain admiration.

The mask is maintained to the last. It is not Irving who proclaims Stuyvesant a hero but Knickerbocker, who, in spite of his own ineffectualness, manages to sow the suspicion that a relatively mean world may not be thoroughly ignoble after all. There can be no sentimentalizing here. The reader knows Knickerbocker too well by this time and can recognize that Stuyvesant is headstrong and stubborn, if not dictatorial. In the general belittling of the colony, his office has not escaped. Knickerbocker allows the reader to expect the governor to lead New Amsterdam in a glorious, if doomed, defense against the British, but Stuyvesant bows ignominiously without a fight. What may stay longer with the reader than the successes or failures of Stuyvesant is Knickerbocker's quixotic desire to believe in the Dutchman's greatness.[28]

[28] For somewhat different views of Stuyvesant's heroism, see Charlton Laird, "Tragedy and Irony in *Knickerbocker's History*," *American Literature*, XII (May, 1940), 159–64; Terence Martin, "Rip, Ichabod, and the American Imagination," *American Literature*, XXXI (May, 1959), 137–49.

IV

The Lintels of the Door-Post: Reflections on an Indigenous Literature

AT the end of the original version of the *History of New York* Knickerbocker, overwhelmed by the sense of ruin and decay, becomes a caricature of "your historian of sensibility." Preparing to face those "most direful and melancholy" phenomena, the "decline and fall of . . . empires" and "the ruins of departed greatness," he pictures the "woe begone historian" mounting a platform like a "well disciplined funeral orator, whose feelings are properly tutored to ebb and flow, to blaze in enthusiastic eulogy, or gush in overwhelming sorrow." He warns his readers to get out their handkerchiefs as he rehearses the successive rise and fall of the Assyrian, Median, Grecian, Roman, and Saracenic empires in preparation for a final comment on the fall of New Netherlands (pp. 440–43).

The satire on sensibility initially seems ludicrous enough, yet the reader, urged to become a sort of traveler "wandering, with mental eye amid the awful and gigantic ruins," may momentarily succumb to the decadent viewpoint, to "the sublimity of the . . . horrors" through which one forgets "private misery" in contemplating the inevitability of universal ruin. Mock this response as he might through overstatement, Irving could not altogether dispel the suspicion that there might in reality be no getting around the "one vast immoveable idea." How fared the young American republic, for instance, in the "night mare" of "the present convulsions of the globe"? It was ridiculous for

86

Knickerbocker to make the French Revolution and the Napoleonic Wars links in "a subtle chain of events, originating at the capture of Fort Casimer" (an incident in the campaign of New Netherlands against New Sweden), but the factionalism of American politics hardly promised exemption for the United States from "the inavertable stroke of fate" (pp. 441–45).[1]

Knickerbocker offers refuge neither in a hope for the future nor a sense of the past. Irving, if not his historian, is caught in a time trap. The vision of New York in Oloffe's dream goes up in smoke, although that does not prevent the Dutch, who for once are as much led on by the promise of history as Barlow's Columbus, from founding the city. The historian sees ruined empires both ahead and behind and longs for a total release from the flux of time. His moment of greatest fulfillment comes not in the course of historical narrative but in the recollection of an autumn day in 1804 when he went for a walk along the Battery. At first he remembers being oppressed (this is Irving kidding his own sentimentality) by the thought that "the dark forests which once clothed these shores had been violated by the savage hand of cultivation, and their tangled mazes, and impracticable thickets, had degenerated into teeming orchards and waving fields of grain." But he says that after "lamenting the melancholy progress of improvement" for some time, he gradually began to discover the beauty of the present moment. And as he recalls the total tranquility of the scene—the sea glassy, a fleet of canoes at anchor, the leaves of the trees still, the drum and guns of the battery silent, his own soul slumbering—he almost slips into eternity (pp. 149–51), or, as Philip Young has said of Rip Van Winkle,[2] falls from time, like Melville's pantheist Ishmael meditating at the masthead. It is the moment of release from tension toward which Irving's work repeatedly moves.

One still ponders the realization that the first contribution to American fiction that has endured was a mock-history. Beyond

[1] Irving subsequently eliminated from the ending of the *History* most of the rhapsody on the theme of ruins. Cf. *Knickerbocker* (New York, 1863), pp. 467–72.

[2] "Fallen from Time: The Mythic Rip Van Winkle," *Kenyon Review*, XXII (Autumn, 1960), 547–73.

Knickerbocker extends a long series of satiric or seriocomic stories and novels which deflate the American dream by presenting "progress" as illusion, zealous humanitarianism as self-deception or hypocrisy. The end product of history projected in such works as "The Celestial Railroad," "Earth's Holocaust," *The Monikins, The Crater,* "Mellonta Tauta," *Mardi, The Confidence-Man, The Bostonians,* and *The Connecticut Yankee* is, at least by implication, a barren present. Some of this fiction has roots in the same broad comic tradition as *Knickerbocker.* If *Mardi,* for instance, in its concern for history owes nothing directly to Irving, certain similarities are at least worth nothing.[3] Melville's "old antiquary" Oh-Oh seems a flagrant caricature of Knickerbocker or of the typical grubbing scholar in Irving. He is "crooked, and dwarfed" and humped, has piggish eyes and a prodigious snout, burrows in a library called "the catacombs" among "mummyish parcels" and "crumbling, illegible, black-letter sheets." What Oh-Oh treasures is a past that is totally lost to understanding. Yet *known* history has little more meaning in *Mardi* than in *Knickerbocker.* For when, in the course of his futile allegorical quest for the perfect society, Taji reaches Vivenza (the United States), Melville deliberately mocks the "conceit that . . . all preceding events were ordained, to bring about . . . a universal and permanent Republic." And a mysterious "voice" intones, "Could time be reversed, and the future change places with the past, the past would cry out against us, and our future, full as loudly, as we against the ages foregone."[4]

Even closer to Irving, Poe's "Mellonta Tauta" is in one sense almost a miniature version of *Knickerbocker.* Set in 2848 A.D., this story views nineteenth-century America as a part of ancient history. The perspective, like that of the "lunatics" imagined by

<hr>

[3] Edward H. Rosenberry (*Melville and the Comic Spirit* [Cambridge, Mass., 1955], p. 18) mentions Melville's interest in Irving, particularly in *Knickerbocker,* passages of which he marked in the copy he owned. Occasionally in *Moby-Dick* also, it may be worth noting, one is startled by blatant reminders of Irving, as when Stubb kills a whale that is first seen "spouting his vapory jet . . . like a portly burgher smoking his pipe of a warm afternoon" (chap. lxi).

[4] Melville, *Mardi: and a Voyage Thither,* chaps. cxxii, cxxiii, clxi.

Knickerbocker, enables Poe to present the inhabitants of the United States as savages and their democratic institutions as the products of a hideous superstition destined for destruction through mob tyranny—New York City having belonged to the "Knickerbocker tribe of savages" who worshiped the "two idols that went by the name of Wealth and Fashion." Destroyed by an earthquake in 2050, the island of Manhattan has now apparently reverted to a state of nature and is considered the "Paradise" of the twenty-ninth century.

One thinks ahead to the ending of *The Great Gatsby* and the narrator's vision of what "the old island" (not Manhattan but the next thing to it, Long Island) had originally been "for Dutch sailors' eyes—a fresh, green breast of the new world." While there has been as yet no earthquake, this paradise has given way by Fitzgerald's time to "Gatsby's house" and that "waste land" and "valley of ashes," the metropolitan dump. Ever thus the dream of the future is "borne back ceaselessly into the past." Again in "Mellonta Tauta," as in *Knickerbocker* and *Mardi*, the humor leaves no refuge. The alternative to democratic savagery is a future which has accepted "War and Pestilence" not only as inevitable but as beneficent and which shows no real advancement over the past, in spite of a superficial scientific progress. The narrative voice that comes to us out of the future is that of a frivolous gossip. And Pundit, Poe's twenty-ninth-century antiquarian, is no more able to construct a faithful view of the past than was the narrator of the *History of New York*.

The mock-heroic reversal, which focuses on deterioration rather than advancement in human affairs, was potentially subversive of faith in history. Trained to see Yahoos in the world around them, both Irving and Cooper quickly found comic possibilities in the theory advanced by Erasmus Darwin and other precursors of Charles Darwin that, as Knickerbocker says, "the whole human species are accidentally descended from a remarkable family of monkies" (*K*, p. 46). Far from assuming any evolution or progression in this relationship, Irving, at least for satirical purposes, took such speculation to imply that men are no better than beasts. And Cooper based *The Monikins* (1835)

on the conceit that the monkey is the descendant, not the ante-
cedent, of man. The image of "progress" becomes a society of
monkeys discovered in the polar regions; the three monkey nations, caricatures of France, England, and the United States,
reflect Cooper's sense of what history is coming to. In Leaplow,
the monkey equivalent of the United States, wrangling factions
substitute for orderly government, and an absurdly cumbersome
legal system promotes confusion and injustice.

By the end of *The Prairie* (1827) Cooper's wilderness nobleman, Natty Bumppo, cousin to Jefferson's "natural" aristocrat,
had already appeared doomed, like the forest itself, whose destruction Francis Parkman's history was to lament. And Cooper
had begun to suspect as likewise doomed the ideal of a common
man sufficiently responsive to common sense to be able to govern
himself by the laws of nature. When he abandoned that ideal
altogether, Cooper was left with a conception of history as little
more than a sequence of accidents. Thus *The Crater* (1847) pictures a "free" society as a product of the chance discovery and
settlement of a new world. Lacking the strength to resist the corrupting influences that threaten it, this society exists, as the
metaphor of Cooper's volcanic setting makes clear, on the edge
of extinction. In the end the great experiment is literally swal-
lowed up.

An earlier generation of Americans, including both Jefferson
and John Adams, had already, as Stow Persons has observed,
been subjected to the contradiction between the doctrine of
progress and the "cyclical theory of history" which an "implicit
conservatism" in the Enlightenment engendered. The eighteenth-
century sense of human nature as constant and universal had
contributed to a tendency to reduce history to a periodic alterna-
tion of ups and downs, the rise and fall of empires, "within a
static . . . continuum." Already, says Persons, in the "revolutionary environment" of the 1770's and 1780's "the countervailing weight of American experience" had clashed with this
cyclical view.[5] But with Irving, in an age more sentimental than

[5] "The Cyclical Theory of History in Eighteenth Century America," *American
Quarterly*, VI (Summer, 1954), 163.

philosophical, the vogue for ruins was still gathering momentum. For some, the "countervailing weight of American experience" had yet to tip the balance irrevocably. In Timothy Dwight's *Greenfield Hill* (1794), for instance, the hope that America is rapidly progressing toward a pastoral millenium fights continually with the awareness that the American people labor under a tremendous burden of proof, since the pattern of history has ever been the inability of greatness to sustain itself. For Dwight, as for many Americans, the Calvinistic stress on man's fallen nature served to intensify this awareness.[6]

Nothing is at first sight more anomalous in American literature of the early national period than its obsession with ruin and decay. A plethora of graveyard imagery, broken columns, and moss-grown towers undermines assumptions as to what one should encounter in a new country. Thanatopsis—thoughts of the grave —lie athwart the hope for the future, turning the virgin land into an "Indian Burying Ground" and conjuring up savage ghosts to haunt Freneau's landscapes. Dwight, about to describe a slaughter of the Pequods in seventeenth-century Connecticut, observes that the cultivators of the American wilderness may be walking or ploughing ground on which an Indian nation once flourished.[7] Bryant and Cooper see the prairie sod as but a thin veneer of growth covering the wreckage of unknown civilizations.[8] For them, nature's processional often seems a death rather than a life cycle. Bryant does not so much transmit to America a Wordsworthian feeling for nature as use the continental expanses of forest and prairie for graveyard meditation. According to Charles L. Sanford, "The principle of mutation in nature" suggested to Bryant and his close associate, the painter Thomas Cole, "a cyclical theory of human history in which great empires flourished and passed away. At the same time

[6] See in particular Part IV of *Greenfield Hill* (New York, 1794). Persons comments (p. 153): "it appears that history is virtue teaching by example; and the decline and fall of empires represent a divine judgment upon the corruption of men."

[7] *Greenfield Hill*, p. 96.

[8] See William Cullen Bryant, "The Prairies"; Cooper, *The Prairie*, chap. xxii.

nature's slower rhythms pronounced a judgment on man's 'feeble strife with time. . . .' "[9]

The mutability cantos which Geoffrey Crayon was to include in his *Sketch Book* have often been taken as an anomalous passion for the obsolete, but one ought to look at the general need of nineteenth-century American literature to rudely juxtapose life and death. Poe is not the only American writer for whom the theme or image of premature burial has meaning, or whose work turns houses into tombs. In "The Wedding Knell" Hawthorne reduces an old bachelor to a living corpse dressed in a shroud and carried to his marriage on a bier, and the author's effort to save his character's spirit for immortality is not wholly convincing. The reverberations of the knell, more ominous than the pealing of the organ in Irving's "Westminster Abbey," push the theme of mutability toward its limit. It is as though Irving in his treatment of the Abbey had made a dominant figure of Roubillac's tomb of Mrs. Nightingale, which Geoffrey Crayon finds "horrible rather than sublime," on which the "sheeted skeleton" of death is depicted as emerging from the "marble doors," the "shroud . . . falling from his fleshless frame as he launches his dart at his victim" (*SB*, p. 216).

There also emerges, out of the supposedly life-giving American earth, that bearded and hoary archetype Rip Van Winkle,

[9] *The Quest for Paradise* (Urbana, Ill., 1961), p. 151. Sanford discusses in detail in chapter viii ("National Self-Consciousness and the Concept of the Sublime") the difficulties Bryant and Cole had in reconciling their faith in America with the cyclical conception of history. "Almost always," as he points out, Bryant's "subject was the rise and decline of Indian nations" (p. 152). Articles by Perry Miller and Curtis Dahl also deal with ironies in American literature and art that are related to the one I am suggesting in focusing on decay and dilapidation; inevitably I touch on some matters that they have already observed. Miller, while pointing out the influence of Thomas Cole's series of paintings, "The Course of Empire" (1835), depicting the rise and fall of a civilization, is, like Sanford, particularly concerned with the conflict between the American's desire to believe that what was good in his society came from Nature and his realization that the development of a commercial and industrial society was destroying Nature. See "The Romantic Dilemma in American Nationalism and the Concept of Nature," *Harvard Theological Review*, XLVIII (October, 1955), 239–53. Dahl provides a suggestive catalogue of paintings (including some by Irving's friends Allston and Vanderlyn) and literary works between 1810 and 1845 that feature destruction, especially violent and sudden cataclysm of the sort perhaps best shown in Bulwer-Lytton's *The Last Days of Pompeii*. "The American School of Catastrophe," *American Quarterly*, XI (Fall, 1959), 380–90.

like a moss-covered ruin, who prefigures a line of Wakefields, Clifford Pyncheons, Bartlebys, and Jimmy Roses. Perhaps even Roderick Usher, whose hair, silken and aristocratic as it is, nonetheless wildly covers his face, like the fungi on the façade of his house, belongs in this line of descent, which reaches its climax in the shaggy, wilderness-born, tomb-voiced cynics—American Casper Hausers—of *The Confidence-Man*.[10] Everywhere in Melville failure and despair become monumental ruin or premature burial. The "Pequod," like the "San Dominique," appears a ruined city in the sea. Ishmael meditates on coffin warehouses and finds New Bedford an overgrown country churchyard. And titanic Pierre turns out to be that pyramid Ahab, reduced, not to sheer backbone, but to a single slab of rock—transformed already, that is, into his own tombstone.

An instinct of American literature is to deny the newness of the New World. Whatever hope for the future survives is likely, like the jackal of Ishmael's "Faith," to feed "among the tombs." The very first page of *The Scarlet Letter* plays ominously with an irony close to that with which the *History of New York* belabors the Puritans. "The founders of a new colony, whatever Utopia of human virtue and happiness they might originally project," says Hawthorne, have never been able to do without cemeteries and prisons: "The rust on the ponderous iron-work of [the prison's] oaken door looked more antique than anything else in the New World. Like all that pertains to crime, it seemed never to have known a youthful era."

Hester's search for a new world, a new life, ends with her acceptance of what is in effect the old. The oppressive sense of the weight of an all-but-dead past laid on the present permeates both the novel and the introductory "Custom House" sketch; both Hawthorne and Hester are inextricably involved with remnants of the past, especially with ancient old men. The new society which she finds in trying to escape an old world and an old husband proves to be one which owes "its origin and progress, and its present state of development, not to the impulses of youth,

---

[10] Melville specifically associates forest imagery with the imagery of the ruined city in *The Confidence-Man*, chap. xvii.

but to the stern and tempered energies of manhood, and the
sombre sagacity of age." It is primarily old men who judge her
(for a sin committed with a *young* man), the chief among them
being John Wilson, who looks down at Hester on the scaffold
with "his gray eyes, accustomed to the shaded light of his
study, . . . winking . . . in the unadulterated sunshine." Here is
another dry-as-dust like Chillingworth himself, or Knickerbocker, or the other old men in Irving—old men always essentially sterile, sometimes positively sinister. Such a man, says
Hawthorne, has "no more right" than a face in an antique en-
graving "to step forth . . . and meddle with a question of human
guilt, passion, and anguish."[11]

Thus the promise of American life blossoms only like the
red rose by the prison door, or shines only like a scarlet letter
on the sable tombstone. Man's greatest range of freedom, Hawthorne's Miles Coverdale was soon to discover, is in the recognition of his limitations. Utopia is never achieved, Arcadia never
restored. The only "good society" is in the "fellowship of all
the sons of labor," who are "Adam's posterity."[12] Undoubtedly,
this, in one form or other, is *the* classic tragic realization. Yet
the American form characteristically carries overtones of a
social experiment being betrayed, a new world growing old, or,
as we have so often been reminded, a paradise being lost.

Only the Transcendentalists, viewing the present not in the
perspective of 2848 A.D. or of the moon, but under the aspect
of eternity, could accept the absence of progress with comparative equanimity. "Society never advances," says Emerson in
"Self-Reliance," though at other times he allows himself to be
more optimistic. "It recedes as fast on one side as it gains on the
other. It undergoes continual changes . . . but this change is not
amelioration." Although men may "plume themselves on the
improvement of society, . . . no man improves." After all, if
history is only a fable, there is no need to pretend it is going
anywhere. To get beyond the awareness of *Knickerbocker* is to
go inward, to glimpse some anchorage within the individual for

[11] *The Scarlet Letter*, chap. iii.
[12] *The Blithedale Romance*, chap. xxiv.

riding out what Emerson calls the "wave" of society. "A man will not need to study history," says Thoreau, "to find out what is best for his own culture." The European may migrate to the New World to "get tea and coffee, and meat every day." This to him looks like progress. But "the only true America is that country where you are at liberty to pursue such a mode of life as may enable you to do without these."[13] And this is in solitude at Walden or in the integrity of the individual spirit.

A Philadelphia reviewer observed in 1821 that the people of New York were an "excellent, amiable, and intelligent set" but that "ever since they had to boast of 'Salmagundi' and 'Knickerbocker' as indigenous productions—a propensity to satire and burlesque has been their besetting sin; the passion has been a perfect *mania,* and they have laughed at their own caricature in every variety of shape."[14] Such a statement is typical of a tendency still observable to talk about "Knickerbocker" humor in New York as a relatively isolated phenomenon perpetrated by Paulding and the Irvings and extended by minor writers such as Fitz-Greene Halleck and Joseph Rodman Drake. But this is to forget that such literature emerged from the general background of journalistic humor in the United States at the turn of the century, in which various cities and states participated. Philadelphia itself had had comic papers which anticipated *Salmagundi*;[15] even the comparatively staid Joseph Dennie had engaged in a humor that partially resembles *Oldstyle*.[16] Brackenridge, trying in *Modern Chivalry* to maintain a tightly reined comic style consistent with Swiftian and Addisonian canons of reasonableness, had begun to slide into broad farce and tangled irony several years before *Knickerbocker*. Even some of the Hartford Wits had succumbed as their conflicts with

---

[13] *Walden,* chap. x ("The Baker Farm").

[14] *Literary Gazette,* I (April 7, 1821), 209, quoted by Nelson F. Adkins, *Fitz-Greene Halleck; An Early Knickerbocker Wit and Poet* (New Haven, 1930), p. 125.

[15] STW, II, 264.

[16] Oliver Oldschool, in announcing his "New Weekly Paper" (Prospectus for *Port Folio,* Vol. I [1801]), had argued that "it is right and decorous, and useful to be *partial, bigoted,* adhesive, to old systems"; he promised, among other things, "burlesque translations," parodies, "characteristical and humorous diaries."

what they considered the forces of anarchy intensified, and they attempted to laugh and frighten voters out of the "mobility" and back to the supposed nobility of the Federalist cause.[17]

Whatever the extremes to which Knickerbockerism and related manifestations of American humor went, the literary sources, of course, were ultimately in European traditions, particularly those of eighteenth-century England. There was nothing uniquely American about shrill comic impudence, vulgar invective, hoaxing, travesty, self-mockery, mystification, and grotesquerie. Undoubtedly preromantic and romantic humor in the United States also had certain affinities with what Europeans, particularly the Germans, called romantic irony. But what American humor borrowed often appears to have had a peculiar relevance to the conditions of native culture. Furthermore, there was nothing to prevent imported humor from merging with vernacular or frontier humor in certain situations, and beginning to become indistinguishable from it. Perhaps the best example of sophisticated and frontier elements functioning together is *Modern Chivalry*, but one finds instances of this in the works of others, including Irving. The reader of *Salmagundi* usually overlooks the advertisement at the end of the second number in which the authors, though they decline to give satisfaction in a duel, offer, through two "strapping" extras allegedly hired from the theater, to cudgel and tweak the nose of anyone whom they have provoked to anger and indignation, "this being what we understand by 'the satisfaction of a gentleman.' " Of course they claim that they "intend to offend nobody under heaven." And their vaunted stage "heroes" are undoubtedly another hoax. Yet facetious as it is, the advertisement acknowledges that someone may well be

[17] See, for instance, the distracting shifts of tone and point of view which develop in Nos. 11, 12, 15, 16, and 18 of "The Echo." *The Echo, with Other Poems* (n.p., 1807). In No. 15 the confusion is so far-reaching that the deliberate nonsense of Knickerbockerism seems anticipated, even though the underlying attitude of the author remains clear because inscriptive verses establish it at the beginning and because the reader assumes it to be the opposite of that of the work being *echoed* or burlesqued.

stung by what *Salmagundi* calls its "good-natured villainy" (pp. 47–49).[18]

This partial defiance of the audience was an aspect of Knickerbockerism. Irving and his young colleagues did not intend to be intimidated by good taste even if they envied the assurance of those who seemed to possess it. In their attitude toward gentility and the code of the gentleman derived from Europe, one detects something of the American squatter frightening the dandy. The boasting and hyperbole of the original Preface to *Knickerbocker* brings this out more clearly:

> Here then I cut my bark adrift, and launch it forth to float upon the waters. . . . And you, oh ye great little fish! ye tadpoles, ye sprats, ye minnows, ye chubbs, ye grubs, ye barnacles, and all you small fry of literature, be cautious how you insult my new launched vessel, or swim within my view; lest in a moment of mingled sportiveness and scorn, I sweep you up in a scoop net, and roast half a hundred of you for my breakfast. (*K*, pp. 13–14)[19]

Barrett Wendell suggested, long before the tide of work on American humor began to swell about 1930, that the "grave mixture of fact and nonsense" in *Knickerbocker* put it directly in the native comic tradition extending from Franklin to Mark Twain and Mr. Dooley.[20] Neither Constance Rourke nor Walter Blair, however, saw fit to naturalize Irving.[21] And Wendell himself had doubts about Irving's style, taking the "gracious manner" of *Knickerbocker* to be basically English. What stood between Wendell and an adequate appreciation of Irving's early humor was the image by then prevalent of Irving as the American Goldsmith. Indeed one wonders whether Wendell ever looked

[18] Legend has it that Irving originally wrote "good-natured raillery" but was happy to let the printer's error stand. PMI, I, 176.

[19] In the course of Irving's revisions this passage was omitted.

[20] *A Literary History of America* (New York, 1928), p. 173. "The fun of the thing lies in frequent and often imperceptible lapses from sense to nonsense and back again." The original date of Wendell's book is 1900.

[21] Daniel Hoffman has noted this virtual silence in regard to Irving. *Form and Fable in American Fiction* (New York, 1961), pp. 84–85. But while Hoffman has himself redeemed "The Legend of Sleepy Hollow" for *American* humor, he concludes that it is "anomalous" in relation to the rest of Irving (p. 95).

carefully at the original edition of *Knickerbocker,* with its more
robust and racy style.[22]

But a literature that mocks a genteel manner even in reaching
for it would seem to be cousin german (city cousin to country
cousin) to a humor based on a homely but shrewd Yankee's
murdering the king's English. While there is no danger of
mistaking Irving for a frontier humorist, his irreverence, irresponsibility, and indolence in the face of appeals to respectability
balance in a characteristically American way the longing for
status. An understanding of Knickerbockerism at least partially
substantiates Daniel Hoffman's reading of "The Legend of
Sleepy Hollow" as a conflict between frontier and seaboard attitudes.[23] Indeed in *Knickerbocker,* Irving, who knew something
about "biting, gouging, and other branches of the rough-and-
tumble mode of warfare" on New Amsterdam's "southern
frontier" (*K*, p. 210), had already created a minor hero, Dirk
Schuiler, in the southwestern image:

> He was a tall, lank fellow, swift of foot, and long-winded. He was
> generally equipped in a half Indian dress, with belt, leggings, and
> moccasons. His hair hung in straight gallows locks about his ears,
> and added not a little to his shirking demeanor. It is an old remark,
> that persons of Indian mixture are half civilized, half savage, and
> half devil, a third half being expressly provided for their particular
> convenience. It is for similar reasons, and probably with equal
> truth, that the back-wood-men of Kentucky are styled half man, half
> horse and half alligator, by the settlers on the Mississippi, and held
> accordingly in great respect and abhorrence. (p. 309)[24]

Dirk may drink too much, may be essentially as lazy as Rip Van
Winkle and as much of a poacher of sheep as the gypsy Starlight
Tom in *Bracebridge Hall,* but he is the only Dutchman with the
ingenuity to escape from the Swedes at Fort Casimir and the

[22] Ironically Wendell believed he was paying Irving high tribute in making him
out a better English stylist than most English writers. But Dana had noted long
ago that the early style, in contrast to that of *The Sketch Book*, had not only a
more "natural run" to it but "home qualities" as well, such as a "direct, simple
and plain phraseology." *N. A. Review*, IX, 348.

[23] *Form and Fable*, pp. 83–96.

[24] Professor Lewis Leary of Columbia and his student Michael L. Black have also
noticed, they inform me, that this is a very early (1809) allusion in print to key
imagery in the Mike Fink legend.

energy to bulldoze his way back through the wilderness to New Amsterdam to alert Peter Stuyvesant that his entire garrison has been captured.

The fondness for burlesque, satire, caricature, and extravagant whimsy may have been more of a "mania" among the minor literati of nineteenth-century New York City than elsewhere, but the symptoms of the contagion were hard for American literature in general to live down. The capacity of both Cooper and Melville for lapsing into crude Swiftian comedy has already been noted, and traces of Knickerbocker humor are particularly pronounced in Poe. His Bon-Bon is the old antiquarian Frenchified and gourmandized. In "The Unparalleled Adventure of One Hans Pfall" one finds Irvingesque Dutchmen and fitful bursts of a facetious Knickerbocker prose: "Upon finishing the perusal of this very extraordinary document, Professor Rubadub, it is said, dropped his pipe to the ground in the extremity of his surprise. . . ." There are more Dutch cabbages in "The Devil in the Belfry" than in all of Irving. And when it comes to exposing little great men, such as the narrator of "The Literary Life of Thingum Bob, Esq.," son of "a merchant-barber in the city of Smug" and "Late Editor of the 'Goosetherumfoodle,' " Poe outdoes *Salmagundi* for broadness of satire and scrupulous, almost obsessive, attention to petty detail.

His burlesques curiously comport with his tales in going to fantastic extremes. He is apt to use what might be called, in *Salmagundi*'s terminology, "gothic risibility" to balance gothic terror.[25] Pieces such as "How to Write a Blackwood Article," "A Predicament," "Loss of Breath," and "The Man that Was Used Up" lampoon the kind of horror situation which he takes seriously in his most famous tales. "Berenice," he suggested, was the result of his having on a bet chosen a subject apparently fit only for burlesque and "treated it seriously."[26] As Constance Rourke brilliantly put it,

[25] "In the midst of the burlesque in *Tales of the Folio Club* he reached an antithetical horror, in *Berenice*." Constance Rourke, *American Humor: A Study of National Character* (New York, 1931), p. 184.

[26] Letter to Thomas W. White, 30 April 1835, *The Letters of Edgar Allan Poe*, ed. John W. Ostrom (Cambridge, Mass., 1948), I, 57.

His laughter was of a single order: it was inhuman, and mixed with hysteria. His purpose in the hoaxes was to make his readers absurd, to reduce them to an involuntary imbecility. His objective was triumph, the familiar objective of popular comedy. To this end, in his burlesques and extravaganzas, he showed human traits or lineaments in unbelievable distortion, using that grotesquerie which lies midway between the comic and the terrible; with Poe the terrible was always within view.[27]

Satire and burlesque surely reach an extreme in Poe, and one hesitates to use the term "mania" with him only because of a suspicion that it is almost literally apt. He suggests one of his own characters, the practical-joking aristocrat of "Mystification," who carries the whimsical (he lives "in an atmosphere of whim") almost to the point of the maniacal. Hoaxing, as Constance Rourke implied, seems close to the basis of Poe's art, and his desire to deceive or mystify an audience was also a compulsion and thus, at bottom, at least a partial self-deception. The fascination with practical jokers, diddlers, and confidence men can hardly have been accidental in one who himself often diddled the public. Pieces like "The Balloon Hoax" are only the most obvious examples. He was also fond of parading recondite knowledge in order to exaggerate his expertise as a linguist or cryptographer, and he was apt to declare a "plagiarism" at the first sign of a literary similarity. It is hardly surprising that his overly pat explanation in "The Philosophy of Composition" of the writing of "The Raven" should sometimes be read as only another piece of deliberate mystification.

His burlesques are in effect playful hoaxes, designed to be seen through but given vitality by a dogged attention to consistent impersonation, if it is only at the level of caricature. "Von Kempelen and His Discovery," for instance, uses as seriously as possible the essentially comic device of insisting on the truthfulness of an obviously fictitious narrative, the device which Irving used with his tales "found among the papers of the late Diedrich Knickerbocker." The seeming genuineness of Poe's scientifically informed and authoritative-sounding narrator, who

[27] Rourke, p. 183.

attempts to persuade the reader that a mad alchemist has actually turned base metal into gold and thus made a California gold rush unnecessary, makes the gothic stereotype almost credible. Similarly, Poe's tales of ratiocination depend on pretenses which require as much patient laboring with technical detail as that in which, in his devious extremes, the hero of "Mystification," who is constantly "upon the lookout for the grotesque," indulges himself, taking infinite pains with his elegant but pointless deceptions. And when in his horror stories Poe impersonates the madman trying to hold onto rationality and self-control, one wonders whether he is not enacting an aspect of himself.

Constance Rourke located Poe's extravagant humor in the American frontier tradition. She admitted that his humorous materials, his "legends," were not essentially native and said the reason was that he had no deep roots in American life and "native" literary traditions. Yet in a candid aside she wondered whether any American of the time was really rooted.[28] Perhaps this is where something like Knickerbockerism comes in. Poe, the grand misfit of American culture, is altogether unable to believe in himself as he attempts to communicate with the citizen reader; he may use humor and sheer virtuosity both to laugh at, and to defend himself against, philistine audiences. If this sounds more like the dandy frightening the squatter than the other way around, it only goes to show that we need an explanation of American humor that will deal simultaneously with its "folk" background and its more "literary" sources.

In the absence of such an explanation, one can at least offer a few observations and suggestions. It may be worth noting, for instance, that there is a humorous side to Hawthorne. "Mrs. Bullfrog" may be a mere forced exercise, a work with which he did not feel the temperamental affinity that Poe had with "The Man that Was Used Up." But, like Irving, Poe, and Melville, Hawthorne was willing on occasion to heighten the ludicrous into the grotesque, as we have already noted in the character of the whimsical old bachelor in "The Wedding Knell," who turns

[28] *Ibid.*, p. 182.

his marriage into a funeral ceremony. The story was one which Poe, understandably, admired. Wakefield, the practical joker in spite of himself, is another of Hawthorne's grotesques. And how far is it from the quaint pleasantries of Dr. Heidegger to the macabre cynicism of Rappaccini? Or what is one to make of the almost Knickerbockerish nonsense of the introduction to "Rappaccini's Daughter"?[29] A tendency toward elaborate satire and fantasy, a willingness to experiment with ludicrous carica- ture, is especially strong in *Mosses from an Old Manse*, as though to compensate both Hawthorne and his readers for the habitual intensity of his moral concern and his willingness, during the Brook Farm and Concord period, to take seriously an Idealism that had Transcendental overtones (this is a matter to be touched on again in Chapter VI).

Hawthorne had a fine sense of the proximity of the ridiculous and the sublime, of "good and evil, faith and infidelity, wisdom and nonsense," as his arrangement of the "most incongruous throng" in "The Hall of Fantasy" shows. The Hall of Fantasy is full of wild-eyed projectors harking back to Swift, hobbyhorse riders and victims of whim-wham. And one finds them elsewhere in Hawthorne, in "The Celestial Railroad" and "Earth's Holo- caust," for instance. Yet, like Sterne and Irving, Hawthorne knew that one had better be careful in writing off humorists and fantastics. For who doesn't visit the Hall of Fantasy from time to time? And how at any given instant can one be sure one isn't there? ". . . the fantasies of one day are the deepest realities of a future one." Deal gently then with idlers, dreamers, and re- formers—even Transcendentalists. One cannot hope to use or

---

[29] I refer to the mock-account of the author which makes him out to be a Frenchman, one M. de l'Aubépine (this presumably makes the story a translation), author of such works as "Contes deux fois racontées." The humor here, which depends on the quaint and incongruous look and sound that a known Hawthorne title such as "The New Adam and Eve" acquires in French—"Le nouveau Père Adam et la nouvelle Mère Eve"—has its resemblance to what one finds so often, in Irving and Poe, a willingness to make fun of the French dancing master, cook, or roué. For a discussion of Hawthorne's use of the narrative convention of the author's showing his awareness that he is only telling a story (not reporting real events), see Alfred H. Marks, "German Romantic Irony in Hawthorne's Tales," *Symposium*, II (May, 1953), 291–93.

enjoy or perhaps even conceive of reality except through imagination, which may always turn out to be illusory.

What Henry James called the "Artless Age" in the United States,[30] the pre-Civil War period, relied heavily on more obvious forms of humor, probably because of its uncertainties about the nature and value of art and because it was still looking for more literate forms of expression. Calculated cleverness served as a useful release for a society straining for high culture. The burden was so heavy that even Emerson laughed mildly at himself in 1820 as he began keeping a journal at Harvard, where he was being fully exposed to the kind of rhetorical machinery that had been driving American writers into epic depictions of the national destiny. His mind was awhirl with mythological figures, rhapsodical diction, and elaborate allegories and personifications. The ostensible reason for keeping a commonplace book was to get some of this eloquence on paper: "Mixing with the thousand pursuits & passions & objects of the world as personified by Imagination is profitable & entertaining." Yet the self-mockery with which he continued, playing with the rhythms and phrasings of the high style, suggests his awareness of a certain artificiality in his academic exercises. The journal was to be not only a "record of new thoughts" but "a receptacle of all the old ideas that partial but peculiar peepings at antiquity can furnish or furbish" and a "tablet to save the wear & tear of weak Memory." In the next breath this Harvard Junior invoked "witches" to "enliven or horrify some midnight lucubration or dream (whichever may be found most convenient) to supply this reservoir when other resources fail." He then apologized to "Fairy Land! rich region of fancy & gnomery, elvery, sylphery, & Queen Mab" for not first requesting assistance from that quarter.[31]

Unlike the young Irving and the wags he corresponded with, Emerson soon managed to free himself from mock-heroic bathos;

[30] *Notes of a Son and Brother*, chap. iii.
[31] *The Journals and Miscellaneous Notebooks of Ralph Waldo Emerson*, ed. William H. Gilman *et al.*, I (Cambridge, Mass., 1960), 3–4. For Emerson's personifications see "Grandeur," "Spring," and "Pestilence" (I, 6, 11–12, 15–16).

he later turned up his nose at "the deplorable Dutch wit of 'Knickerbocker.' "[32] Yet not all Brahmin taste was so fastidious, as the appreciations of Irving's humor by Dana, Prescott,[33] and Lowell show. In his *Autocrat* Holmes may have appeared to possess all the authority so pathetically lacking in Diedrich Knickerbocker, yet this Bostonian version of Dr. Johnson, acting as "his own Boswell," gave himself a sovereignty which extended no farther than a boardinghouse breakfast table.

Perry Miller noted, writing primarily about New York City, that "for reasons which sociologists have not yet clarified, a form of humor seized upon the middle of the nineteenth century which makes that era" seem absolutely "remote." This humor, in which, he said, "Melville was trained," involved some of the far-fetched grotesquerie of Dickens and Cruikshank and reveled in local allusions that must have been partially obscure even to contemporaries. But substantially it was an aspect of what New Yorkers in the thirties and forties called "Rabelaisianism." New York "owed it to Irving," though it was the *Knickerbocker*, founded in 1833 (Irving occasionally contributed to the magazine but had nothing to do with its management), which "had perfected it." The editor of the *Knickerbocker* clearly defined Rabelaisianism in the course of noting its presence in the work of a minor writer of the period:

> there is the same extraordinary display of universal learning, the same minute exactness of quotation, the same extravagant spirit of fun, the same capricious and provoking love of digression, the same upsetting of admitted ideas, by which trifles are seriously descanted upon, and bolstered up with endless authorities, until they expand into gigantic proportions, while time-honored truths are shuffled by with the most whimsical contempt.[34]

But sociologists may not be needed here. For Miller himself in *The Raven and the Whale* has suggested how appropriate such

[32] Quoted in STW, II, 275.

[33] [William H. Prescott], "Essay Writing," *N. A. Review*, XIV (April, 1822), 333. The "comic scenes" of *The Sketch Book*, says Prescott, show "the broad caricature of a truly original humor."

[34] Perry Miller, *The Raven and the Whale* (New York, 1956), pp. 67–68, 260. Lewis Gaylord Clark is the editor quoted.

a manner was for a group of writers like the combatants in the
magazine wars in New York at mid-century, who wanted desperately to belong to "culture," but who were prevented, in the
absence of a clearly articulated heritage, from understanding
what culture consists of or how seriously it should be taken in
a commercial society. The Irving attitude, whether in its most
blatantly Knickerbockerish form or toned down to fit the character of Geoffrey Crayon, masks, though it masks transparently
and self-consciously, a personality which does not fully comprehend itself. In Irving the pseudonymous character (the whole
New York school of the artless age loved pen names), presented
as whimsical and at loose ends, serves as superficial ego to an
unauthoritarian author. Underneath, one often feels, lies an
actual self capable, if it could express itself directly, of something close to dismay, fear, or rage, emotions at least partially
sublimated in humor.

Genuine sophistication involves awareness that the world is
in one sense largely show, fashion, style, and make-believe; it
asks only that the pedantry of demonstrating this awareness be
abandoned. Yet the shrilly voiced contradictions of an almost
admittedly self-deceiving culture in some ways anticipate the
complex integrity of the Transcendentalists, of Poe, Hawthorne,
Melville, and Whitman. Deliberate nonsense often comes close
to the paradoxes of metaphysical or romantic irony. "My life,"
Poe wrote Lowell, "has been *whim*—impulse—passion. . . ."[35]
And there is after all an echo of Knickerbockerism, of Salma-
gundian eccentricity, in the catchword Emerson proposes in
"Self-Reliance" as a sign of outward nonconformity pointing

[35] 2 July 1844, *The Letters of Poe*, I, 257. This assertion may be in part itself
a masquerade, Poe's effort at mystification with Lowell. Yet one suspects that he
at least wanted to believe this about himself. The context in which this statement
occurs is remarkable as evidence of Poe's ability to see his own life in terms
suggestive of, even if more intensely applied than, those Irving used for his: "I
have been too deeply conscious of the mutability and evanescence of temporal
things, to give any continuous effort to anything—to be consistent in anything.
My life has been *whim*—impulse—passion—a longing for solitude—a scorn of all
things present, in an earnest desire for the future." One thinks of Irving, in the
Preface to the revised edition of *The Sketch Book*, quoting one of his letters to
Scott years earlier, which explains that the "desultory" nature of his life has
rendered him unfit "for any periodically recurring task." *SB*, p. 9.

toward an inner individual integrity. "I would write on the lin-
tels of the door-post, *Whim*. I hope it is somewhat better than
whim at last, but we cannot spend all day in explanation." In an
intellectual salmagundi, associations may lead almost anywhere;
the mind is chaotically free because external commonsense
meanings do not bind it. Juxtaposing Irving and Emerson is, I
hope, something more than a whimsical gesture; the universe that
Emerson accepts is as unorganized and undisciplined as Knickerbocker's until the mind creates its own order.

The American writer from Irving to Melville, we have learned,
was apt to feel the attraction of the seventeenth-century English
literary baroque. Yet the tropical and paradoxical style of
Thoreau so nearly approached the habitual language of literary
New York that Evert Duyckinck in denouncing it had to demonstrate carefully that it was only "pseudo-Rabelaisian."[36] Poe
charged Hawthorne with having developed at Brook Farm and
Concord a "*spirit* of 'metaphor-run-mad.'"[37] And Melville's
springboard into the metaphysical conceits of Ishmael was
Rabelaisian fantasticalness. Had the sublibrarian looked back
at the original Preface to the *History of New York*, *Moby-Dick*
might have had still another whaling extract. For Knickerbocker,
in offering his work to the public in 1809, had written (though
Irving had subsequently removed the passage):

> . . . ye mighty Whales, ye grampuses and Sharks of criticism, who
> delight in shipwrecking unfortunate adventurers upon the sea of
> letters, have mercy upon this crazy vessel. Ye may toss it about in
> your sport; or spout your dirty water upon it in showers; but do
> not, for the sake of the unlucky mariner within—do not stave it
> with your tails and send it to the bottom. (*K*, pp. 13–14)

[36] Miller's phrase, *The Raven and the Whale*, p. 263.
[37] "Tale-Writing," *The Complete Works of Edgar Allan Poe*, ed. J. A. Harrison
(New York, 1902), XIII, 155. Hawthorne included Rabelais among the authors
with enduring places in "The Hall of Fantasy."

V

The Romantic Transition

THE nonsense of *Salmagundi* and *Knickerbocker* tended to reduce the world to words, but one went on using words, trying to compose fiction and find order in the records of the past. What Irving needed was a theory of imagination or Transcendental Reason. What he had was a flair for style and a sense of the picturesque. A thoroughgoing organicism might have stabilized the flux of impressions to which his experience seemed reduced. But for those unable to reach a clear intuition of an infinite coherence of parts and parcels within a single Whole, there was apt to be more mutability than stability, and a groping or rioting about in what often seemed merely private associations.[1]

Out of a delight in the images and the "general association of ideas" produced in the mind as one stared at the shapes of the flames in the hearth, took tea or coffee, and contrasted the warmth and comfort of the room with the evils of the outside world might come a familiar essay, such as Leigh Hunt's "A Day by the Fire," which Irving reprinted in the *Analectic Magazine* in 1814 (*AN*, IV, 421–24). This proved a fruitful way of exploiting subjectivity and was obviously related to strategies that Irving was to begin using in *The Sketch Book*. There were, however, less responsible uses of the imagination, as one sees, for instance, in the abandon of a statement by Paulding in a review of a work of history for the *Analectic*:

[1] Writing Brevoort about a "ramble over the scenes hallowed by honest Walton's simple muse," Irving confessed his fear that he was only amusing *himself* "with agreeable recollections, which may be tedious & trifling to those in whom they do not awaken the same associations." Letter of 29 January 1817, *WIHB*, II, 11–12.

> When truth is buried in the rubbish of ages—when all contempo-
> rary testimony is swept away—when detection has quenched her
> taper—and the mists of time . . . have given to distant objects an
> indistinct, mysterious, and exaggerated outline—then it is that
> credulity riots in the fertile fields of the marvellous, and romance
> becomes history. (*AN*, IV, 68)

If Irving was sometimes tempted in this direction, he did not go
so far as to get lost in the mists.[2]

After reducing history almost to blank enigma in *Knickerbocker*, he began to take the past more seriously, yet his change
of attitude hardly amounted to a new conception. The Irving of
The Sketch Book was simply less averse to enjoying in public
his subjective responses to relics of the past—even when he suspected the irrelevancy of his emotions or the inaccuracy, or perhaps unverifiability, of his ideas. If the world seemed to leave
him nothing but the freedom of his own associations, he had at
least to try to take satisfaction in them. Accurate history might
be a virtual impossibility, but palpable remains of the past such
as the items Irving was to investigate in England—old buildings,
paintings, folk tales, traditional ceremonies and customs—had
shape and form and connoted certain qualities of heart and mind
in the people who had created or constructed them. They made
an appeal to the sense of style. They might even tell an imaginative man something about himself, his origins, his everlasting
human-ness.

By 1810 Irving had almost come round to Brydone's amused
and ultracivilized acceptance of folklore. "There is something
indiscribably [sic] charming & fanciful," he wrote in his journal, "in the extravagance—the superstitions and the supernal

---

[2] There was no dearth of discussion of, or references to, associationism in the
Analectic. The most important item in this connection is a review of an apparently
anonymous work, *Essays on the Sources of the Pleasures Received from Literary
Compositions. AN*, III, 353–70. The importance for romanticism of the develop-
ment of associationist psychology, and the general acceptance of associationism in
aesthetics have been carefully studied. See, for instance, William Charvat, *The
Origins of American Critical Thought, 1810–1835* (Philadelphia, 1936), chap. iii;
Walter J. Bate, *From Classic to Romantic* (Cambridge, Mass., 1949), chap. iv.
Leon Howard has commented on the importance of associationism in Irving's
development in *Transitions in American Literary History*, ed. Harry H. Clark
(Durham, N.C., 1953), p. 89.

illusions with which chimerical ignorance once clothed every subject—Those twilight views of nature and of science were infinitely more wild and pleasing than any thing which sobre [sic] truth presents. . . ." As "twilight views" reveals, folklore now qualified as "picturesque." But, although the unreality of the picturesque still slightly disturbed him, he looked for solace in the belief that myths and legends represent the efforts of "the imagination," in periods when "reason" was underdeveloped, "to explain the prodigies of nature."[3]

This is the kind of thinking, just then coming into fashion, that bridges the gap between the early and the later Irving. As editor of the *Analectic*, whose main job, although he wrote and solicited some original material, was to supervise the reprinting of articles and reviews from leading British periodicals, he was exposed to great quantities of it. It was impossible for Irving, the *Analectic*, or the age in general to follow Horne Tooke's bold leap in the direction of pragmatism and the view that truth or knowledge is basically a form of belief, what is "TROWED," rather than what is known for certain.[4] Thus a reviewer of a memoir of the late eighteenth-century politician and philologist became indignant over Tooke's questioning of the existence of absolute metaphysical truth (*AN*, I, 97–98). Yet, ironically, the *Analectic* frequently, though it seldom realized it, raised the question of the relation of knowledge to belief.

Sometimes this happened in a rather simpleminded way, as when the magazine, although it seemed in some ways a storehouse of information, at the same time foisted on its readers the recurring suspicion that too much knowledge or too much disciplined thinking is a dangerous thing. Another reviewer, for instance, who would undoubtedly have seen in the nominalism of Tooke's *Diversions of Purley* the work of a decadent skeptic, is revealed

[3] "Washington Irving's Notebook of 1810," ed. Barbara D. Simison, *Yale University Library Gazette*, XXIV (July, October, 1949), 90. As this notebook shows, Irving was just now reading Burke on the sublime.

[4] ". . . there is nothing but TRUTH in the world. . . . TRUTH supposes mankind: *for whom* and *by whom* alone the world is formed, and *to whom* only it is applicable. . . . There is . . . no such thing as eternal, immutable everlasting TRUTH; unless mankind, *such as they are at present*, be also eternal, immutable, and everlasting." *The Diversions of Purley* (Philadelphia, 1807), II, 339.

as something of an obscurantist when he blames what he takes to be the troubles of the age, among them a strong tendency toward dullness, decadence, and skepticism, on an excess of knowledge: the impoverishment of the working classes, so the argument goes, is a consequence of the industrial revolution currently in progress, which stems in turn from the rapid advances of knowledge in recent generations; demoralization is seen as a by-product of the entire process. "Philosophy," the same writer says later, "which has led to the exact investigation of causes, has robbed the world of much of its sublimity."[5]

Similarly the *Analectic* often implied that it is more interesting to learn in fields where not much knowledge has been accumulated. It grew fat on travel literature and reviews of books of travels, in which readers were encouraged to turn their imaginations loose to feed upon the still undefined connections among geography, history, and local customs. Yet there was a more sophisticated side to this romantic indulgence: when, in reviewing a study of certain aspects of eighteenth-century literature, a writer was finally forced to call Montesquieu's methods unscientific, he nevertheless praised him for "the poetical cast of his imagination, which could not tolerate the appearance of dulness, and delighted in brilliancy and effect." Indeed Montesquieu's tendency to discursiveness, his fondness for whimsy, his habit of alluding to hidden corners of history, and his impatience with slow inductive investigation were all seen by the reviewer as related to his capacity for brilliant insight.[6]

Furthermore there was no ignoring the seriousness with which mythology and folklore were beginning to be treated. The title page of the first number (1813) of the *Analectic* offered "Articles as are most Valuable, Curious, or Entertaining." Some of the strange beliefs and customs recorded in the magazine were obviously intended to be little more than entertaining curiosities. But where the Enlightenment had been prone to see mere quaint

[5] Review of Madame de Staël's *De la littérature considérée dans ses rapports avec les institutions sociales*, AN, II, 193–99, 249–50.

[6] Review of *Tableau de la littérature pendant le dix-huitième siècle*, AN, IV, 190–92.

superstition, writers like Chateaubriand, whose *Les martyrs* and *Génie du Christianisme* were discussed in reviews reprinted in the *Analectic*, were now discovering symbolic significance. Stressing aesthetic considerations (which in itself implied a broader, more sophisticated aesthetic than the eighteenth-century dogma of art as instruction and entertainment), Chateaubriand had concluded that the "true" religion for him was the one which was most beautiful. Its literal truthfulness was largely beside the point; he renounced any effort to demonstrate it. The sheer beauty of Christianity seemed to him to guarantee a better life (on earth) to persons persuaded to it. The origin of its beauty he discovered in its mythology. Christian myths, though they might not say anything exactly new (pagan myths, he showed, had often imperfectly embodied fundamental principles), could give greater clarity to basic human awarenesses because they were better ordered and more harmoniously shaped. The reviewer in the *Analectic* managed to suggest Chateaubriand's impatience with the language of science or natural philosophy in certain contexts. Obviously, for instance, mountains might profitably be talked about as something other than "*protuberances* of *calcareous* or *vitrifiable rock.*" And he made clear Chateaubriand's conviction that "good morals depend on good taste," that "he who is insensible to beauty" is "blind to virtue" (*AN*, II, 118–19).

The *Analectic* was likewise aware of new tendencies in historiography. By the 1820's a virtual school of "narrative" history was to emerge in England and France, ultimately exerting some influence on Irving himself when he turned in earnest to writing history, and, later, on the American historians Prescott, Parkman, and Motley. This tradition was to affect, if it did not altogether take in, such scholars as the Baron de Barante, Augustin Thierry, Adolphe Thiers, François Guizot, Sharon Turner, and Macaulay. Swayed by some of the same romantic forces responsible for Scott's historical fiction, the "narrative" historians ranged themselves more or less directly against the conceptions of the "philosophical" or classicist historiography which stemmed from Bolingbroke, Voltaire, Hume, Robertson, and

Gibbon. Roughly speaking, the difference between the two groups came to turn on the attempt of the writers in the eighteenth-century tradition to expose and define basic causes behind important historical events, as opposed to the concentration of the newer historians upon structural and stylistic devices which would induce in the reader more vivid impressions of the flavor and color of a certain period in history.[7] The "narrative" historians were in some cases willing to forego literal accuracy in order to promote a general "sense" of the past. Thus, as an article in the *Analectic* noted, Joseph Michaud in his *Histoire des croisades* attempted to approximate the style of the medieval chroniclers and even refused to weed out of his account what he knew to be pure fables (*AN*, III, 442–43). And Paulding in another review praised the same kind of history—mixtures of legends and fables, behind which there was no pretense to strict accuracy (IV, 49–50).

Complementing this growing interest in the texture or spirit of past epochs, the historicism of Madame de Staël's *De la littérature considérée dans ses rapports avec les institutions sociales* (a book duly, if not altogether sympathetically, noted in the *Analectic*), tended to turn all literature into a kind of folklore, that is the expression of a folk, of a people or society. In her view, not only did literature preserve an impression of the character of the past, it also exerted a reciprocal influence on the shape of subsequent history. Said her reviewer,

> The professed object of [de Staël's] work is to show that all the peculiarities in the literature of different ages and countries, may be explained by a reference to the condition of society, and the political and religious institutions of each;—and at the same time to point out in what way the progress of letters has in its turn modified and affected the government and religion of those nations among whom they have flourished. (*AN*, II, 180)[8]

---

[7] Elsewhere I have suggested that the distinction between "philosophical" and "narrative" history is far from clear and that the controversy reflects the larger confusions of the pre-romantic era. "The Fiction of History: Washington Irving against a Romantic Transition" (unpublished Ph.D. dissertation, Harvard University, 1954), chap. iv.

[8] Benjamin Spencer has noted the importance of de Staël in helping to break the hold of neoclassicism in the United States after 1815. *Quest for Nationality*

The person who was to have the greatest influence on Irving's interest in the potential usefulness for literary purposes of legendary materials was, of course, Scott. Though not cited in the *Analectic* in this regard, he had some time earlier expressed ideas which reflect some of the same intellectual tendencies observable in the magazine. In stressing the importance of memory in molding a group of people or a mixture of races into a spiritually cohesive community, Scott had written in the Preface to his edition of *Sir Tristrem* that people need to feel themselves related to their environment: "tradition depends upon locality. The scene of a celebrated battle, the ruins of an ancient tower, the 'historic stone' over the grave of a hero, the hill and the valley inhabited by a particular tribe, remind posterity of events which are sometimes recorded in their very names." Even a race translated to a new environment, he continued, tries to connect itself or its ancestors with local tradition.[9] The implications of these remarks are not easy to determine. But Scott may be saying that history, or the past, is what subsequent generations think or remember, or, if not, then at least that a large part of the present is the impression the past makes on its consciousness. The similarity of Scott's attitude toward tradition to that of the American writer who was conscious of the difficulty of creating literature in a landscape devoid of ruins and monuments, is striking. Romantic feeling for history was evolving to the point where its appropriateness to certain American problems was going to become inescapable.

One of the features of the *Analectic* was a series of brief lives of American commanders in the War of 1812, written by the editor himself and his friends Paulding and Gulian Verplanck.

(Syracuse, 1957), p. 91. The *Analectic* had already reprinted her chapter relating Shakespeare to the quasi-barbaric north European character. *AN*, I, 156–63. Irving had met the great lady during his early Italian tour. PMI, I, 137.

[9] Thomas of Erceldoune, *Sir Tristrem; A Metrical Romance of the Thirteenth Century* (Edinburgh, 1811), pp. xxvii–xxviii. Scholars have since concluded that *Sir Tristrem* is not the work of Thomas the Rhymer but is a French poem. From Abbotsford Irving wrote in 1817, "I have rambled about the hills with Scott; visited the haunts of Thomas the Rhymer, and other spots rendered classic by border tale and witching song, and have been in a kind of dream or delirium." Letter to Peter Irving, 1 September, PMI, I, 381.

Though little more than patriotic potboilers, they occasionally reveal in Irving a concern about the function of biography that suggests the new attitudes under discussion. He begins, for instance, to picture himself as a myth-maker.[10] The nation, in the *Analectic*'s view, had a need for heroic images, because, as Paulding said in introducing an account of May Day customs, "Our history is but of yesterday, and of tradition we have scarce a vestige" (*AN*, IV, 252). Thus, although Irving's first impulse, in his comment (I, 250) on a sketch of the life of Robert Treat Paine published in an edition of that author's works, was to try to distinguish biography from heroic literature, he inevitably moved, in a later piece, in the direction of identifying the two genres.[11]

Irving was never to become fully clear in his conception of history. In *The Sketch Book* he was to claim, even in the act of worshiping at the shrine of Stratford on Avon, that the genius of Shakespeare in working with legend and folklore had operated to falsify the "face of nature; to give to things and places a charm and character not their own" (p. 339). Yet he showed clearly enough his belief that in some sense the legendary associations belonged to the land and that Shakespeare, by clothing the English landscape with "airy nothings," had made it more livable, more meaningful, had helped preserve its connection, however tenuous, with its past. Furthermore, by 1814 Irving had written two papers on the American Indians—essays in legendary history;[12] these reappeared in *The Sketch Book*, significantly placed immediately after "Stratford-on-Avon," as though he were suggesting an attempt on his part in "Traits of Indian Character" and "Philip of Pokanoket" to do in some way for his own country what he felt Shakespeare had done for his.

As a document like the Preface to the 1848 edition of *Knickerbocker* suggests, Irving gradually came to see such a motive as the strongest and most significant one behind much

---

[10] See "Biography of Captain James Lawrence," *AN*, II, 135, and "Biographical Notice of the Late Lieutenant Burrows," *AN*, II, 396.

[11] "Biographical Memoir of Commodore Perry," *AN*, II, 494.

[12] *AN*, III, 145–56, 502–15.

of his writing. And though he undoubtedly exaggerated, there is surely a sense in which such stories as "Rip Van Winkle" and "The Legend of Sleepy Hollow," though largely Germanic in origin, are attempts by Irving to equip the American landscape with a kind of mythology, to crystallize a handful of memories, traditions, and a connection with a past already blurred and threatened with extinction.

Following the editorial stint on the *Analectic,* Irving spent the better part of five years priming himself to make a full commitment to professional authorship. These were years of self-appraisal, of anxious tinkering followed by fits of inspiration, of restless searching for material and scrutinizing of prices current in the literary marketplace. When he finally began to publish *The Sketch Book,* he would sometimes, in the effort to satisfy his audience, go too far. The didacticism of "Roscoe," "English Writers on America," and "Rural Life in England" is excessive. And elsewhere, abandoning the sense of the ridiculous, he reverses the mock-heroic process and, seemingly without effort, finds genuine emotions possible in a world at which he had formerly laughed precisely because they were virtually insupportable. The result is sheer sentimentalism.

Irving had deceived even himself with the "pathetic" strain, which he had heard was very popular with the public.[13] He had begun to look for "true" stories, "true" in the Richardsonian sense of being immediately applicable to troubled situations. The need for a literary gospel, for a truth which is not a fiction, for instances of actual life which verify the formulae of literature even led Crayon to—"Shall I confess it?—I believe in broken hearts, and the possibility of dying of disappointed love" (p. 89).

Only women are killed by broken hearts, Irving believed. But men suffer from them, and it is obvious from his *Notes While Preparing Sketch Book* that he thought of himself as still recovering from a nearly mortal wound. Behind Crayon's visits to rural graveyards lies Irving's real sense of isolation, of being

[13] See PMI, I, 430.

cut off from a home and love, floundering in frustration and failure. His notebooks reveal the insecurity that prompted the longing for positive belief noticeable in one side of *The Sketch Book.* For sheer homesick sentimentality the following rhapsody is unsurpassed: "England so richly [?] dight with palaces— earth so studded & gemmed with castles & palaces—so embroi- dered with parks & gardens   So storied so wrought up with pic- tures—Let me wander along the streams of beautiful England & dream of my native rivers [sic] of my beautiful native coun- try."[14] Nothing so heart-wracking as this appears in *The Sketch Book* itself,[15] but the book constantly subdues and rationalizes this divided allegiance.

The career of traveling and sketching on which he had em- barked provided him with a continuous source of images for objectifying his emotional restlessness. In his notebook *Tour in Scotland, 1817,* for instance, he asks, "Why dress we up these our Inns as if they were our homes & are as carefull about a few nights lodgings here as if we designed an everlasting abode?" For the moment, he universalizes his own experience, charac- terizing all mankind as mere "sojourners & pilgrims."[16] Playful as it is in part, *The Sketch Book* also reflects the actuality of Irving's current existence. Year by year he was sinking deeper into his unsettled condition as bachelor, traveler, and anti- quarian.

But though, as Crayon, he might occasionally try to "play" the "preceptor," he was still self-conscious about it: "Methinks I hear the questions asked by my graver readers, 'To what pur- pose is all this—how is the world to be made wiser by this talk?' " Irving could not be sure that his "sagest deductions"— his "mite of wisdom"—were "safe" as "guides" for his readers

---

[14] *NP*, p. 98. The following notes may be fragments of a sketch or story that he was composing; then again they may be direct expressions of Irving's personal feelings; in either case one is not surprised to find them: "now & then a fit of devouring melancholy that eats into my very soul"; "a melancholy that corrodes the spirits & seems to rust all the springs of mental energy." *NP*, p. 79.

[15] "Let me not indulge in this mawkish feeling and sentiment—engendered by literature—which has produced a morbid sensibility and fostered all the melan- choly tendencies &c." *NP*, p. 78.

[16] *TS*, p. 113.

(*SB*, p. 289). Thus to turn his travels to account as literature he personalized them, largely avoided the pretense of objectivity, and capitalized on his private, partially eccentric view.

The character of Irving's best work was always "superficial" —a word used here not in a necessarily derogatory, but in a simpler denotative, sense. Generally, he assumed that he could not have knowledge (which Knickerbockerism had seen only as opinion anyway) of the "inside" of experience unless he started with observations on the surface. True, as his notebooks indicate, he was something of a hunter of proverbial wisdom, and in view of our sense of how he could burlesque just this sort of activity, he is rather pathetic in this role: "From Toffee's mount, where urchins squander their hoarded pence. Emblem of spend-thrift man."[17] Or, looking over a Scottish landscape, he noted that though it was cloudy where he stood, "the heathy mountains down the course of the Tay are in sunshine"; "from the gloom of adversity look out on the prosperity of the world."[18] The extent to which he would ultimately have liked to see into things is revealed in a letter he wrote several years later from Spain. He was trying to relate the effect of the cathedral of Seville at dusk to that of a great American forest: "I cannot compare the scenes, but their sublime and solitary features produce the same dilation of the heart and swelling of the spirit, the same aspiring and longing after something exalted and indefinite; something—I know not what, but something which I feel this world cannot give me."[19] But his in-sights flashed but briefly; his universal-sounding propositions were always dependent on immediate images. Change the outward appearance of the scene or of the world, and his conception of its inner reality had to be revised. His sensibility served him effectively in organizing, in perceiving, the surface of things around dominant impressions, around clusters of related or contrasting images. This was the old faculty of the picturesque.

[17] "Note book, kept while in England, containing memoranda, verses, 3 drawings, etc.," manuscript in the New York Public Library.
[18] *TS*, p. 58.
[19] To Antoinette Bolviller, 20 July 1828, PMI, II, 331. Compare this, however, with the comic treatment of such aspiration, below, n. 25.

His best notebook observations are suggestive rather than
explicit; some of them contain a kind of poetical-prosaic charm:

> Flight of crows far below . . . Road passes below the craig & I hear
> the noise of a cart tho the cart & horse are extremely diminished by
> the hight [sic]—rush of the wind through the trees of the cliff—
> whistles thro the grass that grows on the brow of the precipice—I
> hear the whooping of children but cannot perceive them.[20]

But realism was an epistemological impossibility. If Irving
talked of "describing" things "as they are," it was only to avoid
"pretending to point out how they should be." Theoretical matters—"making converts" to this truth or that—he could only
leave to "abler heads." "The more I have considered the study
of politics, the more I have found it full of perplexity . . ." (*B*,
pp. 14–15). The same was true of religion. The only synonym
of "real" seems to be "significant," and, almost never able to
conclude that in the last analysis any one thing warranted his
undivided attention for very long, Irving had no means of pulling
himself up out of the mire of unreality. Occasionally things
made sense to him, but let it stand out a moment too long and
sense turned sour.

More than many writers', his mind worked on associative or
assimilative principles. He looked for resemblances even when
he could not be sure what to do with them. One sees this clearly
as early as *Salmagundi,* the cosmopolitanism of which is the
freedom of its associations, the willingness (or compulsion) of
its pseudoeditors to let one thing suggest another and to see one
thing as like or unlike another. They refuse to treat provincial
matters as self-contained, unrelated to, or unlike, anything else
that has ever happened. They allow themselves to be reminded
by events in New York of events, actual or imagined, elsewhere
and at any time.

Of course, the kind of wisdom that the magazine sometimes
professes constantly threatens to break down. Fond of "drawing
comparisons between the different divisions of life, and those of
the seasons" (*SAL*, p. 337), the editors are occasionally embarrassed to discover that they have pushed their analogies too

[20] *TS*, p. 51.

far. Langstaff, who is about to begin "a most elaborate and ingenious parallel between authors and travellers," stops short
with the realization that he has arrived at the "balmy season,
which makes men stupid and dogs mad," and he refuses to go
on because "it would be cruel to saddle [readers] with the for-
midable difficulty of putting two ideas together and drawing a
conclusion . . . (p. 264). But Irving's associative tendency endured and developed. Thus, as we shall see in subsequent chapters, imagery and setting are apt to loom larger in his later work
than the characters and actions they reflect.

His sense of the fitness of folklore, tradition, and terrain for
one another is another outgrowth of the same habit of mind.
English fairy stories, Geoffrey Crayon was to say in *Bracebridge
Hall*, "suit these landscapes, which are divided by honeysuckle
hedges into sheltered fields and meadows." Having discovered
a "race" of "little fabled people who haunted the southern sides
of hills and mountains; lurked in flowers and about fountain-
heads; glided through keyholes into ancient halls; watched over
farmhouses and dairies; danced on the green by summer moonlight, and on the kitchen hearth in winter," he suggests that
behind the local habitation and popular superstition lies a "national character." It exists in the fairies' "love of order and
cleanliness," in their

> munificently rewarding, with silver sixpence in shoe, the tidy house-
> maid, but venturing their direful wrath, in midnight bobs and
> pinches, upon the sluttish dairymaid. I think I can trace the good
> effects of this ancient fairy sway over household concerns, in the
> care that prevails to the present day among English housemaids. . . .
> (*B*, pp. 344–45)

In spite of Irving's protestation that he has no head for politics,
there is behind these reflections something that verges on a political philosophy. He makes this clear when he talks about the
"orders of society in all well-constituted governments" being
"mutually bound together, and important to each other." Though
republican by birth, he is "not insensible to the excellence that
may exist in other forms of government; nor to the fact that they
may be more suitable to the situation and circumstances of the

countries in which they exist" (*B*, p. 240). It is not altogether a joke to call this a "picturesque" political science.

One thinks, of course, of Burke's "great mysterious incorporation of the human race," in which conflicting social classes, past and present, customs and ideals are all somehow appropriate to one another, bound together as the distant members of a family are by their common blood.[21] Irving may owe his social relativism to suggestions in any of a number of sources—Montesquieu, Burke, de Staël, Scott, or Blackstone, to name a few.[22] Blackstone, for instance, had seen the law as an institution gradually and constantly being remodeled to fit new needs, like "an old Gothic castle, erected in the days of chivalry," and now "fitted up for a modern inhabitant,"[23] a simile that suggests Irving's account of John Bull's "family mansion." It is an "old castellated manor-house," which "has been built upon no regular plan, but is a vast accumulation of parts, erected in various ages":

> If you point out any part of the building as superfluous, [John Bull] insists that it is material to the strength or decoration of the rest, and the harmony of the whole; and swears that the parts are so built into each other, that if you pull down one, you run the risk of having the whole about your ears. (*SB*, pp. 383, 385)

Blackstone, as Daniel Boorstin points out, had been unable for very long to consider the law separately, as a system of principles based on universal justice and unrelated to local conditions. Legal maxims seemed to him to embody folk wisdom

---

[21] ". . . the whole, at one time, is never old or middle-aged, or young, but in a condition of unchangeable constancy, moves on through the varied tenour of perpetual decay, fall, renovation, and progression." *Reflections on the Revolution in France* (London, 1790), pp. 48–49.

[22] "Every wise government must adopt for the basis of its system, the character of the people subjected to its laws. If the national genius is quick, penetrating and enlightened, the operations of government may be bold; . . . but if the genius is slow, thoughtful, contemplative, legislation must more gradually proceed toward its object. . . ." This passage occurs in François Depons, *Voyage to the Eastern Part of Terra Firma* (New York, 1806), II, 125–26. Irving had helped his brother Peter translate this work into English.

[23] Quoted by Daniel Boorstin, *The Mysterious Science of the Law* (Cambridge, 1941), p. 104.

acquired by a gradual process of trial and error through history.[24]

But above all it was probably Irving's exposure to the vogue for the picturesque that made him responsive to an organic outlook on social problems, eager, for instance, to write an essay on the "effect of natural scenery on character" in America.[25] More and more, the concept of the picturesque was coming to imply a sophisticated sense of harmonious configuration. As William Gilpin, the famous British connoisseur of landscapes, explained, he had

> seen beauty arise even from an unbalanced tree; but it must arise from some peculiar situation, which gives it a local propriety. A tree, for instance, hanging from a rock, though totally unpoised, may be beautiful . . . because it corresponds with its peculiar situation. We do not . . . admire it as a tree; but as an adjunct of an effect. . . .[26]

If "picturesque" had once meant "like certain famous paintings," it now rather, or also, meant the constant reiteration in the various parts of a scene of a single idea or emotion. A passage from Irving's *Tales of a Traveller* suggests both aspects: "The immense solitude around; the wild mountains broken into rocks and precipices, intermingled with vast oaks, corks and

[24] Boorstin, pp. 113–14.

[25] This was in connection with a book of essays that he contemplated in 1825 "on manners and morals as connected with manners" in the United States. *The Journals of Washington Irving (From July, 1815, to July, 1842)*, ed. W. P. Trent and G. S. Hellman (Boston, 1919), II, 185–86. His reluctance, however, to push on to a full-fledged Emersonian sense of Nature as the sole source of human values can be understood by a reading of the following self-mocking passage from a letter written from the Catskills in 1811. *Letters from Washington Irving to Mrs. William Renwick* (n.p., n.d.), p. 5:

I passed a fortnight very agreeably among these noble solitudes. There is something ennobling and elevating in being shut up among stupendous mountains, a man rises into a fine swelling style of thinking. His mind seems to reflect the sublime objects around him, and his ideas become by degrees very grand and mountainous—at least such I found to be my case and I had not been up there above a week before I conceived every thing on a huge shadowy scale, and I . . . verily believe the smallest idea that sprung up in my brain was equal in altitude to Anthony's nose and at least as broad as Dunderbarrack. This may account for one or two attacks I had of the headache—a very unusual complaint with me, and caused no doubt by the gigantic reflections . . . with which my precranium [sic] was continually in labour.

[26] *Remarks on Forest Scenery* (London, 1808), I, 6.

chestnuts; and the groups of banditti in the foreground, reminded me of the savage scenes of Salvator Rosa" (p. 351).

Gilpin had approached the definition of picturesque observation by relating it directly to his awareness that what a person sees in an object is a function of the interests he brings to viewing it. The "picturesque" point of view discovered in nature a kind of harmony which painters liked to create within a picture frame.[27] But this harmony, for Gilpin, was not entirely abstract or geometrical. Light, line, and color turned into hills, clouds, and foliage, combining to produce effects of violence or repose, serenity or ominousness. In Gilpin, associations seemed to spread within the framework of the picture, from one object to another, until they suggested or embodied or symbolized the idea of the whole.

Irving was apparently reading Gilpin's *Remarks on Forest Scenery* when he was preparing *Tales of a Traveller* (1824)[28] and it seems likely, since he was a seasoned traveler and sketcher, that even before that time he had looked into at least one of Gilpin's picturesque tours. But it is not so much a direct connection that needs establishing here as analogous concerns, parts of the gradual push toward romantic organicism. For the picturesque was a concept (as well as a term) constantly invoked by romantic writers. Its influence in an area such as romantic fiction has long been apparent. The prominence of setting and tableau in Scott, Cooper, and Hawthorne, for instance, is widely discussed. But Hawthorne's ability to unify character and action around a central setting, the way in which his fiction seems almost to grow out of, and reflect, settings such as the hollow of the three hills, the town square with prison and scaffold, or the house of seven gables, exemplifies a more heightened and subtle sense of the picturesque.

[27] Gilpin, *Three Essays on Picturesque Beauty* (London, 1808), p. 3. This conception, according to William Templeman (*The Life and Works of William Gilpin* [Urbana, Ill., 1939], p. 135), is central to an understanding of Gilpin, if not to the picturesque in general.
[28] *Journal of Washington Irving (1823–1824)*, ed. Stanley T. Williams (Cambridge, Mass., 1931), p. 206.

In "The Old Apple-Dealer" we find Hawthorne professing himself a "lover of the moral picturesque." The term suggests sudden glimpses of shape, form, or meaning in character or personality, or the opening up in out-of-the-way places of new viewpoints on human nature. Or perhaps it also signifies an interrelationship of individual and native surrounding, for Hawthorne's sense of character and scene as extensions of each other is well exhibited in "The Old Apple-Dealer." As he proceeds to fit his quaint subject into—or outfit him with—an environment, one is reminded of Emerson's discussion, in the chapter on "Beauty" in *Nature*, of the way in which landscape and significant human action reflect one another.

Henry James later picked up Hawthorne's phrase and applied it to "Young Goodman Brown," where he discovered a "moral picturesqueness" in Hawthorne's presentation of the "old secret of mankind in general and of the Puritans in particular, . . . that we are really not by any means so good as a well-regulated society requires us to appear."[29] To James, Hawthorne's art is to a large extent a function of his interest in the picturesque, which, in turn, James seems to see as a reflection of the general drabness of the American scene in Hawthorne's day, of that "large juvenility stamped upon the face of things."[30] While initially perhaps the term means for James simply what is visually striking or spectacular, it becomes clear that the picturesque is closely associated in his mind with a concept of form, style, harmony, or composition, if not quite with imagination itself. Thus for James, Hawthorne does not so much see picturesque objects, scenes, or people and put them into his fiction as he *creates* picturesque effects by his ability to group settings, characters, and images in interesting, fanciful arrangements, thereby making up for a scantiness of intrinsically interesting material.

According to Walter Hipple, "the taste for the picturesque is a taste for a greater complexity and intricacy than either beautiful or sublime affords." There is an instinct at once for rough-

[29] *Hawthorne*, chap. iv.
[30] *Ibid.*, chap. ii.

ness—"the association of the picturesque" in some writers "with age and decay"—and for unity, the tendency to find beauty in a congruity of heterogeneous elements.[31] Thus Emerson could make the Transcendental point of view seem in some respects an extension of the sketcher's search for the picturesque: "There is a property in the horizon which no man has but he whose eye can integrate all the parts. . . ."[32] As James was to say, Emerson's thought was a matter of finding "in the landscape of the soul all sorts of fine sunrise and moonlight effects"; he was a writer "who would help one to take a picturesque view of one's internal responsibilities."[33] In America in the artless age such help proved useful.

To read Gilpin on the singleness of artistic effects in landscape is to be reminded of Poe's aesthetic, since Gilpin makes the picturesque a calculated echoing and re-echoing of resemblance, an idea-lizing of the scene:

> The *blasted tree* has often a fine effect both in natural and in artificial landscape. . . . When the dreary heath is spread before the eye, and the ideas of wildness and desolation are required, what more suitable accompaniment can be imagined, than the blasted oak, ragged, scathed and leafless; shooting it's [sic] peeled, white branches athwart the gathering blackness of some rising storm?[34]

The underlying effects for both Gilpin and Poe are conceived of as "ideas" involving a single intense emotion, "ideas of wildness and desolation," for instance, in Gilpin, or of the terrible, the frightening, the ludicrous, the grotesque, in Poe. Both insist on a connection between atmosphere and emotion. Gilpin does so literally, since his subject is apt to be weather or climate itself, while in Poe the concern for style, mood, manner, *décor*, trappings, costumes, or setting is apt to become the substance of his concern for form itself. His method is based on the exaggeration of resemblances. One might view "The Fall of the House of Usher," for instance, as a picturesque composition, with the

[31] Walter Hipple, *The Beautiful, the Sublime, and the Picturesque* (Carbondale, Ill., 1957), pp. 194 (on Gilpin), 207 (on Uvedale Price), 262–64 (on Richard Payne Knight).

[32] Emerson, *Nature*, chap. i.

[33] *Hawthorne*, chap. iv.

[34] *Forest Scenery*, I, 14–15.

terror developing through the duplication of the image of a unit breaking in two before the narrator's fascinated gaze. Where one starts makes no difference: outside the house or inside the hero's (or the narrator's) mind, it is always a matter of two halves pulling away from each other in the very process of leaning on each other for support. The final collapse and mutual destruction are the inevitable consequence of dwelling in the climate of "fear" which the composition as a whole represents. The house, taking on life as its inhabitants are drained of it, finally comes, almost literally, to personify in its two halves the divided family. And Madeline, a female rather than a male twin, afflicted with what seems a muscular rather than a nervous disorder, still reflects the split in Roderick's personality: she fluctuates between deathlike paralysis and supernatural fits of energy, while his nervous excitement develops out of sullen depression and gives way to it again. His hypersensitivity is calculated to register the least sign of life in her, even after she has been entombed in the vault, and to be overwhelmed by anything like a display of vigorous activity.

The danger of the picturesque is that the viewer's eye, fascinated by a totality, may overlook the parts of which it is composed. In "The House of Usher" the narrator is first impressed by the perfect symmetry of the whole façade and only with concentrated attention is brought to realize that within the composition each individual stone has reached an advanced state of decay. Although, says Gilpin,

> among inferior plants . . . there is great beauty; yet when we consider that these minuter productions are chiefly beautiful as *individuals;* and are not adapted to . . . *composition in landscape;* nor to receive the *effects of light and shade;* they must give place in point of *beauty*—of *picturesque beauty* . . . —to the form and foliage, and ramification of the tree.[35]

Eventually Irving was to lose touch with differences in his overinsistence on resemblance. By the late 1820's, as we shall see, his work was beginning to reduce itself to a single story, and he was having trouble devising new ways of telling it. Mean-

[35] *Ibid.,* I, 1. Poe's "The Domain of Arnheim" makes quite clear his awareness of, and interest in, picturesque landscaping.

while, however, by keeping his distance, and not approaching his subjects so closely as to be distracted by elements that did not belong in the over-all pattern, he was able to compose at least a surface order from his experiences.

To find him saying in *Bracebridge Hall,* "There is an affinity between all nature, animate and inanimate," probably renews the contemporary reader's impatience with him. It looks like the drippings lapped up from the platter of higher romanticism by a poor devil of an author. Irving may have meant by "affinity between all nature" no more than that in some way everything manages to resemble everything else. His tone is somewhat pretentious as he proclaims that "the oak, in the pride and lustihood of its growth, seems . . . to take its range with the lion and the eagle, and to assimilate, in the grandeur of its attributes, to heroic and intellectual man" (p. 92). Yet how much beyond this does the marrow of Transcendental faith in the oneness of nature really or significantly give one the strength to reach?

The oaks on the Bracebridge estate are for Crayon an index to the character of the man who lives among them and cares for them. Such a tree, "its mighty pillar rising straight and direct towards heaven, bearing up its leafy honors from the impurities of earth," becomes "an emblem of what a true nobleman *should be.*" Irving's description compares with Johann Lavater's image of "man," which an American close to the Transcendentalist movement was later to include in his anthology of German literature: "With firm step he advances over the earth's surface, and with erect body he raises his head toward heaven. He looks forward to infinitude. . . ." Man is superior to lower animals, Lavater argues, because he literally stands above them or stands more firmly. The method, as in Irving, may be fundamentally metaphorical, but in Lavater there is a technical term for it, "physiognomy." The "organization of man," he says, actually "distinguishes him from all other earthly beings." But our knowledge of him starts with his "physiognomy, that is to say, the superficies and outlines of this organization."[36]

[36] "On the Nature of Man, Which is the Foundation of the Science of Physiognomy," *Prose Writers of Germany,* ed. Frederic Hedge (Philadelphia, 1848), pp. 191–92.

Physiognomy, regardless of where it eventually leads, begins, according to Lavater, in ordinary observation: "Do we not daily judge of the sky by its physiognomy?" A world of knowledge, like a world of fiction, has virtually to be created by a mere "spectator" on the outside. "No food, not a glass of wine or beer, not a cup of coffee or tea, comes to table, which is not judged by its physiognomy, its exterior, and of which we do not thence deduce some conclusion respecting its interior, good or bad properties."[37] Inevitably, Lavater's science, when pushed to the limit, makes the universe a symbolic index. "Is not all nature," he asks, "physiognomy, superficies and contents; body, and spirit; exterior effect and internal power; invisible beginning and visible ending?"[38] And is not this view of things the beginning of "affinity between all nature"? What is on the surface under direct observation we read, in some context or other, as a sign of what is behind—or ahead. Lavater's statements thus anticipate the career of one wing of nineteenth-century thought soaring toward the Transcendental Idea. And this was an imaginative reconnaissance paralleled, at a lower altitude, by the picturesque flights of fancy within Irving's writings, which moved from acute consciousness that he was only playing with words toward tentative suggestions of something significant or real.

---

[37] *Ibid.*, p. 194. Irving actually satirized Lavater in *Knickerbocker* (*K*, p. 225), as Isaac D'Israeli had in his *Flim-Flams* (I, xvii). As a system-builder, Lavater was an easy target for anti-intellectualist satire. But every caricaturist is his own physiognomist, relating inner character to dominant surface impressions. Later, as a biographer and student of the character and personality of literary men, D'Israeli seemed to convert the concept of the ruling passion into one of, in effect, an underlying Idea. He is a significant analogue to Irving in moving away from extreme irony, burlesque, and grotesquerie toward a more serious prose. In the end he went further than Irving in the direction of Idealism.

[38] Lavater, p. 194. Cf. Melville's despair in *Pierre* (Book XXI, chap. i):

. . . because Pierre began to see through the first superficiality of the world, he fondly weens he has come to the unlayered substance. But, far as any geologist has yet gone down into the world, it is found to consist of nothing but surface stratified on surface. To its axis, the world being nothing but superinduced superficies.

VI

The Alienated Observer

THE realization pervades *The Sketch Book* that in 1819 the United States as yet had no widely acclaimed national literature. While Irving did not deliberately set out to write an "American" book, his view of England constantly focuses on points of contrast with the United States. The consequence is a quaint Janus-faced quality, a tendency to look both ways across the Atlantic at once. The most obvious glance toward home is "English Writers on America," an essay which is today almost unreadable. It is Irving at his ritualistic worst, wallowing in abstractions and stock metaphors. The attitudes of the essay are, at least implicitly, confused. His enthusiasm for "a country in which one of the greatest political experiments in the history of the world is now performing" suggests a high value placed on independence of mind, on a culture unaffected by "national prejudices," which are the "inveterate diseases of old countries" (*SB*, pp. 69, 77). But in almost the same breath he calls upon his countrymen to look back to England for tutelage.

When he raises the question of how a truly native literature can be created, his loudest answer is: look first to Europe and become truly American in due season.

> We are a young people, necessarily an imitative one, and must take our examples and models, in a great degree, from the existing nations of Europe. There is no country more worthy of our study than England. The spirit of her constitution is most analogous to ours. The manners of her people—their intellectual activity—their freedom of opinion—their habits of thinking on those subjects which concern the dearest interests and most sacred charities of private life, are all congenial to the American character. . . . (*SB*, p. 78)

Long before it was refuted in Emerson's "The American Scholar," this doctrine had begun to produce that bias toward Europe known as the genteel tradition. But Irving's own willingness to take the British seriously as his cultural superiors often wavered. By the time he finished his next book, *Bracebridge Hall*, his need for satire was getting the upper hand. And artistically the mere statement of the need to be imitative is not nearly so important as the fact that *The Sketch Book* dramatized that need in the character of Geoffrey Crayon, the persona who becomes the walking, prowling embodiment of Irving's own sense of the incompleteness of American character.

As originally published in New York through an arrangement with Ebenezer Irving, a brother, *The Sketch Book* was issued over a period of a year and a half (1819–20), and was a cross between a book and a periodical. The make-up of later installments was not fully determined until earlier ones had come out. The obvious strategy in assembling the pamphlets was to take advantage of a variety of current fads—the picturesque, the legendary or romantic, the sentimental, and even the sensational or supernatural—so that every reader would be bound to find something to his taste. But the fact that Irving used a pseudonym suggests a desire for a kind of unity in the miscellany. A sense of coherence emerges in patterns of imagery functioning in relation to the central figure of Crayon, the shy spectator who wishes he had close friends or relatives, the aging bachelor who would half like to be married, the American in England searching for a past, the traveler trying to get to something like home. Crayon is a prompter of good feeling among others who finds it impossible to get himself finally settled. He serves as go-between for temporarily estranged husbands and wives, for American readers and British writers; he mediates between present and past; he sympathizes with broken hearts and mourns at funerals in country churchyards. Yet the morbid implications in his own sentimentality frighten him. His interest in the past often seems to him a fascination with gradual decay. His sympathy with the

[1] For a listing of the contents of the various numbers of *The Sketch Book*, see STW, I, 173, 426.

losses of others sometimes masks but thinly an awareness of
something he has lost, or perhaps never had. He is haunted by
the image of the dark, isolated, and forgotten person he may
turn into.

One has to admit Crayon's shortcomings. His avowed sus-
ceptibility to sentiment only in part excuses his sentimentality.
And he ought to know that there are some inconsistencies not
permitted even in a man who pretends to have no head for
philosophy. Nevertheless, a cumulative impression develops in
The Sketch Book which justifies its being read as a whole. There
is a network of relationships among the various items in the
miscellany that catches up again and again and lifts up out of
the murk of the past, tentative, half-formed, anxious attitudes
toward questions of national character, heritage, and culture.
Conflicts of attitude are apparent as early as "The Author's
Account of Himself." Crayon's manner implies that he has been
left either speechless or basically unimpressed by the monumental aspect of Europe. His "idle humor," he tells us, both as
an apology and a boast, has distracted him "from the great objects studied by every regular traveller who would make a book."
He reminds himself of "an unlucky landscape painter," whose
sketchbook on his return from the continent was "crowded with
cottages, and landscapes, and obscure ruins," but who "had
neglected to paint St. Peter's, or the Coliseum; the cascade of
Terni, or the bay of Naples" (p. 16). He waxes broadly ironic
and eloquent by fits and starts. Beginning by lightly mocking
his own provincial boyhood, which encompassed "tours of discovery" to "foreign parts" of his home town, he soon (as though
to compensate for deflating himself) pumps furiously to inflate
the American landscape with conventional rhetoric (pp. 13–14).

As he sketches himself into existence with a few rough strokes,
the net effect is one of debunking—of himself, his country, and
the world at large, which seems to force him to take so small a
view of things. His vague enthusiasms over the "accumulated
treasures of age" in Europe are balanced by the irony of his
decision to go abroad because he wanted to see "the gigantic
race" from which, as an American, he has "degenerated" (pp.

13–15). Crayon, embodiment that he is of the average educated American's cultural uneasiness, comes close to realizing the character of the traveler offered in the inscription from *Euphues* at the beginning of "The Author's Account": "the traveller that stragleth from his owne country is in a short time transformed into so monstrous a shape, that he is faine to alter his mansion with his manners, and to live where he can, not where he would."

In "The Voyage," outward bound from America to Liverpool, Crayon discovers that "a wide sea voyage . . . makes us conscious of being cast loose from the secure anchorage of settled life, and sent adrift upon a doubtful world." Not that being cast loose hasn't a pleasant side to it. Like Ishmael in *Moby-Dick*, he is "delighted to loll over the quarter-railing, or climb to the main-top, . . . and muse for hours together." Escape into day-dream is happy drifting. Yet vision and idle imagination occasionally find the watery world they contemplate populated with "shapeless monsters" in "uncouth gambols" (pp. 18–19). Very early in a book in some ways designed to promote international goodwill, signs of disturbance confront the reader: "the mast of a ship that must have been completely wrecked"; "the remains of handkerchiefs, by which some of the crew had fastened themselves" to the wreckage (pp. 19–20). And what later succeeds these images of fear and destruction is the loneliness of Crayon as he disembarks in a foreign land.

His earliest response to England is only in part determined by "neat cottages, with their trim shrubberies and green grass plots" (p. 23). In "Roscoe," Liverpool serves as a sharp and not entirely pleasant reminder of the society that Crayon has left behind. The port of entry to England and Europe, a natural place for branches of New York firms like the Irvings' to locate, a city strictly oriented toward commerce and the New World, Liverpool, like the newer American cities, was short on culture, and Irving saw it as a kind of American city, facing the problem of trying to get learning and the arts to flourish in a desert of trade.[2]

---

[2] Henry Wansey had said in 1794, "Boston is the Bristol, New York the Liverpool, and Philadelphia the London, of America." *American Social History*, ed. Allan Nevins (New York, 1931), p. 49.

His friend William Roscoe, "elegant historian of the Medici," is a hero to Crayon because he is a writer who began in the market place. Although Roscoe has known failure as well as success in business, Crayon presents him as having survived commercial disaster through devotion to things of the mind; he now lives "with antiquity and posterity" (pp. 26, 29). But the impression his situation makes is a rather sad one, for all Crayon's protests to the contrary. Roscoe's Greek Revival house (which is, to tell the truth, "not in the purest taste") has been sold and is empty now. With the fountain desiccated, it becomes an objectification of the man himself at the end of his career. His devotion to culture in a commercial community makes him, at least in Irving's eyes, a lonely, misunderstood figure, elevated out of the reach of the society he sprang from. Crayon even compares him to a decaying monument, "Pompey's column at Alexandria, towering alone in classic dignity" (p. 32). Roscoe is at last a pathetic intimation of fears which Irving obviously felt for himself.[3]

"Roscoe" is only one of many pieces in the book which are directly concerned with writing or writers. Such essays and sketches as "The Boar's Head Tavern, Eastcheap," "Stratford-on-Avon," "A Royal Poet," and "Westminster Abbey" are obvious bait for the American appetite for British culture. But Irving also has a personal stake in the literary sightseeing. By the time we get to "The Art of Book-Making," we know that Crayon has been ransacking old books for quaint and apt quotations to pretty up his sometimes threadbare remarks. Books and stock images are almost his only reality, although his awareness that this is so, his fear of the consequences, gives him reality as a character. He is haunted by books. In "The Mutability of Literature" old books long forgotten in the dust of the shelves of Westminster Library come alive fantastically and complain of their neglect. In "The Art of Book-Making" he falls asleep in the reading room of the British Museum and dreams of hack

[3] Osborne has noted the personal significance of "Roscoe" in his Ph.D. dissertation (University of North Carolina, 1947), "Irving's Development," p. 282.

writers grubbing among worm-eaten books to dredge up antique material which they can pass off as their own.

What raises "Westminster Abbey" above the level of a monumental echoing of Gray's awareness of what the paths of glory lead to is the special sense Irving manages to convey of the alienation into which, he fears, his calling as a writer may push him. Crayon proceeds by gradual stages from the light of the living present outside the Abbey, through increasing shadows, to an almost total darkness within. In the first stage, going through a "long, low, vaulted passage" to an inner court and cloister enclosing a "scanty plot of grass" (as at the end of Melville's "Bartleby") lit by an autumnal sun, Crayon is confronted by the "gradual dilapidations of time, which yet has something touching and pleasing in its very decay" (*SB*, pp. 210–11). But later, as he wanders among the tombs in the Abbey proper, the afternoon wanes, visitors depart, the few remaining footsteps echo ominously, and faint sounds from the outside clash against the emptiness within. If historic relics have somehow established a temporary contact for him with great spirits of the past, he nonetheless begins to sense the past as also a potential trap for the imagination, where, like the little man in black, he may lose himself. In contemplating a crusader's tomb, says Crayon, one's mind "is apt to kindle with the legendary associations, the romantic fiction, the chivalrous pomp and pageantry, which poetry has spread over the wars for the sepulchre of Christ." But before long the tombs turn into "objects from some strange and distant land, of which we have no certain knowledge," "relics of times utterly gone by; of beings passed from recollection; of customs and manners with which ours have no affinity" (p. 215). And although he has meditated in the Poet's Corner on the writer's service to his public, which sacrifices "the delights of social life" for the prospect of a kind of immortality, in the gathering darkness posthumous recognition appears less meaningful to Crayon: the lonely writer's vigil almost turns to nightmare. Monuments are transformed before his eyes into monstrous ruins, and everywhere he seems to see "the nameless urn" and ivy twined about "the fallen column" (pp. 214, 223).

Like the speaker courting melancholy in Milton's "Il Penseroso" (long passages of which, about this time, Irving diligently copied into a commonplace book), Crayon seems repelled by "Day's garish eye" and attracted to the "lonely tower," the "mossy cell," or the "studious cloister."[4] His loneliness continually drives him into blind alleys and dark corners, through small doorways into courtyards cut off from all but a few muffled sounds of the outside world and perhaps a ray of sunshine. A small plot of grass may give the setting the appearance of a garden, but it is not one where Crayon can stay for long. He passes through further doorways into darker interiors; the womb-like openings take him into chambers of the past. He is drawn by his need as "a man from a young country" (B, p. 14) to be with old things, to feel himself in the presence of his ancestors, lineal or spiritual.

The sense of mutability, as Stanley Williams insisted, is everything in *The Sketch Book*.[5] If it is not old books or buildings, it is old men who, even though he responds to them whimsically, haunt Crayon. Thus, for instance, in exploring "dull monotonous streets" and Gothic gateways—the American writer transformed into a kind of Guy Fawkes, with a "dark lanthorn" —he enters an old building in which he encounters a line of "gray-headed old men, clad in long black cloaks." They file by in silence, each one "turning a pale face" toward him in passing. He tries to amuse himself at first with the fancy that these figures are "the ghosts of departed years." But fears develop when he rambles on "through a labyrinth of interior courts, and corridors, and dilapidated cloisters" to a chamber crammed with

---

[4] Irving's manuscript notebook "Extracts &c 1819–1823" is in the Houghton Library, Harvard University. He copied lines 73–96, 110–20, and 131–74 from "Il Penseroso." His extracts from "L'Allegro" in the same notebook are very brief. His preoccupation with loss, illusion, the passing of time, and earthly vanity, as well as his interest in English folklore continue to show up strongly in this commonplace book in numerous quotations from Renaissance English literature. In contrast, Irving seems also drawn to the kind of poetic statement (in verse or prose) that urges that joy is to be found in humble circumstances and common things. Thus the attraction of Izaak Walton, quoted in the notebook and celebrated by Geoffrey Crayon in "The Angler."

[5] STW, I, 187–88.

"implements of savage warfare; strange idols and stuffed alligators; bottled serpents and monsters." From "the high tester of an old-fashioned bedstead" grins a "human skull, flanked on each side by a dried cat." And, as if these relics weren't enough, Crayon gradually becomes aware of "a human countenance staring . . . from a dusky corner." It is an apparition he would like to take for a mummy, but it inevitably comes alive, revealing itself to be another of the pensioners in what turns out to be an old men's home. Without realizing it Crayon has stumbled into the Charter House (pp. 290–94).[6]

For American literature, the gloomy enclosures into which he is driven prefigure the "haunted chamber" in Salem where Hawthorne spent his twelve years learning to write. Learning from what? From old books, quaint histories of the sort Irving liked, from an occasional ramble, from his own imagination, from staring at the walls of his room, that "dungeon," which he said he had created for himself. Of the outside "real world" he had no more than occasional glimpses "through a peep-hole."[7] Similarly the images that Irving uses in *The Sketch Book* to counterbalance dark courtyards and cloisters and large empty halls suggest those which Hawthorne looked forward to as an escape from the private blackness of such lucubrations as "Fancy's Show Box," "The Haunted Mind," "The Procession of Life," and "The Devil in Manuscript." Lighted windows, houses full of people, crowded inns, blazing hearths, sunshine, green grass, and ample shade trees constantly command Crayon's attention, even though there is a bias away from home in many of Irving's men, including Crayon. "Man is the creature of interest and ambition," Crayon tells us. "His nature leads him forth into the struggle and bustle of the world," where he risks getting lost in

[6] Though apparently written at the time of the original composition of *The Sketch Book* (1817–20) (see STW, I, 421), "London Antiques," together with "A Sunday in London," was not included until the revised edition (1848).
[7] See Hawthorne's letters to Sophia Peabody, 4 October 1840, and H. W. Longfellow, 4 June 1837, *The Portable Hawthorne*, ed. Malcolm Cowley (New York, 1955), pp. 608–9, 611. Of his sketches in *Twice-Told Tales* he says (Preface, 2d ed., 1851), "They are not the talk of a secluded man with his own mind and heart . . . , but his attempts, and very imperfectly successful ones, to open up an intercourse with the world."

travel or bogged down in trade. But the "heart" is woman's "world" (p. 90). Irving likes to associate women, hearts, and homes, and he can turn a broken heart into a deserted house.

Not surprisingly, then, in "The Wife," as he pictures the single man in "waste and self-neglect," his "heart" falling to "ruin" like a "deserted mansion" (p. 35), Crayon sounds like Hawthorne talking about marriage as virtual salvation, at least for the husband. To Crayon, the ideal wife is like "the vine, which has long twined its graceful foliage about the oak" (p. 34). And the young couple in "The Wife," as a way of terminating troubles that have initially beset their marriage, move to a cottage in the suburbs, "up a narrow lane . . . shaded with forest trees" and "overrun" "with a profusion of foliage." Eating strawberries under a "beautiful tree behind the cottage" becomes the symbol of marital bliss; and Crayon himself is apparently to be served by the wife in this almost sacramental repast at the end (pp. 42–43).

How far is this cottage from Miles Coverdale's hermitage in a vine-covered tree? Symbol of his solitariness, the bower of bliss, which so obviously recalls his name, also ironically mirrors his longings and desires. Coverdale thinks of it as a honeymoon retreat and daydreams (with an intensity that carries obvious sexual overtones) of the ripening of grapes on the vine, the harvesting and pressing of them to make wine.[8] But there are at the same time some disturbing elements in this vision. Coverdale sees the vines clinging to the branches of the trees in a deathlike embrace. And when he contemplates the bacchanalian revel in which he would like to take part after the harvest, he envisions his mouth stained with grapes as though with blood.

There are also disturbances in "The Wife," where men are consistently pictured in a near-ruinous condition, the function of women being to pull them back from the brink. Marriage has meaning for Crayon chiefly in relation to a world of troubles; it is most appropriate when the "hardy" oak of manhood has been "rifted by the thunderbolt." Then the vine's "caressing tendrils" can "bind up . . . shattered boughs" (pp. 34–35). In the end the

---

[8] Hawthorne, *Blithedale Romance*, chap. xii.

supposed treatment for ruined manhood begins to look like the real cause. The woman as "ministering angel"—actually equipped with harp and dressed in white—becomes less a wife than a mother (pp. 39–42).

Again and again Irving affirms the values of hearth and home, yet he seems to have doubts and questions about the family that, as a bachelor, he can't dispel or answer completely. This may be in part why the specter of economic failure (and thus of success) plagues *The Sketch Book*. We have already mentioned "Roscoe." And in "The Wife," only a few months after his marriage, business reverses in the city have overwhelmed the young husband. What frightens him most is the idea that his bride will be unable to live without the house, clothes, and furniture to which she is accustomed.

It is in "Rip Van Winkle," however, for all its humor, that the questioning becomes most intense. "If left to himself," Rip Van Winkle "would have whistled life away in perfect contentment; but his wife kept continually dinning in his ears about his idleness, his carelessness, and the ruin he was bringing on his family." Rip's wife is the spirit of industry, a *Poor Richard's Almanac* made flesh, a combination of puritan conscience and Protestant ethic. He himself is a "simple good-natured man" and a "kind neighbor," but he is "hen-pecked." He seeks refuge at the inn, in the shade of a great tree, "talking listlessly over village gossip, or telling endless sleepy stories about nothing." He has some imagination, likes to hear the schoolmaster using big words, is aware of the past, of being descended from one of Peter Stuyvesant's men. He has "inherited, however, but little of the martial character of his ancestors" (pp. 46–50).

His long walk into the hills one lovely day is a retreat from a woman who is the antithesis of the motherly figure in "The Wife," the preceding piece in the book.[9] Retreat to what? To

[9] Elsewhere in the book one notices similar ironic juxtapositions: the mock-ghost story "The Spectre Bridegroom" appears immediately after "Rural Funerals" at the end of Part IV ("The Inn Kitchen" merely introduces "Spectre"), and "Sleepy Hollow," which in subsequent editions concludes the entire book (except for the brief "L'Envoy"), holds a similar position in Part VI, after a maudlin piece, "The Pride of the Village," which deals with a very different kind of community.

nature, a nature which is not the West of frontier adventure but
a region of fantasy, a benign, if half-wild, landscape that
throughout the nineteenth century was to feed starved American
imaginations. Irving's Dolph Heyliger (in *Bracebridge Hall*),
for instance, when lost in the forests that lined the Hudson River,
would begin to realize within himself the force of character he
needed to enable him to come to terms with his ancestry. But
Rip, as it turns out, in going to nature encounters a vague past
and withdraws into it. In a way, the meagerness of his heritage
mocks him. Even so, it is preferable to life with Dame Van
Winkle.

What he encounters—the temptation that he is half-right to
succumb to—is Henry Hudson's crew playing at ninepins in
the Catskills. He has heard the legend which connects them with
the thunder. They are not the elves or goblins that later versions
of the story turned them into. They are figures out of "an old
Flemish painting" that Rip has seen "in the parlor . . . of the
village parson, and which had been brought over from Holland
at the time of the settlement" (p. 54). They are small and
comical, one suspects, because they are in a sense mock-heroic
images of Rip himself; they represent his unconscious recognition of his lack of stature, and his willingness to put up with himself as he is even though he sees how little he amounts to.

Before his surrender to oblivion, however, his adventure gives
him a scare or two. Hardly a Thoreau, he becomes uneasy too
far beyond the settlements. Late in the afternoon, as he turns
his glance down the side of a mountain which faces away from
home and the Hudson, he stares for a while into a "deep . . . glen,
wild, lonely, and shagged, the bottom filled with fragments from
the impending cliffs." Withdrawal into the wilderness now
seems as unhappy a choice as going home and "encountering the
terrors of Dame Van Winkle." Nature, suddenly ceasing to be a
solace, begins to seem a mirror reflecting the ordeal of his daily
life. Before long he hears an ominous voice from the glen calling
his name.

The femaleness of the landscape suggests that in transferring
a German folk legend to an American setting Irving has by no

means obliterated all traces of the sexual fears and desires which
the basic myth of a long sleep, found in many forms in many
countries, usually seems to embody.[10] Rip has thrown himself
on a bosomy "green knoll." An old man who is laboring in the
glen under a heavy load ("a stout keg") directs Rip to help him
and leads him up a dry stream bed into a cliff-walled, tree-
thatched "amphitheatre." His eventual reawakening back on the
knoll, together with his discovery afterwards that the womblike
amphitheater is impenetrable, perhaps means that Rip never
actually entered it but only dreamed of his encounter with the
old men bowling. Of course, the fact that the "dream" occurs
during a twenty years' sleep makes the status of events in the
story somewhat uncertain, and it may be just as easy to assume
that the bowlers bring him back after he falls asleep in the amphitheater. To see the experience as a dream is to have its unreality
emphasized. But this scarcely matters, since apparently escape
has now become Rip's reality.

As he follows his guide through the desolate glen, he hears
the rumble of thunder, but it turns out to be merely the strange
men bowling. He avoids the rain; the amphitheater becomes his
refuge from the storm. The bowlers frighten him at first but soon
prove cordial, if silent. They ply him with "excellent Hollands,"
and he gradually dozes off. His life has become a sleep—within,
perhaps, a dream. When he awakes, his dog Wolf has left him.
A powerful sense of sterility and decay now develops. Rip
"looked round for his gun, but in place of the clean well-oiled
fowling-piece, he found an old firelock lying by him, the barrel
incrusted with rust, the lock falling off, and the stock worm-
eaten" (p. 51–55). When he tries to get into the amphitheater
where he thinks the old man took him the night before, his way

---

[10] Heiman (*American Imago*, XVI, 3–47) and Young (*Kenyon Review*, XXII,
547–73) should be consulted. They have both probed deeply in an attempt to
interpret the unconscious sexual imagery of the story. Heiman's primary concern
is the psychological significance of "Rip Van Winkle" for Irving, Young's, the
more general or universal significance of the myth. In "Dolph Heylinger" (*B*)
Irving was to become more explicit in feminizing landscape. For the basic discussion of the German sources of "Rip," as well as of "The Legend of Sleepy
Hollow," see Henry Pochmann, "Irving's German Sources in *The Sketch Book*,"
Studies in Philology, XXVII (July, 1930), 477–507.

is blocked by a raging torrent. The green knoll, the softness and benevolence of the landscape where he wakes up, seems a maternal bosom. He has slept there for twenty years, unless (which is much the same thing) he has spent the time in the amphitheater. The dried-up pool or stream bed where little men play games, drink, and doze becomes in the final analysis a way of avoiding the more rampantly female aspects of nature.

Here, as in many of Irving's stories and sketches, a prevailingly comic tone does not prevent the narrative from turning upon a few moments in which the lonely protagonist is overtaken by fear. Rip's dream, or the bowlers' magic, does not lift him beyond reality forever. Life goes on even in his deathlike sleep. The closest thing to terror in "Rip Van Winkle" occurs not so much when the strange bowlers appear in the glen as when Rip wakes up to the fact of change. The story, as several commentators have observed, is concerned with the loss of identity. Coming back from the hills, an old man, though he doesn't quite realize it, he finds his house "gone to decay—the roof fallen in, the windows shattered, and the doors off the hinges." Desolate, his "connubial fears" temporarily overcome, he calls for his family; "the lonely chambers" ring momentarily "with his voice, and then all again" is "silence." The village inn, where Rip and his cronies used to gather, is gone, replaced by the new hotel, a "large rickety wooden building . . . with great gaping windows." And the "great tree" in front of the inn, possibly another unconscious phallic symbol, has been cut down. In its place stands a "tall, naked" liberty pole. Rip's country has changed its name. On the hotel sign George III has given way to George Washington. Rip is no longer even Rip Van Winkle; his own son now answers to that designation (pp. 58–59).

If in the end the story remains comic rather than tragic, it is because Rip is able to parlay his loss into a positive asset, to make a success of inadequacy or failure. He acquires a new identity as a result of having a tale to tell. True enough, in this story the reader cannot altogether rejoice in the losing of oneself that becomes a finding. Yet Irving's village loafer proves to have a permanent appeal to the American flair for irresponsibility, a trait which compensates the nation for its often un-flagging puritanism.[11]

Technically, the narrator of both "Rip Van Winkle" and "The Legend of Sleepy Hollow" is Diedrich Knickerbocker, but one suspects that Irving was merely trying to capitalize on his earlier reputation in order to stimulate the sales of *The Sketch Book*. There is not much of Knickerbocker in the tone of these stories. "Rip" may contain a few phrases that recall the eccentricities of the old historian, but the essential quality of Knickerbocker, the rather desperate need to inflate limp subjects with a flourish of rhetoric, is quite lacking.[12] It is, in effect, Geoffrey Crayon who is telling the stories, that is, an American who is in England and who has aspirations to an English style of gentility but who never-theless has fond recollections of settings which he frequented as a boy and a young man. The beginning of "Sleepy Hollow" almost makes this explicit, and in the context of the book as a whole, after Irving has been at such pains to construct the character of Crayon as a partially displaced American, it is difficult to avoid looking at things from his point of view. Crayon, who is far enough from America to see the details as somewhat blurred, the harsh edges smoothed round in a slight haze, remains primarily sympathetic. Because he is a little, but not overpoweringly, homesick, he can respond to America to a considerable extent as terrain or scene.[13]

"The Legend of Sleepy Hollow," like "Rip," is a story about a home and a way of settling down. Ichabod Crane, a variation of the type Geoffrey Crayon (their last names look like puns on each other), is another solitary interloper in foreign terrain, a half-starved bachelor with no permanent home who boards

---

[11] See Louis Le Fevre, "Paul Bunyan and Rip Van Winkle," *Yale Review*, XXXVI (Autumn, 1946), 66–76.

[12] In "Sleepy Hollow" Knickerbocker effaces himself almost completely, claiming to give the story "almost in the precise words in which I heard it related at a corporation meeting." *SB*, p. 455.

[13] Irving himself tended to see "Sleepy Hollow" this way, although he is overly modest, if not evasive (in view of the German sources), in calling it "a random thing, suggested by recollections of scenes and stories about Tarrytown. The story is a mere whimsical band to connect descriptions of scenery, customs, man-ners, &c." Letter to Ebenezer Irving, 29 December 1819, PMI, I, 448.

around the neighborhood, spending a week at a time with one
family and then going on to the next. What he wants is simply a
home, like anyone else. He dreams of buying large tracts of
land in Kentucky or Tennessee and heading west. But he isn't
the kind of man who simply heads west on his own and gets his
land by fighting for it. He is not a fighter (won't settle things
with Brom Bones in single combat) but a dreamer, a mock-
Quixote on a borrowed horse that is ironically named Gun-
powder, "gaunt and shagged, with a ewe neck and a head like a
hammer" (p. 436). His Dulcinea is a bouncing farmer's daughter, and his aim is not to right wrongs for her but to have her
father set up the two of them in Kentucky.

The story suggests that a large imagination may be only a
means of camouflaging narrow capacities. Too much dreaming,
even of the great American dream, appears to induce impotence.
Small wonder that Ichabod's love for Katrina Van Tassel blurs
eating and sex.[14] He is just as much in love with the plump
pigeons and ducks in her father's barnyard as with her; he has
visions of fowl "snugly put to bed in a comfortable pie, and
tucked in with a coverlet of crust" or "pairing cosily in dishes,
like snug married couples" (p. 428). The most revealing moment of the story comes when he arrives at the Van Tassel's
quilting party after riding through a countryside "rich and
golden" in its "abundance" (p. 437). "Fain would I pause,"
says the narrator, "to dwell upon the world of charms that burst
upon the enraptured gaze of my hero, as he entered the state
parlor of the Van Tassels' mansion. Not those of the bevy of
buxom lasses . . . but the ample charms of a genuine Dutch
country tea-table, in the sumptuous time of autumn." Whereupon
follows the famous enumeration of the pastries and meats that
Ichabod samples before his last ride in Sleepy Hollow (pp.
439–40).

To a large extent the method of this story is to heap up images
of abundance and contrast Sleepy Hollow's amplitude with the
meagreness of Ichabod Crane's body and spirit. Irving seems to

[14] See Martin, "Rip, Ichabod, and the American Imagination," *American Literature*, XXXI, 143–44.

be trying to exorcise the Craneish tendencies in himself, to laugh off the superstitious fears and solitary dreaming that leave a man unable to see anything in the world around him but the projection of his own dread and desire. The sympathy of the narrator, though it often touches Ichabod Crane, rests finally with Brom Bones.[15] Crane has to go. The harvest in Tarrytown, the whole well-fed, workaday American world, belongs to those with just enough imagination to enjoy working for it.

Often Crayon gives the impression that he, like Ichabod or Rip, would like to retire to a sleepy hollow (Irving later would choose to be buried in the one in Tarrytown), to a quiet niche, a patch of the past, a terrain where everything is properly in its place, stationary, comprehensible, traditional. Given the chance, he would curl up and let history pass him by. While life moves him on, he finds only occasionally, in "John Bull" and "Little Britain," the good-natured humor to accept the mutability of things.

The orderly landscaping of the English countryside and the neatness of the British housekeepers tend to develop England, with its aura of tradition and age, as the chief symbol or repository of symbols for home. Sleepy Hollow may be the native land of housewifery, but England often seems a mother country to the American traveler. And there is room for fathers in the larger domestic metaphor, a role for England as a virtual fatherland in Irving's political economy. The imagery develops effectively through the fatherly figure of Squire Bracebridge in the Christmas sketches, until inevitably Irving's greatest tribute to England is presented in the metaphor of a thoroughly lived-in house, John Bull's mansion, the symbol of permanence in the midst of change.

On the whole in *The Sketch Book* the city yields images of decaying buildings, dark narrow streets, and dismal commerce. But in both "John Bull" and "Little Britain" it comes to life

---

[15] See Daniel Hoffman's interpretation of "Sleepy Hollow" in terms of American folklore and native humor (*Form and Fable*, chap. iv). For a contrasting interpretation, see Robert Bone, "Irving's Headless Hessian: Prosperity and the Inner Life," *American Quarterly*, XV (Summer, 1963), 167–75.

with cockney vulgarity. "Little Britain" may have its prophet
of doom in an apothecary with "a cadaverous countenance, full
of cavities and projections" (p. 301). And fashion may shake
the neighborhood; "its golden simplicity of manners" is "threatened with total subversion, by the aspiring family of a retired
butcher" (p. 310). But the piece takes social confusion as entirely natural and therefore amusing, serene in the faith that if
Little Britain is going to the dogs there are other neighborhoods
where pure and unadulterated cockneyism can flourish.

Nevertheless, if John Bull's house is one that Crayon can admire, it is not one he can really inhabit for long. He remains
largely a solitary figure. The only satisfactory settlement he
can make of his need to be near other people is to be a temporary
guest in a house or a traveler who chats with casual acquaintances
at an inn. With the old bachelor of "The Angler," for instance,
he shares a love of fishing in quiet country streams—which, for
Crayon, an indifferent fisherman, is a love of retirement. Having
been to America, failed in business, and lost a leg in a naval
battle, the angler now lives on his pension and simply fishes. He
loves the world, particularly the young people of his village;
he is the bachelor equivalent of Rip Van Winkle. He has a neat
cottage, goes regularly to church (though he sleeps through the
service), and waits to be buried in the green spot where his
mother and father lie. Crayon's sympathetic amusement at this
figure sums up much of the feeling of *The Sketch Book.*

Looking back from "The Angler" to one of Goldsmith's
periodical essay *récits,* "The Distresses of a Common Soldier,"
one sees a contrast that helps clarify Irving's approach to fiction.
As with "Westminster Abbey" and "The Boar's Head Tavern,"
one suspects that the choice of the disabled veteran as subject derives from Goldsmith.[16] But "The Distresses of a Common
Soldier" is merely an *exemplum,* a personification of a moral

---

[16] "The Distresses of a Common Soldier" is Essay XXIV, and in an earlier
version, Letter CXIX of *Citizen of the World.* For Goldsmith on the Abbey and
the Boar's Head see *Citizen,* Letter XIII, and Essay XIX, "A Reverie at the Boar's
Head Tavern in Eastcheap." Addison also wrote an essay on Westminster Abbey
(*Spectator,* No. 26).

abstraction: "he who in the vale of obscurity, can brave adversity; who without friends to encourage, acquaintances to pity, or even without hope to alleviate his misfortunes, can behave with tranquility and indifference, is truly great. . . ." When taken as a representation of an actual person whom the author had known long ago in the country, "honest and industrious," but now "begging at one of the outlets of the town, with a wooden leg," the disabled soldier is quite unconvincing. He has more life as a caricature, as an ironic symbol of how institutional indifference may ruin a life, though on the whole Goldsmith seems to want to take him seriously as a human being. There is no suggestion of a personal life or feeling in him, nothing faintly resembling doubt, no hint of private interior resources which might console him against misfortune. Everything is ludicrously public and trimmed to fit the abstraction: "I had almost forgotten to tell you, that in that engagement, I was wounded in two places; I lost four fingers off the left hand, and my leg was shot off." Yet he concludes idiotically as he limps away, "I enjoy good heath, and will ever love liberty and old England."

The emphasis in "The Distresses of a Common Soldier" is on action in the form of a rapid succession of external events. In "The Angler," however, Irving eliminates action altogether. Next to nothing "happens." The piece is little more than a description of the subject in and around his village home. The emphasis is on scene or setting and on the present appearance, behavior, and interests of the angler. Although his life has been almost as full of trials as that of Goldsmith's soldier, Irving focuses on its end, letting that serve as an indication of the whole. And Crayon's sympathy becomes an active complicating factor; one is not sure whether the main concern is the angler or the observer. It is the subjective, reflective ingredient, as much as the attention to scenic and sensuous detail, that marks the development.

The handbooks say that *The Sketch Book* in some way or other marks a crucial stage in the development of short fiction—that indeed the short story itself actually begins with "Rip Van Winkle" and "The Legend of Sleepy Hollow." But the nature

of the achievement remains obscure. As yet no one has seriously
attempted to define the sketch or explain its relationship to the
short story. A typical critic says of the sketch, "differentiating it
from the tale," that it depends on "its emphasis upon atmosphere
and scene, its subordination of action and adventure." But as a
genre developed by Irving and perhaps perfected by Hawthorne,
the sketch is surely more than simply a "romantic means of
catching the atmosphere of remote places."[17] It is fundamentally the expression of a Crayon-like narrator. It consists of brief
observations by a narrator speaking (sometimes literally) from
an isolated chamber.

Many of the items in *The Sketch Book*, of course, are not
sketches in this sense. But Irving's general tendency is to avoid
the detailed and relatively objective descriptions of people and
places in which someone like Mary Russell Mitford specialized,
and instead to create a kind of fiction in which something that
happens or does not happen to Crayon is of primary concern, in
which his responses to people and places are as important or
more important than the people and places are in themselves.
There are certainly some similarities of tone and interest relating
Irving's work to that of the British essayists of the romantic
period. But even the bachelor voice of Lamb (or Elia) on the
whole sounds more detached from the observations it makes than
does that of Crayon, for Crayon, at least in *The Sketch Book*,
almost always manages to get himself into a specific scene.
Irving's mode is primarily narrative. He tends to put whatever
he has to say in the form of a story, even if he has no other
character than his narrator and no action except the narrator's
observations. Compared to Irving's, the observations of Hunt
and Lamb, for instance, are much more generalized. The latter,
for all their sensitivity to concrete impressions, primarily write
familiar essays, even when they call them sketches. On the whole,
however, Irving writes a kind of fiction.

One reason for Crayon's importance is that his character is
diametrically opposed to that of the narrative voice which

[17] Ray B. West, Jr., *The Short Story in America* (Chicago, 1952), p. 2.

dominated fiction in the eighteenth century. It is not coincidental that Irving uses as an inscription on the title page of *The Sketch Book* a quotation from Burton in which he characterizes himself as a "spectator." For unlike Addison, Crayon is uneasy and insecure; he is a spectator who, like the author of *The Anatomy of Melancholy*, has to watch his moods and humors; he is one whom the world can upset. His loneliness tends to make his surroundings reflect his own image. The convenience for Irving of the sketch, its intimate connection with his personality, can hardly be overstated.

Picturesqueness also distinguishes the sketch, which is based less on belief in the objective reality of an observed scene than on the associations read into it by a spectator. Although it is visual, exploiting what can be seen and taking as its point of departure a physical setting, the sketch makes no attempt to distinguish sharply between nature or the landscape as a thing in itself and nature as experience molded by the observer's imagination. It hardly trusts or conceives of either nature in the raw or the naked eye. Its tone half-apologizes to the reader for not being able to break out of the limitations of a personal point of view. The sketch represents the somewhat puzzled and alienated observer, someone who, like Irving, constantly tries to adjust American eyes to English views, or can never actually be sure that he is looking at his own country in the right way.

But for all its dependence on the narrator's presence in the scene, sketching tends to keep him at a distance from his subject. In the classic example, Hawthorne's "Sights from a Steeple," for instance, the narrator is located high above the spectacle he is viewing. In the church steeple he is cut off from the world below in every sense but sight, and even sight from such a distance is dim. He would like to be a spiritual Paul Pry and come to know, close up and inside, the figures he observes, but perhaps moving in and down on them would mean losing the broader perspective. As he looks down, he sees a sunlit world threatened by an encroaching storm, little boys playing soldiers juxtaposed with a funeral cortege, two blooming girls in the company of a handsome youth about to collide at a street corner with a haughty merchant returning from the wharf where he has been overseeing the unloading of a cargo. The distant observer here is as limited to broad outlines and obvious impressions as is Crayon the tourist, who browses through memorials and sees in Westminster Abbey or Stratford little more than the mere hop, skip, and jump that separate birth and death—even though in Hawthorne human beings have replaced sepulchers and coronation chairs as the symbols and we are closer to story than to essay. As the storm breaks, an ominous mercantilism seems to come between young lovers: the old gentleman from the wharf wrenches his daughters away from the youth and hurries them home.

Action cannot develop further because the observer cannot see through the walls of the houses where his characters take cover, cannot hear what they say. He seems a stranger in the community; he does not know his characters by name. Yet the reader does get one vivid sustained impression, that of the alienated observer's efforts to see life. One senses that he would like to be down in the street immersed in the experiences he is reporting, but a desire to see everything seems to strand him suspended above the town. One admires his consistency. He reports nothing that he cannot observe at first hand. Hawthorne preserves the point of view meticulously, and, in the absence of familiarity with his subject, this guarantees an illusion of real life. The author of the sketch knows how to make the best of what he doesn't know.[18]

[18] What I am calling Hawthorne's sketches F. L. Pattee (*The Development of the American Short Story* [New York, 1923], p. 99) designated *"Studies in Personality,"* a particular species, since Hawthorne was adept at several kinds of not fully fictional narrative. Such studies consist of "observations upon moving sections of life during a typical hour with intense focus, the procession that files by a solitary man who records what he sees and draws what conclusions he may, even to the discerning of plot and dénouement." Pattee believed this genre "peculiarly the creation of Hawthorne," a view which I would dispute. Thomas Walsh has pursued the study of Hawthorne's sketches in detail in "Hawthorne's Handling of Point of View in His Tales and Sketches," (unpublished Ph.D. dissertation, University of Wisconsin, 1957). He has refined on Pattee's system of classification and offers discussions of Hawthorne's technique in both the simple "sketch in personality" and what Walsh calls the "Narcissistic pieces," the latter being intensifications, such as "Monsieur du Miroir" and "The Vision of the Fountain," which virtually turn the sketch into a story (pp. 33–147).

The sketch, then, views the world from a distance. In *The Alhambra*, in a sketch called "The Balcony," which in some respects is very close to "Sights from a Steeple," Irving was to present himself as positioned high above Granada looking out over the city and trying to make out what was going on below. And we have already seen Crayon, in "The Voyage," up in the crow's nest, meditating on the monsters of the deep. As his ship docks in Liverpool, he stands alone at the rail, playing the spectator, and catches glimpses of typical human activities and interests. The merchant waiting for his cargo paces the pier, "restless" and "calculating." Recognition scenes between friends and relatives on ship and shore play themselves out before Crayon's sympathetic view. One encounter that is described at length—a dying sailor's reunion with his wife—though it comes straight out of sentimental fiction, takes on some validity because the underlying feeling refers back to Crayon's own situation. The sailor is "so wasted, so pale, so ghastly" that at first, though he has lived through the voyage only for the last look at her, his wife fails to recognize him. He is obviously destined for the delicious agony of dying in her arms, but instead of seeing him through to the bittersweet end, we shift, as in "Sights from a Steeple," back to the narrator-observer, who is going through his own ordeal: "I stepped upon the land of my forefathers—but felt that I was a stranger in the land" (pp. 23–24).

Another comparison between Irving and Hawthorne will further clarify the nature of the sketch. In Irving's "A Sunday in London"[19] the contrast between a congregating community and a solitary observer, although largely implicit, approaches that in Hawthorne's "Sunday at Home," in which we are given a narrator hiding behind a window curtain, watching people enter and leave the church, listening to the muffled sounds of worship, and feeling guilty at his inability to join the worshipers. In Irving's sketch, after the throngs have entered the churches and the "ringing of bells is at an end," Crayon is outside by himself. The

[19] See above, n. 6.

"rumbling of the carriage has ceased; the pattering of feet is heard no more," and he listens to "the deep, pervading sound of the organ, rolling and vibrating through the empty lanes and courts . . ." (p. 141). This sketch ends on a joyous note with Crayon melting spiritually into the crowds bound for suburban parks on Sunday afternoon. But what the observations in a sketch usually manage to do is to remind the reader, if not the narrator himself, of a difference between the viewer and the world. In "The Stage Coach," for instance, Crayon sits all day and happily watches and listens to "three fine rosy-cheeked boys . . . returning home for the holidays in high glee" (pp. 231–32). After a long ride however, when the boys excitedly reach their destination, the mood changes. "I looked after them," Crayon says, "with a feeling in which I do not know whether pleasure or melancholy predominated; for I was reminded of those days when, like them, I had neither known care nor sorrow, and a holiday was the summit of earthly felicity." As the coach moves on he catches sight of a woman and two girls, obviously the boys' mother and sisters, "in the portico" of "a neat country seat." He leans out of the window for a view of "the happy meeting." But, he says, "a grove of trees shut it from my sight" (pp. 236–37).[20]

It is a modification of this kind of effect that Irving used as a climax when in "The Stout Gentleman" (*Bracebridge Hall*) he transformed the sketch into a bona fide short story. Here the narrator, who is not Crayon but another "nervous gentleman," alone at an inn during rainy weather, amuses himself by trying to guess the identity of a mysterious fellow guest who can be heard upstairs and is constantly being waited upon by servants but who never appears. The story turns out to be a joke on the narrator. He never finds out who the man is. At the climax he gets only a fleeting glimpse of his subject's posteriors as he climbs

[20] One can get some sense of the difference between Irving and Leigh Hunt by comparing pieces they wrote on identical subjects, for instance, Hunt's "Coaches" and "May-Day" with Irving's "The Stage Coach" (*SB*) and "May-Day" (*B*). Hunt may well have helped arouse Irving to a sense of the literary possibilities in certain English manners and customs, past and present. But Irving's tendency toward narrative prevents his becoming a mere imitator of Hunt's essays.

into a coach to leave. His observations have amounted to absolutely nothing.[21]

In Irving and Hawthorne the sketch becomes a formal device whereby the mystery and suspense that dominated gothic fiction are transmuted, toned down, and given some psychological authenticity. The sketch tends to draw the reader's attention away from the expected sensational disclosure and raise questions about the relation between the observer and the outcome he is looking for or anticipating. The usual tone of the sketch is the sadness or melancholy of partial alienation, but the impression can be modulated in various directions—toward the joy of temporarily overcoming separation, toward comic frustration, as in "The Stout Gentleman," or toward fear, terror, or despair. Thus in "The Art of Book-Making," a typical sketch-verging-on-story, Crayon's situation in the scene he is observing in the British Museum is dramatically reversed: by laughing inadvertently, he finds *himself* turned into a curiosity at whom others stare. Much of the time Crayon has been asleep, dreaming about modern authors rummaging about for odd literary remnants. Now he sneaks away, frightened and embarrassed, leaving the reader with the suspicion that he has seen something of himself in the grubbing hacks in the library.[22]

One of the chief concerns of American fiction (if not of American literature in general) is with the irony embodied in the seeker, searcher, viewer, sometimes virtual voyeur, whose observations or researches end by revealing, to the reader if not to the protagonist himself, more about the onlooker than about an observed world. This is an irony almost implicit in the form of fiction once an interest develops in point of view, in the relativity of what is seen or experienced to the individual awareness. Thus, for example, the Walpurgis Night that Hawthorne's Good-

---

[21] The sketch developed into story in Hawthorne can also turn into a sort of joke at the narrator's expense, as the two "Narcissistic pieces" mentioned in n. 18 above show.

[22] In "Fragments from the Journal of a Solitary Man" (*The Complete Works of Nathaniel Hawthorne*, ed. G. P. Lathrop [Boston, 1891], XXIII, 30) Hawthorne has his poet-protagonist, a greater recluse than Crayon and even more fearful of being cut off from reality and the present, dream that he is "promenading Broadway," in his shroud.

man Brown witnesses becomes on one level (with the device of
the dream again lending credibility) a projection of his own
doubts about his society and himself. The formal manifestation
of this epistemological probing is a fairly constant refinement
from Irving through James in the manipulation of point of
view, although often, as in "Ethan Brand," the probing, the
investigation of the limitation or ambiguities of a point of view,
may itself become the major theme.

Hawthorne picks up (especially in his sketches, though one may
encounter the traces almost anywhere) the Irvingesque image of
the writer as bachelor, traveler, and self-conscious antiquarian.[23]
In "Chippings with a Chisel" the workshop of his sculptor of
tombstones at Edgartown on Martha's Vineyard substitutes for
"The Country Church" and "Rural Funerals" in Crayon's England. And there are hints that a "certain church in the city of
New York" substitutes for Westminster Abbey.[24] Perhaps because Hawthorne was unable to go to England until late in life
and could only read about it (in, for example, *The Sketch Book*),
he was able to voice even more poignantly than Irving the
American writer's "homesickness for the fatherland":

> Once I had fancied that my sleep would not be quiet in the grave
> unless I should return, as it were, to my home of past ages, and see
> the very cities, and castles, and battle-fields of history, and stand
> within the holy gloom of its cathedrals, and kneel at the shrines of its
> immortal poets, there asserting myself their hereditary countryman.
> This feeling lay among the deepest in my heart.[25]

[23] Pattee felt the influence of Irving, especially on the early Hawthorne, to be
fairly strong: "one cannot but feel that the two groups of sketches are very
closely related" (pp. 99–100). Poe, in his review of *Twice-Told Tales* (*Graham's
Magazine*, XX [May, 1842], 298) said, "The Essays of Hawthorne have much of
the character of Irving, with more originality, and less finish. . . ." What Poe
calls "Essays" are in several cases what would be more commonly called sketches.
Poe thought the "repose" in Hawthorne was much the same as in Irving. He
saw Hawthorne's as a "truly imaginative intellect, restrained, and in some measure
repressed, by fastidiousness of taste, by constitutional melancholy and by indolence." For Hawthorne's opinion of Irving, see STW, II, 101, 205–6, 278.

[24] See the beginning of "The Wedding Knell" and the graveyard imagery connected with St. Paul's in New York in the dream of the "Solitary Man" (*Complete
Works*, XXIII, 30).

[25] Hawthorne, *Complete Works*, XXIII, 26.

True, technically this is the sentiment of the poet Oberon in "Journal of a Solitary Man" rather than that of Hawthorne himself, but Oberon surely represents, both here and in the grotesque whimsy of "The Devil in Manuscript," Hawthorne's own fears that his "peep-hole" approach to reality may prove artistically unfruitful. "Night Sketches," with Hawthorne speaking more nearly in his own voice, gives very clearly the ordeal of the solitary chamber, the writer's ambivalence toward dream and reality, privacy and exposure. Cooped up all day with his shadowy fantasies, by nightfall he begins to doubt the substantiality of the outside world. And when he goes out to check up on reality, it is only furtively and fearfully. The darkness both frightens and protects him from involvement. At the same time it gives the world an intriguing, mysterious cast. One is reminded of Crayon's exploration of the gloomy recesses of London and comparison of himself to Guy Fawkes with his dark lantern. True, the "solitary" lantern carrier on whom Hawthorne's hopes ride is a man striding "fearlessly into the unknown gloom," trusting that his light, feeble as it is, will guide him home to the hearth where it was kindled. Yet one wonders if what makes this figure appealing to the writer is not after all the fancifulness of the "circular pattern" of light which the "punched holes" of the lantern throw "on the ground before him."[26]

Miles Coverdale is essentially an extension and amplification of the narrator of the sketch. Curiousness, standoffishness, and a flair for mystery are among his distinguishing characteristics. He too is a bachelor, on the surface a confidant to parties more actively engaged in affairs than himself. Yet at the end of *The Blithedale Romance* he fully reveals the extent of his involvement in the story he has told, enabling us to view the whole narrative on one level as the consequence of his need (though he may seem to deny it) to talk about himself.[27] To look ahead momen-

---

[26] There is a similar ambivalence toward life in the literary narrator of "The Village Uncle."

[27] In the Preface to *Twice-Told Tales* (2d ed.) Hawthorne speaks of himself as the author, who, on the internal evidence of his sketches, came to be regarded as a mild, shy, gentle, melancholic, exceedingly sensitive, and not very forcible man, hiding his blushes under an assumed name, the quaintness of which was

tarily in order to instance first person narrators in Henry James
(*The Aspern Papers, The Sacred Fount*), observers who capitalize on qualities like Coverdale's—who are educated, gentlemanly, dignified, scrupulous, more or less artistic, and perhaps
too observant for their own good—is only to begin to suggest the
richness of the vein Irving fell into in presenting himself as
Geoffrey Crayon, seer of sights.

   The image of the writer in Hawthorne, so close to Irving at
the beginning, undergoes more than one significant metamor-
phosis. Though he might smile at misguided idealists and
Utopian reformers, he took to Nature and shunned conventional
society almost as eagerly as a Transcendentalist, at least if one
is to judge by such sketches, early and late, as "Footprints on the
Sea-Shore," "Buds and Bird Voices," and "The Old Manse."
Annoyances at Brook Farm were not strong enough to keep him
away from Concord. A certain lethargy of spirit might tempt
him to remain indoors; in "Snowflakes" he scrutinizes natural
phenomena minutely but through the window. But once outside,
he could often accept the contemplation of Nature as a substitute
for private fantasy. In "The Old Manse" he does even better by
himself than he manages to do by his old apple-dealer, as he
seems almost to "put on" the house, the village, their past, the
surrounding landscape, and the cycle of the seasons like the well-
worn suit of clothes about which Thoreau was to talk in
"Economy."

   Irvingesque traces remain. If the cadence of Hawthorne's
prose as he talks about growing beans anticipates Thoreau's
"Bean Field" in *Walden*, he can, within a page, come back to
"Dutch cabbage" swelling "to a monstrous circumference" and
ready to be devoured by appetites as big as those of Brom Bones

---

supposed, somehow or other, to symbolize his personal and literary traits. He
is by no means certain that some of his subsequent productions have not been
influenced and modified by a natural desire to fill up so amiable an outline,
and to act in consonance with the character assigned to him; nor, even now,
could he forfeit it without a few tears of tender sensibility.

One is intrigued by the thought of Nathaniel Hawthorne being a pen name like
Geoffrey Crayon. The Preface was written in 1851. *Blithedale* came the following
year. I have discussed Coverdale more fully in "Hawthorne's *Blithedale*: The
Problem of the Narrator," *Nineteenth-Century Fiction*, XIV (March, 1960), 303–16.

and Ichabod Crane.[28] He can still play the antiquarian, musing
on worthless and forgotten books in the attic of the old manse.
But the main pull here is to the outside, for a walk in the woods,
or a row with Ellery Channing on that tributary of the Concord
River, the Assabeth. And in the "sacred solitude" of the forest
there come moments when it is possible "to utter the extremest
nonsense or the profoundest wisdom, or that ethereal product of
the mind which partakes of both, and may become one or the
other, in accordance with the faith and insight of the auditor."[29]

Is Hawthorne on the verge of pseudo-Rabelaisianism?—so
close to Thoreau that the next moment "the leaves of the trees
that overhang the Assabeth were whispering to us, 'Be free! be
free!' " Thus beyond the Irvingesque observer, half-desirous of
conventional social involvement but willing enough to watch the
procession or pageant of life play itself out in representative
scenes beneath his gaze, one glimpses a Transcendental observer
eager to see reflections in the world's physiognomy of a more
essential spirit, or Nature, or self. Hawthorne comes to peer into
the mirror of the Assabeth as intently as Thoreau into Walden
for eternity, or the narcissistic Ishmael into the ocean for "the
ungraspable phantom of life." The river, "flowing softly through
the midmost privacy and deepest heart" of the woods, "sleeps
along its course and dreams of the sky and of the clustering
foliage." To Hawthorne the "disembodied images" in the "dream
picture," which are the "apotheosis" of actual woods and sky,
seem more real than those "objects palpable to our grosser
senses." They "stand in closer relation to the soul. . . . I could
have fancied that this river had strayed forth out of the rich
scenery of my companion's [Channing's] inner world."[30]

[28] Hawthorne, *Mosses from the Old Manse*, Vol. III of *Complete Works*, 23–25.
[29] *Ibid.*, III, 35.
[30] *Complete Works*, III, 32. F. O. Matthiessen, speaking of the original draft
of this passage in Hawthorne's notebook, found the idealistic doctrine or speculation in "The Old Manse" artistically dangerous. *American Renaissance* (New
York, n.d.), p. 259. Hawthorne's sense of the connection between mirror imagery
and the artist's desire for self-discovery is apparent in "Monsieur du Miroir" and
"The Vision of the Fountain," an obvious embodiment of the narcissistic theme
which Irving's "Mountjoy" (1839—see his *Wolfert's Roost*) similarly develops,
though in a grossly sentimentalized form. It is customary to see Hawthorne and

Melville's Ishmael is not presented as one who shyly pries into other people's business from a distance, but he too is a bachelor and a homeless traveler. Often but a thin disguise for Melville himself, he is left alone at the end of the voyage, sole survivor of an action which is far too mysterious for him to comprehend. Many of the chapters of *Moby-Dick* give us, instead of narrative, a spectator's observations on a whaling world. Ishmael in the crow's nest, even more than Crayon at the quarter rail or in the Abbey, Coverdale in the vine-covered tree, or Hawthorne on the Assabeth, runs the risk of being lost to reality, of taking the final plunge into imagination.[31] His meditations on things in general have a way of turning back to remind him of his own situation as one who meditates and never connects with final meanings. Ishmael's technique in the non-narrative chapters is sketching carried to a logical extreme, concerning itself not with people and events but with static facts, the bare statistics of the whaling industry, the contemplation of which, the raising of them to the status of symbols, becomes a kind of action.

The "conceited" prose of *Moby-Dick,* surely in part an off-shoot of Knickerbockerism, reflects Ishmael's neurotic temperament and establishes the metaphysical texture of the whole novel in the fantastic but "linked" analogies which Melville, through his characters, reads into the voyage. Ishmael sees something amusing in his own imaginativeness; his very tone constantly implies it, if indeed in labored moments he does not flaunt it at the reader. He can mock his own quest for a final answer, the urgency of which so thoroughly animates his narrative. He

---

Transcendentalism as basically antagonistic to each other, but the opposition, I believe, has been pushed much too far. As Frank Davidson has shown, for instance, there is good reason to believe that his friendship with Thoreau had an influence on Hawthorne. "Thoreau's Contribution to Hawthorne's *Mosses,*" *New England Quarterly,* XX (December, 1947), 535–42. Raymond Adams also sees a relationship between Transcendentalism and the fiction of the *Mosses.* "Hawthorne: The Old Manse Period," *Tulane Studies in English,* VII (1958), 115–51. And B. R. McElderry points out that in his own time Hawthorne was associated with the Concord group as another idealist. "The Transcendental Hawthorne," *Midwest Quarterly,* II (July, 1961), 307–23.

[31] As Crayon's position aloft relates him to the nobly Roman Roscoe ("Pompey's column . . . towering alone"), so "The Mast-Head" (chap. xxxv) in *Moby-Dick,* with its discussion of statues of heroes standing on high columns, associates Ishmael's tendency to withdrawal with Ahab's inaccessibility.

oscillates between faith and doubt, for all his ties to Queequeg—in contrast to Ahab, who, positive of the evil of existence, cannot laugh at himself. Ahab has conviction at the price of madness. He perishes while Ishmael survives to pursue the endless search, making jokes to keep his courage afloat.

In *Walden* a new sense of authority, a brashness, replaces the uneasiness and insecurity of Crayon, Coverdale, and Ishmael. But there is in Thoreau an even greater insistence on solitude and the disconnection of the writer from the rest of the conventional world. This is the very source of the authority: the building within the hut at Walden (or within Thoreau's own imagination) of a universe of discourse to compensate him for the world well lost. He makes himself a kind of sightseer and observer, although he has seen even less of the ordinary world than Irving or Hawthorne. He has traveled much in Concord, he blithely says; he is able to make his journey to Walden a voyage of discovery. He is a writer with nothing to write about but his own limited experience, which he reads universally and to some extent fictionalizes, casting his work in pseudonarrative forms centering on the small actions he has performed or the limited movements he has made, the trip on the Concord and Merrimack or the assumption of residence at Walden.

It is well to remind ourselves how strong the autobiographical element is in American literature generally. The early fiction of Melville, Mark Twain, and Howells is often scarcely more than autobiography in disguise. And their narrators or protagonists are usually travelers of one sort or another, even if they are only Howells' Basil March taking the excursion of *Their Wedding Journey* or Howells himself taking "A Pedestrian Tour" around Cambridge in *Suburban Sketches*. It took time to develop the American businessman as a tragic hero out of the comic stereotype of the *nouveau riche* tradesman, to distinguish the fresh and independent American girl from the stock heroine of sentimental fiction, or the innocent American youth from the country bumpkin. But one thing the American writer had from the beginning was a sense of the strangeness of his own situation, caught somewhere in the middle between the wildness of the frontier and the cultivation of Europe, the vast expanses on either side of him demanding to be explored. To refuse to explore them—except in imagination—took the microcosmopolitan daring and metaphysical conceitedness of a Transcendentalist, who would insist that an understanding of the province of the inner life could be achieved by confining one's attention to the immediate external environment (Concord). Otherwise, exposing oneself to either the frontier or culture meant facing risks; in effect, the writer had to personify himself as innocence thrust into a mysterious world. While this is a role that a few major American writers, like Cooper, tried to avoid, most of them, from Irving on, at least half-adopted it. Ultimately Mark Twain was to go to the logical limit, making himself both innocence abroad and, as Henry Nash Smith has shown,[32] tenderfoot being initiated into the far West.

The first person narrator in American fiction is characteristically not an assured, experienced, authoritative man of the world but a tenderfoot exploring an unfamiliar country, telling a story that threatens to become a joke at his own expense.[33] And he is first cousin to another favorite American construction, the uninitiated person as central intelligence. When we realize how close the narrator in "Bartleby the Scrivener" is to Amasa Delano in "Benito Cereno"; Miles Coverdale to James's Rowland Mallett, Frederick Winterbourne, John Marcher, and Lambert Strether; and Huck Finn to James's Maisie, we sense the intimacy of the connection between the theme of innocence in American literature and the question of how much an observer can see. The gothic tendencies in American fiction, the interest in romance, in the unreal, all make sense. The narrator of "The Fall of the House of Usher," who is simultaneously fascinated

[32] "Mark Twain as an Interpreter of the Far West: The Structure of Roughing It," in *The Frontier in Perspective*, ed. Walker D. Wyman and Clifton B. Kroeber (Madison, Wis., 1957), pp. 206–28.

[33] Marius Bewley has commented: "There was really only one subject available to the nineteenth-century American novelist—his own unhappy plight. And the essence of that plight was his isolation." *The Eccentric Design* (New York, 1959), p. 15. The significance of the persistence of the point of view of the alienated observer-narrator in twentieth-century American fiction, in, for instance, *The Sun Also Rises, The Great Gatsby, Dangling Man, The Catcher in the Rye,* and *Goodbye, Columbus,* may also be worth pondering.

and horrified by decadence, is in one sense symptomatic of an American point of view. We see this as early as the novels of Charles Brockden Brown, although, in spite of his interest in character complexity, Brown still tends to maintain his narrator-initiates as innocent victims exposed to, and not intrinsically implicated in, external villainy. Like Brown's, Poe's first person narrators undoubtedly come directly out of the conventions of the gothic tale and the sensational anecdote. They have in them less of the Crayon-like diffidence than of the authority of a man who has survived a unique and dangerous experience and who is able to give the firsthand account of it. They always speak as eyewitnesses to unusual events. Even so, we find a tenderfoot quality emerging in many of Poe's tales, such as "Usher," "Berenice," "Ligeia," "Morella," and "The Tell-Tale Heart," where the story gets away from the narrator or reflects his own instability as he waits and watches for the destined horror to transpire.

A look at Melville's "The Paradise of Bachelors and the Tartarus of Maids" brings Irving, Melville, and Poe together in a connection which suggests even more strongly how primary a figure to American fiction is the solitary narrator exploring a mysterious world. The first half of this sketch, or rather of two sketches put back to back, must be in part a parody of Irving. The parallels between the opening paragraphs of "The Paradise of Bachelors" and the beginning of Irving's "London Antiques" (Crayon, escaping the rush of the city, discovers a cool courtyard—with "grassplot"—and the chapel of the Knights Templars before going on to the Charter House) are too striking to leave any doubt on this score. Crayon says, for instance, "I was like an Arab, who had suddenly come upon an oasis amid the panting sterility of the desert" (*SB*, p. 291). And Melville, "Sweet are the oases in Sahara . . . but sweeter, still more charming, most delectable, the dreamy Paradise of Bachelors, found in the stony heart of stunning London." There are echoes of Irving all through the sketch. Superficially "The Paradise of Bachelors" warms to enthusiasm over the life of the Templars

snugly installed in bachelor quarters and joined in the conviviality of bachelor banquets. But through the glow one gets an
impression of emptiness and irresponsibility. The bachelors
simply deny the existence of pain and trouble (as the crew of
the ship "Bachelor" in *Moby-Dick* refuse to believe in the
existence of the white whale).

Yet it is perhaps not so much Irving himself who is being
parodied as it is the popular image of Irving and the vogue of
the genial and sentimental bachelor-escapist in pre-Civil War
American literature, best typified in D. G. Mitchell's *Reveries of
a Bachelor* (1850). For in going from the paradise of bachelors
to the Tartarus of maids, Melville is dramatizing a dilemma
closely related to the one that confronted Crayon when (whether
in *The Sketch Book* or later works) he looked from his wizened
black old men (usually, of course, bachelors) to the excessively
idealized sweetheart, the motherly wife, or the termagant like
Dame Van Winkle. Melville has caught the sexual overtones of
the imagery of narrow passageways, secluded courtyards, and
snug chambers. He parallels images in the opening of "The
Paradise of Bachelors" with the "Dantean gateway," the "Black
Notch," and the "dangerously narrow wheel-road" in "the bottom
of the gorge" at the start of "The Tartarus of Maids." And the
more than claustrophobic fear of confining enclosures here suggests a Poe story as interpreted by Marie Bonaparte. Working
with the contrast between grassy valleys (sleepy hollows) and
sepulchral recesses used by both Irving and Poe, Melville ex-
plores symbolically in these sketches the alternatives of with-
drawing from life into the equivalent of a protective womb and
involving himself in a more active life which has something aggressively and threateningly female about it. Somewhat like
Crayon at the end, he is "all alone with inscrutable nature," ex-
claiming, "Oh! Paradise of Bachelors! and oh! Tartarus of
Maids!" It is not surprising that years later, in "Rip Van
Winkle's Lilac," Melville revealed, as Leslie Fiedler has suggested,[34] that he had responded to some of the elusive implica-

---

[34] *Love and Death in the American Novel* (New York, 1960), p. 336.

tions of Irving's most famous story, which contemporary symbolic readings have picked up.

Crayon is seldom made directly responsible for the stories (as opposed to the sketches) that he puts into his books, but the people who allegedly tell him the stories or supply him with them are almost always, like the "nervous" narrator of "The Stout Gentleman," significant analogues of himself. The essential characteristic of Irving's stories is that they are told by a man who is not altogether sure of himself. Hence they take the form of legends, of hearsay; they are stories picked up at second or third hand, not eyewitness accounts. The disavowal of responsibility carries over into the more or less whimsical tone that persists in most of Irving's fiction. There is an element of spoofing in all three of the tales in *The Sketch Book.* The specter of "The Spectre Bridegroom" turns out to be flesh and blood, as the alert reader will have anticipated almost from the beginning. In the mock-gothic tone of this story Irving is for the moment shrugging off all the claptrap of aristocratic connections, customs, and traditions to which Crayon is so susceptible on certain occasions. Here the old baronial family seems quaint and oddly decadent. The ghost is only a trick resorted to by an energetic young man with a contemporary outlook in order to free a beautiful girl from the clutches of a tyrannical, tradition-ridden father. The story is a joke on the reader looking for real ghosts. Similarly the headless horseman in "Sleepy Hollow" turns out to be Brom Bones. To have expected anything else is to have read the story the wrong way.

Irving's is a fiction of dreams, fantasies, symbolic projections; it is heavily loaded with imagery functioning as metaphor. Its heroes or protagonists tend to be variations of, or foils to, the personality of the Crayonesque observer or the author behind the story. It alternately sympathizes with, laughs at, and turns in fear from the stranger, the homeless or orphaned young man, the provincial abroad, the recluse, the eccentric scholar, the dreamer, the enthusiast, and the teller of tales. Whether these heroes come to good or bad ends, are lucky or unlucky, succeed or fail, come home or get lost seems to depend largely on the precise shade of

Crayon that they have in them. They have adversaries: women who are too strong for them in one way or another, who laugh at them, nag them and provoke them; young men who are more practical than they are; and old men who are often the fathers of the heroes themselves or of the women they court—either tyrants or old men in whom life has largely dried up, even when they are not bachelors.

Beyond Irving we come to Hawthorne's versions of the estranged hero. We notice, for instance, the obvious similarities between Rip Van Winkle's disappearance and Wakefield's "long whimwham," twenty years lost to himself and his wife in the wilderness of London streets.[35] For all their longings for permanent establishments of one sort or another, longings which are in large measure what such protagonists as Peter Goldthwaite, Goodman Brown, Owen Warland, and Aylmer represent, a regular home, a more or less normal life usually proves a responsibility that they are, for better or for worse, unequal to. The wife proves a worry almost as often as she is a comfort and a protection. Brown, like Wakefield and Rip Van Winkle, leaves his wife guiltily. If Irving's Tom Walker lets his go to the devil, Aylmer destroys his in trying to improve on her. And Giovanni, in "Rappaccini's Daughter," loses the chance to save his intended bride because he is basically afraid of her.

Then one thinks of the first person narratives of Poe, which constantly worry wives into early graves, only to be haunted by ghosts and reincarnations and plagued by guilt feelings. The narrator is finally sure only of the reality of his fantasies. Poe gets rid of hesitancy and vagueness in his narratives and avoids giving the impression of not taking responsibility for the truth of what he says only by insisting in his eyewitness manner upon the actuality of experiences which are obviously fantastic. The strategy is a step further back into the isolated chamber. The final step is into the solitary confinement of Rip Van Winkle's distant relative, Bartleby, the scrivener.

[35] William Austin's "Peter Rugg" (1824), with its Rip Van Winkle motif (Pattee, p. 38), may be a connecting link here.

American storytelling, at least in the nineteenth century, becomes very often for the author an elaborate way of talking about himself. The world at large may be left behind or may fade out and come through only in symbol. Distant or special settings—a ship at sea, a private garden, an alchemist's laboratory—serve as theaters for movements that have a balletic formality. In the midst of massed stage effects—rich *décor*, pageantry, and procession—a few conflicts which are of especial concern to Crayonesque narrators or observers, first carefully abstracted from the sphere of ordinary daily life, are acted out. But it is hard for such fiction to believe in itself all the time. The strain of pretending that the fanciful and fantastic are in some way credible can become too great. Thus humor and whimsy persist as ways out, as reminders to the reader that he is encountering fiction and not the actual world.

In "The Art of Fiction" Henry James protests against the sketchiness of fiction that calls attention to the fact that it is only fiction. In effect he rules out the device of calling a story a legend or romance, a device which Irving and Hawthorne used to avoid insisting too strongly on the inescapability of everything they had to say. But if James strengthens the hold of the author or narrator on his story, he at the same time unblushingly takes over the tentative and diffident observer and his observations as primary subjects for fiction. And in his concern for point of view, in the rarefied atmosphere in which he immerses his observers, in the almost lyrical way he approaches motive and attitude through elaborate metaphor, James's work, significantly, often seems an extension of the earlier fiction.

VII

The Ancestral Mansion and
the Haunted House

THE beginning of *Bracebridge Hall* (1822) shows an Irving highly conscious of the mask he had created for himself in *The Sketch Book*. The title-page motto magnifies Crayon into a world traveler, and in "The Author" he pulls out all the stops to harmonize again on the theme of national differences. "It has been a matter of marvel, to my European readers," he says, "that a man from the wilds of America should express himself in tolerable English." He fears that he has been overpraised and that his English topics aren't very original but hopes that they at least will continue to be of interest "when discussed by the pen of a stranger." For "England is as classic ground to an American, as Italy is to an Englishman; and old London teems with as much historical association as mighty Rome" (pp. 10–11). There follows one of American literature's more memorable declarations of the attraction of "an old state of society" for a man from a new world:

> Accustomed always to scenes where history was, in a manner, anticipation; where everything in art was new and progressive, and pointed to the future rather than to the past; where in short, the works of man gave no ideas but those of young existence, and prospective improvement; there was something inexpressibly touching in the sight of enormous piles of architecture, gray with antiquity, and sinking to decay.

His feelings were what might have been expected of an American raised on English history, on poetic allusions to larks and nightingales, on magazine illustrations of London landmarks, on English books which made him "familiar with the names of . . . streets and squares, and public places" in London before he knew those of New York. "Having been brought up also," he says a bit later, "in the comparative simplicity of a republic, I am apt to be struck with even the ordinary circumstances incident to an aristocratical state of society" (pp. 12–14).

Irving was trying to stay in character, to work out a literary destiny as a representative American in Europe. He had been successful in the part in *The Sketch Book*. He had won the acceptance not only of the *Edinburgh Review* (which was perhaps not surprising in view of his acquaintances with Scott and with the Francis Jeffrey circle in Edinburgh) but also of that particular scourge of American authors, William Gifford of the *Quarterly*. Already he was something of a celebrity in London. John Murray was his publisher, and he counted such authors as Isaac D'Israeli, Thomas Moore, Thomas Campbell, and Samuel Rogers among his friends. Uncertain as to his next literary venture, he had responded to Moore's suggestion that he follow up Crayon's Christmas visit to Bracebridge Hall in *The Sketch Book* with a book-length sojourn.[1]

But writing sketchbooks proved to be something Irving could not do automatically. *Bracebridge Hall* ran into difficulties, and, though generally well received, it was thought to be a falling-off from its predecessor. One disappointment is the diminution of the personal, wistful quality, a consequence of Irving's not utilizing fully the Crayonesque viewpoint. The emphasis is again on place, landscape, environment, atmosphere, manners, customs. But, whereas the Christmas sketches, which started with Geoffrey Crayon on the road and stopping over at random inns, had rescued him from solitude and found him a temporary home, *Bracebridge* largely dispenses with this narrative prop. Crayon is present as a guest during the festivities leading up to the marriage of one of the Squire's sons. We find him at the very beginning contemplating the "prospect" from his window (p.

[1] STW, I, 202.

17). With general consistency the book moves outward from his room to the Bracebridge estate, the nearby village, and the surrounding countryside, all leading more or less in the direction of a consideration of the national character. But there is not sufficient concern with the personal attitudes and reactions of Crayon to guarantee *Bracebridge Hall* the kind of unity implicit in *The Sketch Book*. This unity Irving did not achieve again until *The Alhambra*.

In *The Sketch Book* Irving had used the Bracebridge estate as a place of refuge for Crayon at a time when "nature" lay "wrapped in her shroud of snow." The function of Christmas had been to fill up houses, brighten hearths, and shut out darkness and ill feeling, like a roaring fire diffusing "an artificial summer and sunshine through the room" (*SB*, pp. 226–27). In contrast to the solitary Crayon, the figure of a coachman, with his vehicle jammed with passengers "bound to the mansions of relations or friends, to eat the Christmas dinner," presides over the early part of the Christmas sequence in *The Sketch Book*. His "jolly dimensions," a swelling brought on "by frequent potations of malt liquors" and extended by his being "buried like a cauliflower" in a "multiplicity of coats," are a part of the largesse of feeling attached to the season (pp. 231–33). A day's ride with this fat god of good tidings and connections made prepares Crayon for an accidental meeting with young Frank Bracebridge at an inn, whence he is hustled away to Bracebridge Hall, to a magical Christmas-card world. There, under the eye of the benign Squire, everything tends to become song, sport, pageant, or ritual.

It is primarily the novelty of festival pastimes, the keeping up of "the old games of hoodman blind, shoe the wild mare, hot cockles" (p. 245), that gives Bracebridge Hall importance in *The Sketch Book*. Crayon's temporary homecoming becomes in part the American writer's discovery of traditional forms and symbols whose absence from his own country he laments. They become so palpable as to turn, almost literally, into dramatis personae. In the Christmas sermon, for instance, the parson gets "completely embroiled in the sectarian controversies of the

Revolution, when the Puritans made such a fierce assault upon the ceremonies of the church, and poor old Christmas was driven out of the land by proclamation." These were the times of "the fiery persecution of poor mince-pie throughout the land," the denunciation of "plum porridge . . . as 'mere popery,' and roast-beef as anti-christian." No relief came until Christmas was "brought in again triumphantly with the merry court of King Charles at the Restoration" (pp. 265–66).

The martial imagery here, the overtones of battle, both echo Butler's *Hudibras*[2] and suggest what Hawthorne was to do in "The May-Pole of Merry Mount" with the device of having puritans make war on ceremony and ritual. After the Christmas dinner several of the figures from the sermon actually material-ize, as the guests at Bracebridge Hall perform a "burlesque imi-tation of an antique mask," based, we are informed by Crayon, on Ben Jonson's *Masque of Christmas*. Master Simon, the Squire's relative, plays the lead as Ancient Christmas, while Dame Mince Pie, Roast Beef and Plum Pudding join in the procession, oddly mixed with such characters as Robin Hood and Maid Marian. The "medley of costumes" makes it appear that "the old family portraits" have "skipped down from their frames to join in the sport. Different centuries [are] figuring at cross hands and right and left; the dark ages . . . cutting pirouettes and rigadoons; and the days of Queen Bess jigging merrily down the middle, through a line of succeeding generations" (pp. 286–88). Thirty years later Miles Coverdale was to witness at Blithedale, though with less pleasure than Crayon, a masquerade in which there was a similar quaint mixture of figures from various settings, creatures out of Greek and Christian myths juxtaposed with each other and with native American heroes.[3]

Such parallels suggest not only the excitment that Irving's exploration of English folklore and tradition helped to generate, especially in Hawthorne, but also an important connection be-tween that sort of excitement and the American concern for the

[2] Canto I.
[3] Hawthorne, *Blithedale*, chap. xxiv.

Puritan past.[4] There was, for instance, a deeper significance for nineteenth-century Americans in Crayon's description of "Yule clogs" and mistletoe than is usually noticed today. Christmas was still a subject of controversy in the United States. As the sailing of the "Pequod" on Christmas in *Moby-Dick* makes clear, the day, for some industrious Christians, was not an occasion for celebration at all but an incentive to harder work. "Puritan opposition" to Christmas did not disappear, nor was the day formally recognized as a "national holiday" or accepted as a "folk festival" until well into the century.[5] Meanwhile sects which did and did not observe Christmas still eyed each other suspiciously.

But while the Squire's interest in traditions is a reflection of Irving's reading in old almanacs, song books, handbooks for gentlemen, and compendia of ancient customs such as Joseph Strutt's *English Sports and Pastimes,* Irving refuses to allow the interest to degenerate into mere antiquarianism. In the Christmas series, using a pair of dubious figures, he directs a steady under-current of humor against the very flair for the traditional which is so vital to the work. One of these figures is Master Simon, "a tight brisk little man, with the air of an arrant old bachelor." His nose is "shaped like the bill of a parrot; his face slightly pitted with the small-pox, with a dry perpetual bloom on it, like a frost-bitten leaf in autumn." He has a quick, vivacious, and droll eye and can "cut an orange into such a ludicrous caricature that the young folks . . . die with laughing." Yet Simon is a

[4] Daniel Hoffman's discussion of "The May-Pole of Merry Mount" (*Form and Fable,* chap. vii) brings out strongly Hawthorne's interest in English folk custom. He stresses Hawthorne's reliance on Joseph Strutt's *English Sports and Pastimes* and especially on William Hone's *The Every Day Book.* But I suspect Irving may have been equally important, at least as an original stimulus to further investigation by Hawthorne. To reread the Christmas series in *The Sketch Book* and "May-Day Customs" (partly reproduced in Hone) and "May-Day" from *Bracebridge Hall* is to be struck by the frequency with which costumes, customs, gestures, and rituals that Irving describes, passages of English verse that he quotes, and comments that he makes relate to aspects of Hawthorne's knowledge and awareness which Hoffman sees fit to discuss.

[5] During the colonial period communities "dominated by Quakers, Baptists, Congregationalists, and Presbyterians" had "vigorously denounced" Christmas as essentially pagan or papist. James H. Barnett, *The American Christmas: A Study in National Character* (New York, 1954), pp. 5, 20.

sterile offshoot of the family, particularly in contrast to the Squire. Having no immediate connection with any of the others, he revolves "through the family system like a vagrant comet in its orbit," is essentially flighty and frivolous, flirts with all the ladies, talks much of marrying, but backs away at the crisis. While the Squire superintends his estate, raises his family, and cultivates venerable traditions in order to implant manly feelings in his sons, the interest Master Simon takes "in the genealogy, history, and intermarriages of the whole house of Bracebridge" stems from his having essentially nothing to do (pp. 248–49).

If Simon's attitude toward the past is frivolous, the parson's is unhealthy. He is portrayed as another Knickerbocker, a "little, meagre, black-looking man," with an ill-fitting, "grizzled wig" and a head that seems "to have shrunk away within it, like a dried filbert in its shell." The Squire, realizing the parson's love of old books, has set him to doing research into "the festive rites and holiday customs of former times." The parson complies zealously, but it is "merely with that plodding spirit with which men of adust temperament follow up any track of study, merely because it is denominated learning" (pp. 261–62). On the whole, in the Christmas series Crayon, who is allied with the Squire, can laugh off in the holiday spirit the threat of dryness and sterility in the behavior of Simon and the parson. Irving does not let the reader become aware enough of character to ask the kinds of questions that were bound to come up in a longer work, questions as to the moral and social implications of the Squire's interest in tradition.

But the festive interest in itself was not enough to sustain a whole book about the Hall. Although Irving tried in *Bracebridge Hall* to give the Squire another good excuse for reviving ancient rites and pastimes by building toward a climax in a rousing May Day celebration, the emphasis on spring, rebirth, and pro-creation required at least a pair of lovers and a marriage—and one pair of lovers attracted others. Still composing by contrast and complement, Irving began adding stereotyped characters out of British comedy and sentimental fiction: Lady Lillycraft, the rich but antiquated widow, whose mind dwells only on her debutante days before her looks were ruined by smallpox, who loves lovers and love stories and who flutters the feeble pulse of Master Simon; General Harbottle, retired, another bachelor, who eats inordinately, ogles Lady Lillycraft, is bored by love stories, and talks endlessly about campaigns in India; Hannah, an aging spinster and maid to Lady Lillycraft; Christy, the crusty old-bachelor huntsman; and Phoebe Wilkins, the house-keeper's niece, educated above her station and in love with the son of a prosperous yeoman who, everyone fears, will not tolerate an alliance between his family and the servant class.

Adding them all up, we get in *Bracebridge Hall* the rough outlines of a quadruple plot: an upper-class romance between the Squire's son and his fiancée, the fair Julia; a comic counterpart to this in the Lillycraft-Simon-Harbottle triangle; a middle-class intrigue turning on Phoebe; and at the end, on a still lower social level, the surprise engagement of Hannah and Christy. Mean-while titillating suggestions of sexuality hover about a band of gypsies in the vicinity, whom the bachelors make occasional jaunts to see. Crayon, Simon, and Harbottle relish the romantic innuendo that goes with the rituals of fortune-telling and arrang-ing for false fortunes as practical jokes.

To prolong the activity, Irving has the fair Julia take a bad enough fall from her horse to have to postpone the wedding until later in the month. And this is about all that happens to her, except that she is crowned by the Queen of the May and finally married. Among the other couples, however, there are con-ventional maneuverings which provide pretexts for spinning things out to greater length. Thus *Bracebridge Hall,* though it is another collection of essays, sketches, and tales, comes close to turning into a novel.

But Irving, with what in one sense seems sound instinct (though he is flirting with literary suicide) refuses to be drawn into developing a single sustained complication as a rack on which to hang his scenes and characters. He offers no suspense, no real action.[6] What could he have done but produce a faint imitation

---

[6] ". . . I am not writing a novel, and have nothing of intricate plot or marvelous adventure to promise the reader." *B*, p. 18.

of Fielding, Jane Austen, Scott, or any of the dozens of writers who had made the country gentleman, the manor, and the village the staples of English fiction? Not pretending to originality of character, he could at least draw freely on the stereotypes of that fiction and treat them with a certain playfulness. The light, frequently mocking touch keeps the reader at a distance, free from involvement with character. And as he piles up stock characters, he unconsciously produces something close to a parody of a novel. In this sense, one sometimes wishes he had gone further.

The sentimentality, the heavy emphasis on home and harmony that one might have expected after *The Sketch Book,* on the whole fails to materialize in *Bracebridge.* Irving does provide a few outright sops for sentimental readers, including two of the four interpolated tales in the book, the pathetic "Annette Delarbre" and "The Student of Salamanca," a dreadful gothic melodrama.[7] But for the most part contemporary readers had to satisfy their appetite for sentiment by ignoring, or discounting the full import of, the quasi-satirical humor that surrounds all the flocking about the nest (and this was a feat of which a good many of Irving's admirers appear to have been capable).[8]

The surprising thing is that the twentieth-century reader tends to read the book in much the same way, except that because he disapproves of sentimentality he finds it difficult to tolerate *Bracebridge Hall.* Stanley Williams put it bluntly: this "insipid" book serves "an interest long since dead"; Irving, in his "determination to de-Americanize himself," employs "orthodox rhetoric," unites "an approved style with an approved subject," and romantically idealizes "English village life" in conformity with a "tendency still alive in reactionary literary groups."[9] But a close look will not bear out the interpretation. The social orders in *Bracebridge* prove not to be so mutually subservient to, and respectful of, one another as one would expect. And Irving, far

[7] And "St. Mark's Eve" is full of sentimental regret at Crayon's inability to believe literally in the existence of spirits and guardian angels.

[8] See, for instance, the review of *Bracebridge Hall* in the *Edinburgh Magazine,* XI (June, 1822), 91–96, or that in the *Monthly Review; or Literary Journal,* XCVIII (August, 1822), 400–414.

[9] STW, I, 211.

from uncritically endorsing all of the Squire's views, leans rather toward exposing him as an ineffectual, if lovable, Quixote.

> The Squire has something of the old feudal feeling. He looks back with regret to the "good old times," when journeys were only made on horseback, and the extraordinary difficulties of travelling, owing to bad roads, bad accommodations, and highway robbers, seemed to separate each village and hamlet from the rest of the world. The lord of the manor was then a kind of monarch in the little realm around him.

Benevolent as the Squire's despotism may be at Bracebridge Hall, it is in no way made to seem an adequate compensation for perpetuating anarchy on the highways. The Squire actually prefers wretched traveling conditions because they promise him "adventures." When he sallies forth on horseback, he fancies himself "a knight-errant on an enterprise." He prefers to the "more spacious and modern inns" the older establishments, "ancient houses of wood and plaster." And he "would cheerfully put up with bad cheer and bad accommodations in the gratification of his humor" (B, pp. 332–35).[10]

He also keeps gypsies in the vicinity of the Hall in spite of the protests of the community, in order to add color to country life. They become his allies in superstition and adherence to old customs, his examples of natural boldness and manly courage. But they take advantage of him by robbing his sheep, the arch sheep-stealer being Starlight Tom, the jolliest and the most daring gypsy of all and the one most willing to help the Squire promote ancient sports and pastimes. When Tom is caught by Ready-Money Jack, the yeoman farmer, the Squire, as justice

[10] Williams wrote that Irving "anxiously debates the dreadful question of whether the passion for coaches will destroy the temper of the old English gentry." STW, I, 211–12. But there is no anxiety in Crayon. Only to the slightly quixotic Squire is the question a "dreadful" one. In "Horsemanship" Crayon's sympathy for the Squire's insistence that being a good rider is essential to manliness is qualified by views we get of the recklessness of the Squire's sons as riders, and of the greater interest one son at Oxford shows in keeping a horse than in keeping a tutor. By the time we get to "Travelling," a much later essay, the Squire's character as a fond lover of old fashions who vainly fights the future and is not really capable of dealing effectively with the present has been so firmly established that Crayon in the first sentence can present the Squire's concern with horsemanship as at best an ability for riding a delightful hobby horse.

of the peace, has to preside at the trial, and in the courtroom order comes close to breaking down completely. The Squire has no stomach for the job and unfortunately is supported in sympathy for the culprit by most of the women of his household who, under the influence of the fiction they read and the fortunes they hear from the gypsy women, are all too eager to take Tom for a romantic desperado. Slingsby, the good-natured school-master, willingly undertakes to defend Tom, summoning up arguments more from the "heart" than the "head." And, in spite of anything Master Simon, as clerk of the court, can do, dignity and decorum go by the board.

Irving describes the scene with a gusto reminiscent of that in some of the scenes of furious confusion in *Salmagundi* and *Knickerbocker*. If he had been able to work up to such out-bursts more frequently, *Bracebridge Hall* might have become a successful comic novel. The Squire is forced to convict Starlight Tom, only to discover that he has no jail in which to house him. Christy and the gamekeeper, who represent the forces really bent on stopping the gypsy depredations, volunteer to stand guard all night with a "fowling-piece" and an "ancient blunderbuss." But although Starlight Tom is shut up in an old tower on the estate, by morning he has flown the coop—an apt metaphor in this case, since Tom has been seen already as a "hawk entrapped in a dove-cote," and hawks, as we shall see, exist as something more than figures of speech at Bracebridge Hall (pp. 348–55).

Irving probably discusses topics such as the absenteeism of the landed gentry because it was conventional to touch on them in English novels of country life, just as it was conventional to create scenes in which squires acted as justices of the peace.[11] He was hardly a profound or original social thinker. But even at this stage in his career one can easily exaggerate Irving's conservatism. He may show dislike of the village "radical," who reads Cobbett and the newspapers, by giving him a "long, pale, bilious face; a black beard, so ill-shaven as to leave marks of blood on his shirt-collar; a feverish eye." But the radical's

[11] See Kenneth C. Slagle, *The English Country Squire as Depicted in English Fiction from 1740 to 1800* (Philadelphia, 1938), pp. 114, 132.

aristocratic and middle-class antagonists are hardly made a
match for him. He terrifies Master Simon, saddens the Squire,
who hates to see politics intruded into the quiet complacency
of the village, and arouses the violent and wholly irrational
hostility of Ready-Money Jack Tibbets. Irving's tone implies that
politics and talk about reform have come to the village to stay.
Opposition to the radical is ironically defined as a fear that the
community, which is the Squire's personal protectorate, will be
transformed into an "unhappy, thinking" one (pp. 280–83).[12]

When *Bracebridge Hall* appeared in the spring of 1822,
Cooper was hard at work on *The Pioneers*, the first of his Leatherstocking novels. Though the two books are fundamentally different in attitude, and as different in structure as a novel and a loose
collection of essays and sketches can be, nevertheless, because of
their heavy indebtednesses to certain conventions of the English
novel, they have a good many resemblances to each other. Each
presents a comprehensive view of a small, rural, relatively isolated community, taking care to include representatives of the
various prominent social types. In spite of the fact that one is
British and the other American, the two communities have much
in common: both are dominated by paternalistic landlords who
seek through force of character and personal example to encourage on all social levels a respect for law, order, custom, and
ceremony. Both Squire Bracebridge and Cooper's Judge Temple,
as conservators of traditional values and natural resources, are
opponents of selfish commercialism.

In the matter of particular parallels (though the details mentioned here do not always have the same kind or degree of significance for both authors), both books deal with the wanton
destruction of trees and contain scenes in which flocks of birds
are slaughtered; both the Squire and the Judge have imported
into their domains Anglican clergymen who are (in different
ways) pedantic and literal-minded, although good-natured and
well-meaning; and both landlords are assisted and at the same
time often thwarted by relatives (Master Simon and Richard

---

[12] Williams, however, found "The Village Politician" not only "banal" but reactionary. STW, I, 211.

Jones, the Judge's brother-in-law) who, not really understanding the Squire's and the Judge's visions of the ideal society, act largely out of purely personal motives. There are characters in both books who, in contrast to the landlords, are overzealous about exacting the penalty of the law, and each contains a tavern-haunting village malcontent or agitator.[13]

Most interesting of all, the relationship between Judge Temple and Natty Bumppo bears resemblance to that between the Squire and Starlight Tom, the gypsy sheep-stealer. The gypsies, like Natty and Indian John, represent a way of life outside the normal social order, a life closer to nature and therefore more robust and spontaneous.[14] While the landlords tolerate, and indeed encourage, the presence of the outsiders as "squatters" on their lands, both Natty and Tom run afoul of the law and become "outlaws," the one by stealing sheep, the other by killing a deer out of season; in each case the culprit is apprehended not by the landlord himself but by characters who occupy intermediary positions on the social scale. Although the landlords sympathize with the defendants, both are forced to apply the law, hold trials, and serve as judges. At bottom, Judge Temple recognizes in Natty's stubborn insistence on his natural rights a sense of freedom more substantial, because less self-centered, than that implicit in the behavior of many law-abiding citizens who use their connection with law-enforcement agencies to promote their own importance. Squire Bracebridge's sympathy for Starlight Tom is more sentimental; Tom is a less reputable character than Natty. Nevertheless, even in Tom there is an element of manly strength. Finally, both Irving and Cooper stage jailbreaks which expose the incompetence of (in some cases self-appointed) petty officials and the resourcefulness of the "outcasts."[15]

[13] A similarity of names, Cooper's Judge Temple and Irving's Julia Templeton, is simply another reminder of how convention-ridden English and American fiction was at the beginning of the nineteenth century. Probably both writers had Susanna Rowson's *Charlotte Temple* (1791) somewhere in mind.
[14] Crayon talks about the "primitive independence" of the gypsies and specifically compares them with the American Indians. *B*, pp. 258–59.
[15] On the English novel's conventional concern with poaching, see Slagle, pp. 60–64.

The comparison suggests how close Irving was to writing a novel and yet how far he was from doing so. In *Bracebridge Hall* the tensions are eased arbitrarily and unconvincingly, as though he hadn't the patience to see them through. Instead of finally representing a social *order,* the book simply delights in disorder. One even doubts whether, had Irving as an American been foolish enough to try to write an English novel, he could have found a consistent attitude toward society on which to base it.

Crayon declares in "English Country Gentlemen" that he is "more and more confirmed in republican principles by every year's observation and experience." In viewing "the mixed nature of the government" of England, and "its representative form," he seems to prize the "rural establishments" of the gentry and nobility only to the extent that they promise to promote and preserve English "freedom." The function of the English gentleman, as Irving sees it, should be to eschew absenteeism and "lavish expenditure" and to superintend the welfare of his home community and to reside on his estate, except when he is serving in "legislative assemblies" (pp. 240–41). Irving justifies the system in theory, in spite of his loyalty to republicanism, by appealing to the Burkean and Montesquieuvian conception of the suitability of different social and governmental institutions to different peoples. When it is operating properly, the British system ought to alleviate economic distress and bring the various classes of society into closer relationship to one another.

But speaking about the privileges and responsibilities of the landed gentry, Crayon admits to being "both surprised and disappointed" to find that he was "often indulging in an Utopian dream, rather than a well-founded opinion." Times are growing harder. The "fine estates" are "too often involved, and mortgaged, or placed in the hands of creditors, and the owners exiled." Among the upper classes "heedless, joyous dissipation" and addiction to French pleasures are increasing. Theoretically, more squires like Bracebridge would solve the problem. In fact Crayon argues that "the virtue and welfare of the nation" depend on "the rural habits of the . . . nobility and gentry, on the manner in which they discharge their duties on their patrimonial possessions" (pp. 240–42). But the increasing quirkiness of Squire Bracebridge suggests that Irving did not have much hope that his solution could be effected.[16]

Interesting in this connection is "English Gravity," an essay dealing with another commonplace of English fiction, the conflict between the country gentleman and the retired bourgeois. In spite of his name, Mr. Faddy is not satirized so much for his addiction to outlandish nouveau modes as for excessive earnestness and Puritanism. He wants to put a stop to the idle pastimes, sports, and festivals that the Squire promotes. He would encourage sober industry and "plans for public utility" (p. 250) in the neighborhood. Crayon obviously finds Faddy's aggressiveness distasteful but cannot gainsay a certain merit in some of his plans. The Squire's reaction, on the other hand, is to fulminate less at Faddy himself than at the contemporary expansion of trade and manufactures. Crayon sympathizes up to a point, but in the end brushes off as a mere "whimsical lamentation" a long tirade in which the Squire uses imagery derived from epic descriptions of hell or gothic scenes in alchemists' laboratories to dramatize his fear that "manufacturers will be the ruin of our rural manners" (p. 251).

Crayon, while agreeing that English character has changed since the time when the phrase "merry England" gained cur-

[16] "English Country Gentlemen" is thus hardly the paean to an "outworn feudal system" that Williams implied it is. STW, I, 211. The recognition of similarities between Irving's Bracebridge pieces and the de Coverley papers, similarities of character and situation, seems to have prepared some readers for an ultra-conservative Irving (see William Hazlitt, "Elia, and Geoffrey Crayon," *The Spirit of the Age*). A careful comparison, however, I believe, would reveal Irving's Squire as almost as much a parody of Sir Roger as *Salmagundi* is of the *Spectator*. Francis Jeffrey, reviewing *Bracebridge* in the *Edinburgh Review* (XXXVII [Nov., 1822], 340–43), though missing a good deal of the satire, at least saw the essential "neutrality" of Irving's position in regard to English politics. This is notable in view of Jeffrey's strong Whig commitment. He did not, like several reviewers, dismiss Irving's representation of English life as a century or two outdated. Confessing that he was initially disturbed to see Irving using a Tory family as an "emblem of old English character," he finally concluded that Irving really helped the Whig cause by trying to promote "benevolence" and "philanthropy," the foundations of freedom. Jeffrey's tendency is always to see Irving as the peace-maker—his role in "English Writers on America"—or the American cultural ambassador to Europe. The oversimplification in this view, of course, misses the subtlety of Irving, but it does not seriously misinterpret basic attitudes.

rency, attributes the difference not so much to "growing hardships" or to commercialism as (going back to the idea Irving had
picked up in 1805) to "the gradual increase of the liberty of the
subject, and the growing freedom and activity of opinion"
(p. 254). Once again he speaks as the self-conscious, New World
republican. His statements about gravity may not actually account for English character, but they reflect his American background: freer institutions promote heavy responsibilities; it is
not easy for a Faddy, either in England or America, to act as an
independent citizen. The conception belongs in the tradition
which was to culminate in Tocqueville's remarks nearly twenty
years later on the "astonishing gravity" of Americans.[17]

Cooper, who was desirous of preserving in the United States
the power and authority of large property-holders like his father
in eighteenth-century Cooperstown, New York, found the manor-
house ideal useful in fiction. Stripped of hereditary titles and
privileges, but still brimful of *noblesse oblige,* the English squire
proved adaptable to the American setting. The view of society
that called on the well-to-do to set the tone of American civilization theoretically justified the extreme gentility or sensibility of
upper-class females in fiction, a trait which Irving, in spite of
sentimental leanings, was quick to satirize. And Cooper could
use unblushingly a dialogue convention in which elegance and
propriety of speech instantly defined the aristocrat, while dialect
and bad grammar permanently froze the lower-class character in
his place.

---

[17] "I thought that the English constituted the most serious nation on the face
of the earth, but I have since seen the Americans. . . ." Alexis de Tocqueville,
Democracy in America, chap. xxxi. According to Tocqueville, "All free people
are serious, because their minds are habitually absorbed by the contemplation of
some dangerous or difficult purpose. This is more especially the case among
those free nations which form democratic communities." Cf. Irving (*B,* p. 254):

A free people are apt to be grave and thoughtful. They have high and important matters to occupy their minds. They feel it their right, and their
duty to mingle in public concerns, and to watch over the general welfare.
The continual exercise of the mind on political topics gives intenser habits of
thinking, and a more serious and earnest demeanor. A nation becomes less
gay, but more intellectually active and vigorous. It evinces less play of the
fancy, but more power of the imagination; less taste and elegance, but more
grandeur of mind; less animated vivacity, but deeper enthusiasm.

The beauty of the formula of the Leatherstocking series was that it separated democratic faith from middle-class ambition, left freedom and equality shining on the frontier, and, as Henry Nash Smith has shown,[18] tended to define the central conflict in American life as one between grand abstractions such as natural law and man-made law, wilderness and civilization, rather than as one between groups within society opposed for reasons that fell somewhat short of philosophical principle. In *The Pioneers* Cooper conveniently disposes of the potentially obstreperous small independent farmer or village shop-keeper by giving the moral supremacy to Judge Temple and by making Natty the repository of human dignity among the lower orders.

Irving was certainly sensitive to parvenuism and fearful of the blemish the factory might make on the landscape, but as an urbanite and an inhabitant of several years' standing in a country further advanced industrially than his own, he could not blink the future, even in his fondness for the past. Had he written a novel that actually represented the social situation as he saw it in Britain, it would have centered on a conflict between middle- and upper-class characters. The real issue in *Bracebridge* is between what Irving would like to think of as a benevolent authority, still potentially enforceable by the gentry, and what is in fact the erosion of that authority in the wake of the Industrial Revolution.

Without quite realizing it, Irving in *Bracebridge Hall* joins in that prolonged American search for a middle-class hero that reaches fruition in Howells and James. It is a complicated quest, and when the hero finally evolves, he comes trailing clouded origins behind him, compounding qualities that in the beginning belonged to stations both lower and higher than his own. He is asked to do the nearly impossible—which is perhaps what makes him heroic—to be middle class without being morally middlebrow, to be neither pure farmer nor pure bourgeois, but somehow a combination of rural innocence and urban know-how, to synthesize the apparently opposed but

[18] Introduction to Cooper, *The Prairie* (New York, 1950), pp. xii–xx.

nonetheless essential components often fictionalized in "nature's nobleman" and the "good squire." *Bracebridge Hall* does not advance American literature very far in this quest. But it does refuse, finally, to take the landed gentry seriously as the guardians and custodians of the social welfare. Its most substantial characters belong, curiously enough, to the middle classes.

In "The Rookery" Irving allegorizes the gentry as little better than scavenger birds, for all their pretensions to dignity. He may have intended to write about the rooks as a typical concomitant of the English manor, but once the satire starts, it seems to develop naturally. "The rooks," says Crayon, "are looked upon by the Squire as a very ancient and honorable line of gentry, highly aristocratical in their notions, fond of place, and attached to church and state. . . ." Much of the time they are to be seen "looking down with sovereign contempt upon the humble crawlers upon earth." In spite of certain attractive qualities, they prove to be robber barons, who sometimes "defraud and plunder each other" and sometimes come down to perch on the heads of sheep, who bear it like "sheep." Whether the birds "requited" this "submission . . . by levying a contribution" on the "fleece," Crayon cannot tell, but he presumes that they "followed the usual custom of protecting powers" (pp. 284–88).[19]

It is difficult not to read the behavior of the people of the village toward these birds as evidence of a latent hostility toward the gentry. The villagers try to slaughter young rooks late in May. The Squire won't allow shooting on his estate, and his agent, the parson, tries to prevent it in the village, but he can't keep order. Though the commoners aren't very good shots, they swarm about "the old church" in large numbers, and there is great rejoicing when they get a "squab rook" (pp. 288–89).

---

[19] "Having the true baronial spirit of the good old feudal times, they are apt now and then to issue forth from their castles on a foray, and lay the plebeian fields under contribution. . . ." *B*, p. 290.

Bird imagery elsewhere in *Bracebridge* complements the implications of "The Rookery." The Squire tries to honor an ancient custom by keeping hawks. Assisted by Simon, he pursues researches into old books to ascertain how hawks should be trained. But Christy and Simon, who are given, or simply take, charge of the birds, get into squabbles over methods of feeding and training. When a hawking expedition is finally undertaken by the whole company of the Hall, Christy makes the mistake of letting the hawk fly at a crow. It misses and then soars away. The inability of the Bracebridges and their servant to control the hawks suggests an aristocracy which, like the falcon, has outlived its original function. These gentry more closely resemble rooks, an inferior and seemingly degenerate line of scavengers, perhaps little better than the crows that Irving's imagery identifies with the gypsies.[20] Ironically Starlight Tom, who ought to be classified with the crows, proves to be the only man possessed of hawklike daring and agility. And old Christy (and behind him the Squire) can no more control Tom than he can the hawk.

"May-Day," following hard upon "The Rookery," is further proof of the irrevocability, in Irving's eyes, of the passing of the old order. As the organized activity which the Squire seeks to inspire gets out of control, his desire to revive ancient customs is revealed as more quixotic than ever. Master Simon chooses as the May Queen a bashful, inarticulate country girl; she is supposed to crown the Squire's prospective daughter-in-law, Julia, with flowers, but the ceremony breaks down when the May Queen drops the crown and forgets the verses she was to recite, which is good fortune anyway, since she murders the king's English. The village radical, standing on the sidelines, reminds those who listen to him that elsewhere Englishmen are starving and denounces May Day as a social evil. Simon and General Harbottle try to out-talk him but are driven off, the General swelling into a veritable Colonel Blimp as he retreats. The festivities culminate in a grand free-for-all when athletes from

[20] ". . . as to the poor crows, they are a kind of vagabond, predatory, gypsy race. . . ." *B*, p. 285.

a rival village crash the sports, and even the more important townspeople and the higher servants from the Hall, including Christy and Mistress Hannah, get involved in the fight. Significantly, it is Ready-Money Jack, the yeoman farmer, not one of the gentry, who finally asserts authority sufficient to quell the turmoil.

A small, independent, middle-class farmer with a sense of civic responsibility, Jack Tibbets combines the industry of the Yankee with the jollity and heartiness of Irving's New York Dutchman. The satire on the gentry means that to some extent he encroaches on the Squire's preserve as the symbol of social and political authority. Not only is he the one who restores order at the May Day brawl; he also has the good sense to set his son's love life in order after his wife and the genteel atmosphere of the Hall have nearly ruined it. Tibbets' wife thinks Phoebe Wilkins not good enough to marry into the family; at the same time Phoebe's situation at the Hall as niece of the housekeeper has softened her and given her certain artificial manners which have alienated her lover. The father, however, letting no petty scruples stand in the way, promises to push through the marriage.

Ready-Money Jack is Irving's closest approach to an English hero in *Bracebridge*. He is a sort of rural middle-class John Bull. Irving's attitude toward him is akin to the feeling in "Little Britain" for the London cit, for all the unpleasant aggressiveness of certain tradesmen. Any middle-class hero would, for Irving, have to be above the earnest industriousness of a Robinson Crusoe, as well as the moral casuistry in which the Richardsonian heroine anchored her hopes for improving her social status. Although Tibbets at times seems merely a tight-fisted yeoman, he is a "ready-money" Jack when it comes to festive occasions, and his liberality gives him an affinity with both upper and lower classes.

But if Irving at times seems envious of those who have a clearly designated room or niche in John Bull's mansion, he also has recollections, many of them fond, of a different order at home. "Dolph Heyliger" represents Irving's attachment to a view of life largely opposed to his original conception of the Hall. One could argue that it is thrown in merely as a sop to the American audience. But Irving has a penchant for putting American stories in final or climactic positions in his books. There are weaknesses in "Dolph Heyliger": it is long and imperfectly constructed, the hero being too slight a figure to support so much narrative. Symbolically, however, his behavior is richly interpretable; in a shorter tale the lack of depth in his character would actually have proved an asset. For it is important that his actions seem largely unpremeditated. He is essentially a drifter, one whose good fortune depends on his not being too determined to possess it; he is not a hounded man.

Dolph is the real hero of *Bracebridge Hall,* a middle-class hero who marries a land-owner's daughter, a traveler who discovers on an extended journey how to establish himself securely at home. He is also an early American boy, or boyish hero, who runs away to river and wilderness and the manly company of hunters and Indians. The picaresque narrative sets him loose in a rugged but ultimately benevolent American terrain, where a sense of spaciousness and boundless opportunity predominates. Though somewhat roguish, Dolph is basically good-natured, and, partly for his good nature, he is at last rewarded. There is an element of magic in his success.

But more is required for his success than pluck and luck, though he is notably endowed with these Horatio Alger assets. At bottom what is at issue is his relation to the past—the influence in his life of his ancestry, his parentage. His unconscious strategy is to ignore the past, to deny any excessive claims it makes on him. And in doing this, ironically, he makes the past yield him his proper heritage.

The action of the story, as in most of Irving's tales, is largely an externalization of what is essentially a process of self-discovery. Dolph is a spiritual orphan: from his widowed mother, who lives in genteel poverty in New York, he has received distorted notions of the family past. Her ancestors have been mercantile adventurers and her husband a ship captain, but she cherishes aristocratic pretensions which are imaged

in "the family arms," "painted and framed," hanging "over
her mantel-piece" (p. 376). Her pride, her horror of trade,
and her "hoity-toity" cat make her something of a forerunner
of Hawthorne's Hepzibah Pyncheon.[21] Dame Heyliger does not
actually live in a haunted ancestral mansion, but she proves to
be closely connected with one.

In her pathetic pride she envisions her son as a professional
man, a doctor, but the practitioner to whom she apprentices
him, Doctor Knipperhausen, is a quack, little better than a
crack-pate alchemist. Dolph has no aptitude for medicine anyway. When the doctor buys an old house in the neighborhood
and discovers that people won't go near it because it is haunted,
Dolph, who is bored and yearning for excitement, volunteers to
stand guard there. He has the courage to hold his ground when
an enigmatic ghost appears at the house. Later, however, a dis-
quieting dream lures him away to the riverside, and, in what
seems a combination of nightmare and daydream, he boards a
ship on the Hudson for Albany, only to be swept overboard before long. Scrambling ashore, he at first gets lost in the forest
and then is rescued by a hunting party, which he eventually
accompanies to Albany. There he discovers the ghost's identity:
it is his own ancestor, a wealthy man who formerly owned the
house which he now haunts.

In Freudian terms, the story is an unconscious quest for a
father and rejection of an oversolicitous mother. Various aspects or degrees of fatherliness and motherliness are suggested
in the narrative. Knipperhausen, whose household is a repository of contrasting symbols of sterility and fertility, is a
kind of stepfather to Dolph, but, surrounded by the conventional
props that Irving uses to indicate desiccation—skulls, a pre-

[21] Like Hepzibah, Dolph's mother, in her reduced circumstances, has to "cast
about her for some mode of doing something for herself." And her solution likewise is a cent-shop, which she opens in her own house—her neighbors being
surprised to see in her window "a grand array of gingerbread kings and queens."
If Dame Heyliger is, on the surface, a fairly friendly person, what she lacks
of Hepzibah's scowling countenance is compensated for by her cat, the embodiment of her pride, a creature who at the appearance of an "idle vagabond
dog" becomes as "indignant as ever was an ancient and ugly spinster on the
approach of some graceless profligate." B, pp. 375–76.

served fetus, stuffed lizards and snakes—he turns into the embodiment of male impotence. The balance of power in the doctor's establishment—that is, in young Dolph's life—is on the female side. The "strings of red pepper and corpulent cucumbers, carefully preserved for seed" (p. 380) by the old bachelor Knipperhausen's industrious housekeeper, suggest more vitality than he can ever muster. A lame, half-blind ship captain appears in the youth's dream the night before he goes down to the river and embarks. The next day he actually materializes on the deck of a vessel about to set sail, and issues an abrupt summons to the hesitant Dolph: "Step on board young man, or you'll be left behind!" (p. 403). This commander, who is apparently an obscure reminder of the youth's real father, himself a ship captain, cut off in the prime of life, represents both the fear (in Dolph) of, and the need for, an adventurous life, something Dolph's mother has explicitly denied him.

Dolph has his affinities with Huck Finn—although the haunted mansion from which he escapes houses nothing like the horror in the squatter's shack where Pap confines Huck. Each boy is a virtual orphan, with one real but quite inadequate parent and a variety of guardians functioning as the other parent. Both are plagued by "sivilizing" influences on the one hand and a lawless violence in nature or human nature on the other, although the threat of brutality in Irving is largely a specter, an illusion, a product of Dolph's immaturity, whereas Huck's fears are real. Both find temporary refuge and an almost idyllic contentment on the river; and even the mythic stillness which pervades some of Huck's descriptions of the Mississippi occasionally develops in "Dolph Heyliger":

> In the second day of the voyage they came to the highlands. It was the latter part of a calm, sultry day, that they floated gently with the tide between these stern mountains. There was that perfect quiet which prevails over nature in the languor of summer heat: the turning of a plank, or the accidental falling of an oar on deck, was echoed from the mountain side, and reverberated along the shores; and if by chance the captain gave a shout of command, there were airy tongues which mocked it from every cliff. (p. 404)

Though Dolph manages to save himself from drowning, his only refuge is the dark forest, where, after nightfall, he has the typical folk hero's terrifying encounter with evil, nearly walking into a nest of writhing adders. Like Goodman Brown, who fears an Indian behind every tree, he moves on, "full of this new horror," seeing "an adder in every curling vine." When he happens upon a campfire, "the glare falling on painted features, and glittering on silver ornaments" warns him of Indians and gives him a further scare (pp. 408–10).

Fully lost now, he at last is ripe for finding. Anthony Vander Heyden, the Albany hunter, is the older man who helps Dolph complete his initiation into maturity and under whom he serves an apprenticeship, like a youth in Cooper who ranges the woods with Leatherstocking and Chingachgook. Vander Heyden, who is a teller of tall tales,[22] dresses in a backwoods outfit, carries a tomahawk in his belt, befriends Indians, and, though a wealthy landowner, makes a boon companion of the vagabond Dolph. In the end Vander Heyden turns out to be a distant relative, in whose home Dolph, as though by magic, identifies the subject of an ancestral portrait as the ghost of the haunted house. Returning to New York, he recovers a treasure buried on the property years before by his ancestor. By establishing or discovering his own identity, he has made himself a rightful heir, a son to redeem his branch of the family from false pride. He marries Vander Heyden's daughter and prospers the rest of his life.

Dolph is Irving's perfect comic hero. Something of an idler, like Rip, he wastes time but not life. There are an essential energy and courage in him, though these qualities are not exaggerated. He has imagination, loves a good story, but does not let legends frighten him. His greatest talent is for making ghosts work for him. In *Bracebridge Hall* the search for tradi-

[22] He tells the stories in the interlude called "The Storm-Ship." He is not a regular frontier hoaxer. He does not use a vernacular style, and it is not in his character to pretend seriously to believe the fantasies he relates. But if he aims primarily at being appreciated for his ability to embroider a legend, he is not unwilling for the more naïve members of his audience to be duped, at least temporarily, into accepting his tales as truth.

tion in effect ends with Dolph, the representative of the present, succeeding nicely by refusing to be haunted by the past.

As in *The House of the Seven Gables*, a central concern in "Dolph Heyliger" is the bringing out of his exclusiveness and pretentiousness a dispossessed character living too much in the shadow of the past. Misfortune and humiliation do part of the job.[23] The good nature, openness, courage, and common sense of a near relation—Dolph or Phoebe Pyncheon—do the rest. The story (though with a change of location it might have been shifted ahead a hundred years) takes place in the early eighteenth century, when Albany was merely a rural village. Country cousins like Phoebe, the Vander Heydens, by their freshness, conviviality, and freedom from affectation, offset the stifling nature of the town. Irving stresses the mercantile orientation of New York City; like Hawthorne, he situates in a seaport town his gloomy, secret-haunted house, built by a powerful and aggressive businessman.[24] The preservation of a family pride basically rooted in greed has brought on, as with the Pyncheons, a moral and spiritual deterioration paralleling the physical decay of the house.

The disinherited Dolph, like Phoebe, is rewarded for the modesty of his pretensions. In both works, money magically allies itself with youth, open-mindedness, and good nature, regardless of the social station of the legatee. The cousinly relations which connect Dolph and Phoebe with wealthy families are not ways of giving these characters fancy pedigrees, not guarantees that they come from "good stock." The relations are rather metaphors, suggesting an equality of talents and moral worth which can transcend artificial social barriers. Significantly, Dolph's country cousins have largely disposed of family, class, and racial prejudices. His marriage with Vander Heyden's daughter recognizes the phenomenon of social

[23] Dame Heyliger's house, by a symbolic coincidence, burns down in Dolph's absence. She becomes helpless and destitute. Even her cat, its proudly worn whiskers singed in the fire, is humbled into a better disposition. *B*, pp. 440–43.

[24] Considering the fact that Dolph has lost his ship-captain father, the resemblance of his background to Hawthorne's as it gave rise to *The House of the Seven Gables* is striking.

mobility in America and repudiates tendencies toward aristocratic exclusiveness. There are vulgar instincts in the one-time apprentice, if not, as in Holgrave, plebeian blood. Irving's hero does not threaten, any more than do Holgrave or Vander Heyden, to try to play the fine gentleman.

The Dolph who emerges in a brief glimpse at the end of the story, the mature man and "distinguished citizen" (p. 447), is a generous, well-fed, heavy-drinking burgher. Only his rural contacts seem to have saved him from deteriorating altogether into a fat alderman with Gargantuan appetites like those depicted in *Salmagundi* and *Knickerbocker*. Irving's prose at the end treads a thin line between admiration and ridicule without straying in either direction for more than a phrase or two. And the final hint that the whole story may be nothing but a tall tale made up by Dolph suggests that his money-accruing propensity may be his most essential characteristic, that the story may be a way of softening or disguising it. Then one would admire the story more than the man, his vision of what he would like to have been or be more than what he has actually become. It is not with the whole solid middle class that Irving aligns himself, any more than with the rural gentry, but with the individual in either class whose spirit is not consumed in the grind of commercial competition or the effort to dignify, or preserve the dignity of, a family name.

Vander Heyden, who is, of course, a landowner, not a merchant, functions as an American foil to Irving's English squire. He also contrasts strikingly with that other upstate New York proprietor, Judge Temple. Temple loves the land as much as Vander Heyden does and goes on hunting trips and has kind words for Natty and John Mohegan, but, conscious of his inherited position, he patronizes the town politically and keeps the lower orders at a distance socially. Irving sees Vander Heyden not as the bulwark of a social order but as something closer to the image of the completely fulfilled and free individual, who owes his identity more to his close relationship to what the romantics would call "nature" than to his connection with a particular social or political institution.

The image of a native land discernible in "Dolph," "Rip Van Winkle," "Sleepy Hollow," and the American stories in *Tales of a Traveller* (1824) largely anticipates the pleasure Irving was to take in his homecoming ten years after *Bracebridge Hall*. Like Dolph, in a sense he had had to leave home in order to discover it. The country he was to see in 1832 was the one his wishful thinking had been envisioning from Europe, and in contrast to Europe—a prosperous, expansive, warm-hearted land which guaranteed a considerable range of individual freedom, a land notably different from the nation of vulgarian conformists that Cooper would find awaiting him only a year later.

By the 1820's time and distance had enabled Irving in his American stories to transform the reality he had satirized in *Salmagundi* and *Knickerbocker* into dream or myth or (to use his own term) legend. In spite of the rampant insecurities which possess Ichabod Crane, Dame Heyliger, and Tom Walker and his wife, Irving was now projecting American life as more of a promise than a frustration. True, a modified mock-heroic was still his soundest approach to native subjects; he was still debunking overly intense Americanism. The Revolutionary War, for example, is slighted in "Rip Van Winkle," not because Federalist sympathies made Irving secretly long for a return to good old colonial days—the happy ending belies such an interpretation—but because, like "Dolph Heyliger" and "Sleepy Hollow," the story offers a world where strenuous heroism is beside the point. Irving's American dream is of a land which simply takes care of its own as long as it is not cared for covetously. Thus in "Sleepy Hollow" it overwhelms with abundance. The American stories reach toward a myth of deliverance from the Protestant ethic. The hero is the American who can be miraculously easygoing and industrious at the same time, who can enjoy life without resorting to "sordid, dusty, soul killing" routines or participating in sanctimonious status-seeking. This myth, as we shall see more clearly at the end of the next chapter, is in one sense a de-puritanized variation of the common one that glorifies rural America by somewhat nostalgically associating innocence, goodness, and happiness with nature and a teeming land. Instead of pastoral, however, Irving offers comedy, a comedy flexible enough to shift from celebration to criticism whenever what Richard Hofstadter calls the "commercial realities" behind the "agrarian myth" present themselves.[25]

Cooper in 1833 had been away from the United States for seven years. He was angered by changes that had occurred in his absence, whereas Irving, his feelings softened from seventeen years abroad, was pleased at finding "home," regardless of changes, much the same as he remembered it. Each year Cooper's vision of Cooperstown as the ideal society was receding further into the past. Irving, however, from the beginning had been under no illusions about the purity or nobility of American motives. He was aware of economic and political tensions. His view that the "serving of one's country" was apt to be "a nauseous piece of business"[26] had developed early. Recollecting the contentiousness of American politics in the first decade of the century, he may have been less inclined than others to see in the aggressiveness of the Jacksonian hangers-on the beginning of an entirely new era in American political behavior. Whig and Democrat appear to have given him as little to choose between as had Federalist and Republican. He retained connections in both parties, enjoying the political privileges conferred on him as an American citizen, and he responded to the obvious material advantages of American life, without, however, expecting free institutions and abundant land and natural resources to change human nature. As *Salmagundi* and *Knickerbocker* show, he had had his doubts early. Some of them had survived, but so had the nation. He had not cared much for Jefferson, but something in Andrew Jackson appealed to him.[27]

[25] Hofstadter, *The Age of Reform* (New York, 1955), chap. i.

[26] Letter to Mary Fairlie, 2 May 1807, quoted in STW, I, 96. See the explanation in STW (I, 95) of the misreading of this passage in PMI (I, 187).

[27] Letter to Peter Irving, 16 June 1832, PMI, III, 22.

VIII

The Way the Story Is Told

IRVING'S next work was supposed to have been his German
sketchbook. With Crayon beginning to feel pinched for
English subjects, Irving, a half-convert—in the standard view—
to the new faith of romanticism, had dutifully gone to Germany
in 1822 to replenish his muse at a pure source.[1] Instead of
settling down to the systematic study of language and literature
or the collection of legends and folktales, however, he had been
undone by a variety of distractions, particularly in Dresden,
where he found a group of new companions, the stimulation of
opera and theater, and a social life which involved him to some
extent with the royal family of Saxony as well as with such
German intellectuals and artists as Ludwig Tieck and Carl
Maria von Weber. At the same time he seems to have fallen
in love again, at the age of 40, with a young English girl named
Emily Foster. It was perhaps the deepening of this attachment
and of his anxiety about the outcome of it that had more than
anything else to do with his inability to write the book people
expected.[2] Emily proved unable to return his love, and Irving
retreated forlornly to Paris. There he composed most of *Tales
of a Traveller*.

When it finally appeared in 1824, it had nothing to do with
the "German localities, manners, characters" that he had been

---

[1] The reviews, says F. L. Pattee, show that "England expected a German book."
The American Short Story (New York, 1923), p. 14.
[2] See Walter Reichart, *Washington Irving and Germany* (Ann Arbor, 1957),
pp. 94, 143–44. This book gives a full account of the German tour.

turning over in his mind even after leaving Germany.[3] Nor
was it a sketchbook. British and American readers were greatly
disappointed. For many the book had nothing distinctive about
it; the fiction seemed little, if at all, better than the standard
light reading then being dispensed by the popular press. Critics
who had felt all along that there was no great originality in
Geoffrey Crayon now reveled in I-told-you-so's.[4] Not only did
many of the tales have a familiar ring, but Irving's relaxed and
half-humorous manner on the whole tended to detract from the
kind of excitement and sensation that popular fiction was supposed to generate.

Today Irving's backing off from Germany in his fiction has
become a mark of his comparative unromanticalness. True, he
may have read widely first and last in Schiller, Goethe, Jean
Paul, Tieck, and lesser German romantics, and undoubtedly the
"*Märchen* world" had "laid powerfully hold" of his "imagination." But (so the argument runs) his work finally lacks "the
wild extravagance" of Hoffmann; or, "one cannot feel that
Irving" in his lighter fantasies is "sincerely romantic."[5]

But to look for German romanticism in *Tales of a Traveller*
is simply to court disappointment and to be distracted by what
the book is not from seeing what it is. Misreadings of this
sort have been common, though the controlling preconception
has not always been the same. It was the failure of Irving to live
up to the image of Geoffrey Crayon that outraged some of his
contemporaries. John Neal, for instance, charged him with a
betrayal of trust, with attempting "to smuggle impurity" into
the English home through certain "equivocal" remarks "that no

[3] Letter to Peter Irving, 4 September 1823, PMI, II, 166. German influences
can be detected here and there, but the German background to the *Tales* is trifling
compared to the English, Italian, and American backgrounds. There is little that
is Germanic about the texture of the book. For a detailed discussion of sources see
Reichart, chap. vi; Pochmann, "Irving's German Tour and Its Influence on His
Tales," *PMLA*, XLV (December, 1930), 1150–87; STW, II, 286–96.
[4] For discussions of the contemporary reaction to the *Tales*, see STW, II, 294–
95; Reichart, pp. 157–64.
[5] Pattee, pp. 13–15. Or see Pochmann (ed.), *Irving* (New York, 1934), p.
lxxvi. Pochmann does believe that Irving took a deep plunge into romanticism in
Spain with *The Alhambra*.

woman could bear to read . . . aloud." Complaints about the risqué humor of the *Tales* were common. The trouble, Neal said, was not that such humor in itself was absolutely objectionable; after all, *Salmagundi* and *Knickerbocker* had from time to time reveled in "droll indecencies." But critics had touted Geoffrey Crayon "as an immaculate creature for this profligate age.—He knew this. He knew that any book with his name to it, would be permitted by fathers, husbands, brothers, to pass without examination: that it would be read aloud in family circles, all over our country."[6]

In view of the general disapproval expressed for the *Tales*, it is curious that Irving's most quoted remarks about the nature of fiction occur in a letter to Henry Brevoort in which he defends the book, well aware that it had "met with some handling from the press."[7] The letter is generally cited as evidence of a certain artistic self-consciousness in Irving and of his willingness to experiment with a new and still vaguely defined form. Earlier, when he was only planning *Tales of a Traveller*, he had written of feeling a need to steer clear of "Scott's manner," to "strike out some way of my own, suited to my own way of thinking and writing"; he had been determined to avoid falling "into the commonplace of the day," exemplified in the "legendary and romantic tales now littering from the press both in England and Germany." And he had hoped to find his way through "style," rather than mere "narrative," which he believed to be "evanescent."[8] Now, in the wake of the bad reviews, he said in writing to Brevoort, "I fancy much of what I value myself upon in writing, escapes the observation of the great mass of my readers: who are intent more upon the story than the way in

[6] "American Writers, No. IV," *Blackwood's* XVII, 67. The review in the *United States Literary Gazette* (I [15 November 1824], 229) also feared lest the book offend the "private eye of the young and innocent." The *Eclectic Review* noted that Irving was now less careful than in his two previous works "to avoid any thing bordering on either coarseness or profaneness" and wondered whether he now "thinks worse of the public" or was himself "*worsened* by his travels." The reviewer was even upset by Irving's levity in dealing with "Tom Walker's master." XXIV (July, 1825), p. 74.

[7] 11 December 1824, *WIHB*, II, 184.

[8] Letter to Peter Irving, 4 September 1823, PMI, II, 166.

which it is told." His chief concerns, he insisted, were "the play of thought, and sentiment, and language; the weaving in of characters, lightly yet expressively delineated; . . . the half-concealed vein of humour that is often playing through the whole."[9]

Tales of a Traveller is the work of a short-story writer who had not quite discovered his form, even though he had already, partly by chance, written two or three stories that are destined to survive. An instinct for the form seems almost miraculously in control in "Rip Van Winkle," "The Legend of Sleepy Hollow," and "The Stout Gentleman," where in each case the story is essentially the extension or development of a single episode or moment in which character is decisively exposed. But there was very little precedent for such economy in prose fiction. For all practical purposes the short story did not yet exist because, although pieces more or less corresponding to our sense of the term had been written, there was no clear conception of the genre. Consciously Irving was attempting to write, not short stories, but a series of relatively short narratives that could somehow be combined into a book. He thought of himself as a bookman, not as a magazine hack. A few years later it was to the advantage of Hawthorne and Poe to be forced to begin by publishing pieces individually in periodicals. They moved more easily toward a realization of the short story as a self-contained fictional form. Yet their early aspiration was also to publish booklength collections of short items tied together by one device or another.

That Poe professed to admire the *Tales*[10] may come as a surprise, because on the whole he saw in Irving simply that darling of the 1840's, the sentimental essayist, and he considered

---

[9] He admitted that the book had been composed hastily but said, ". . . I am convinced that a great part of it was written in a free and happier vein than almost any of my other writings." *WIHB*, II, 185–86.

[10] See "Tale-Writing," *Complete Works* (1902), XIII, 153–54. Poe speaks of the "graceful and impressive narratives" in the *Tales*, though he finds the stories individually not so neat and compact or climactic as he would have liked. Longfellow and Robert Louis Stevenson were also supporters of the *Tales* (see STW, II, 295–96).

him "much overrated."[11] But of course his concern for what Irving, in the famous letter to Brevoort, called the "nicety of execution"[12]—the proper telling of the tale—went even farther than Irving's. What is perhaps more important is what the two writers had in common: it was a necessary strategy for them to attempt to clarify their intentions in the story or tale by exposing the false assumptions underlying what Poe called the puerile *"intensities"* or *"bizarreries"* of popular fiction.[13] On the one hand for instance, *Bracebridge Hall* in its interpolated tales had veered toward mystery and gothic excitement; on the other, Irving had made the Hall itself an anti-gothic mansion, equipped with "neither trapdoor, nor sliding-panel, nor donjon-keep." In "Dolph Heyliger" he deliberately passed up a "fine opportunity for weaving in strange adventures among these wild mountains . . . and, after involving my hero in a variety of perils and difficulties, rescuing him . . . by some miraculous contrivance" (*B*, pp. 18, 427). Similarly, although Poe repeatedly burlesqued the magazine thrillers of his day, some of his finer stories fulfill the formula for romantic fiction which he gave facetiously in "How to Write a Blackwood Article": ". . . get yourself into such a scrape as no one ever got into before"; "should you ever be drowned or hung, be sure to make a note of your sensations—they will be worth to you ten guineas a sheet."

The keynote of *Tales of a Traveller* is the recognition of a certain fraudulent quality in fiction. Crayon will not let his readers forget that he is only telling them stories: ". . . I am an old traveller. I have read somewhat, heard and seen more, and dreamt more than all. My brain is filled therefore, with all kinds of odds and ends . . . and I am always at a loss to know how much to believe of my own stories" (p. ix). The implication is that stories are not actualities; one needn't pretend that they really happened or be duped into taking them

---

[11] Poe to Nathan C. Brooks, 4 September 1838, *Letters of Poe*, ed. Ostrom (Cambridge, Mass., 1948), I, 112.

[12] *WIHB*, II, 186.

[13] "How to Write a Blackwood Article."

the wrong way. Part I consists of "Strange Stories" for which the same "nervous gentleman" whom Crayon encountered at Bracebridge Hall is made responsible, and it is the spirit of "The Stout Gentleman" that presides over the beginning of the *Tales,* a spirit perhaps best epitomized in the final sentences of the original story: "The skirts of a brown coat parted behind, and gave me a full view of the broad disk of a pair of drab breeches . . . and that was all I ever saw of the stout gentleman!" (*B,* p. 86).[14] The story as such, the point, the sensational disclosure gets away. What is left is simply storytelling, the "way" the story is told. "The Stout Gentleman" is, as one reviewer pointed out, a spoof on the "writers of the Radcliffe school"[15] and, as Irving himself made clear, on readers who expect something in the vein of the "Wandering Jew," the "Man with the Iron Mask," or the "Invisible Girl" (*B,* p. 73). Burlesque, then, is the mode in which the new book, the *Tales,* starts.

At "The Hunting Dinner," which is the setting for all the stories in Part I, the "nervous" narrator observes "a thin, hatchet-faced gentleman, with projecting eyes like a lobster," "one of those incessant questioners, who have a craving, unhealthy appetite in conversation." He is "never . . . satisfied with the whole of a story," and, instead of joining in the laughter at a joke, he puts it "to the question" (*TT,* p. 20). An "Irish captain of dragoons," inspecting family portraits in the "ancient rook-haunted" country house (p. 17) where the dinner guests are stranded for the night because of inclement weather, says that he wouldn't be surprised to "find the ghost of one of those long-waisted ladies" in his bed, whereupon the hatchet-faced man quizzes, "Do you believe in ghosts, then?" (p. 20) *Tales of a Traveller* repeatedly mocks such literal-minded re-

[14] According to his nephew, Irving, on once hearing it said that his "most comical pieces have always a serious end in view," quipped that "the moral of the Stout Gentleman" had finally been "detected." PMI, II, 57. In the *Tales* Crayon's attitude toward his "simple" reader becomes that of a horse-doctor toward a sick animal. He is willing that the patient, while "listening with open mouth to a ghost or a love story . . . have a bolus of sound morality popped down his throat, and be never the wiser for the fraud." *TT,* p. ix.

[15] *Edinburgh Magazine,* XI, 96.

sponses to wit and imagination. Several narrators deliberately tell stories to baffle readers like the hatchet-faced man. One reviewer, upset by these tactics, complained that the tales were generally

> wanting in those satisfactory conclusions for which we pant so ardently, when our curiosity has been put to the rack, and our sympathies worked to a considerable fermentation. They often break off suddenly, like those broken skeins of incident, of which our dreams are composed.[16]

But, as we shall see, this is to miss the point.

The frame narratives of Parts I, III, and IV of the *Tales* provide contexts for storytelling which seem ready-made for the thrill-seeker: an old mansion on a stormy night; an isolated inn in a bandit-infested region in Italy; the shore of Long Island Sound, purportedly the haunt of Captain Kidd. But Irving produces the ghost, the sensation, the intensity only on his own terms. In "The Adventure of My Uncle," the first story in Part I, a ghost actually appears, but when the suspense has been screwed tight, the protagonist abruptly turns his back, draws the bedclothes about his head, and falls asleep. In the morning, when he identifies the ghost as that of a great lady whose portrait hangs in the gallery below, his host begins a story which seems likely to account for the ghost, only to excuse himself from continuing after having aroused curiosity— family pride will not permit him to go into sordid details.

"The Adventure of My Uncle" thus proves merely a trap for the hatchet-faced man, who at the end exclaims, "Well, . . .

---

[16] *Eclectic Review*, XXIV, 65–66. *Blackwood's* said of the ghost stories in the *Tales*, "The tone in which Mr. Irving does them up, is quite wrong. A ghost story *ought* to be a ghost story. Something like seriousness is absolutely necessary . . . and the sort of half-witty vein, the little dancing quirks, &c. &c. with which these are set forth, entirely destroy the whole matter." "Letters of Timothy Tickler, Esq., No. XVIII," *Blackwood's*, XVI (September, 1824), 295. The *Blackwood's* review was devastating. Obviously disappointed at not finding a German sketch-book, the reviewer saw everything but the American section of the *Tales* as shopworn and artificial. Making no effort to respond to Irving's particular manner of treating familiar materials, he simply dismissed him as unable to find the passion and intensity for a ghost story or love story, unable to summon up interest in the classical past—a prerequisite for dealing with Italy—and unqualified as an American to say anything important about England or Europe.

and what did your uncle say then?" The answer is "Nothing" (p. 37).[17] Real ghosts do not appear on such trivial and trumped-up pretexts and for the mere curiosity of a sight-seer like "my uncle." Ghosts appear, as Henry James's Ralph Touchett was later to tell Isabel Archer, only to those who have suffered enough—to the German student, in a later story in the *Tales*, for instance, who, instead of turning his back and going to sleep on his vision, leaps to embrace her. For Irving, the way out of the earlier situation is through "French" jests. "My uncle" (the phrase still ludicrously echoes *Tristram Shandy*) talks about the ghost as the lady who "paid me a visit in my bed-chamber" (p. 37). And the valet says that it is "not for him to know any thing of *les bonnes fortunes* of Monsieur" (p. 31).

Before it is finished, the next piece, "The Adventure of My Aunt," dissolves in risqué *double-entendres*, and "The Bold Dragoon," another joke on the hatchet-faced man, becomes in addition a racy comic fantasy about a hero in the lusty line of Sterne's Slawkenbergius and *Knickerbocker*'s trumpeter, Antony Van Corlear, whose "instrument" stirred up untold excitement among the lasses of Connecticut (*K*, p. 266). The bold dragoon's adventures are "untold" too, but the reader's imagination is given a good deal to work on. The "haunted chamber," we are made to understand, is not the only room in the inn in which the protagonist spends time during the night of his "ordeal." Seen as part of a tall tale, the "pirouetting" of the furniture, "like so many devils" (*TT*, p. 53) in his room, becomes a graphic way of suggesting the dragoon's sexual prowess—his exploits nearly turn the house upside down.[18]

---

[17] Said the *Eclectic*, this story "provokingly breaks off just where it ought to have gone on. Our Author is, apparently, much enamoured of these experiments upon our love for the marvellous; for he seems to have no other end in raising our curiosity, than suddenly to let it down to disappoint us." XXIV, 67.

[18] Of this story the *U.S. Literary Gazette* said, ". . . if Mr. Geoffrey Crayon is not a thought more careful, the more recondite meaning of his double entendres will become a little too apparent." I (September, 1824), 16. "Tall tale" is, I believe, the correct term for "The Bold Dragoon," which depends a great deal on the pleasure the narrator takes in his own ingenuity and inventiveness, but which

After "The Bold Dragoon," however, Part I of *Tales of a Traveller* moves, and quite deliberately, from vivid demonstrations of what a ghost story ought not to be, to suggestions of what it can be, an arrangement that makes the "Adventure of the German Student" pivotal. This brief tale occupies such a delicately balanced situation in the book that it loses much of its force when it is lifted out of context and anthologized, as it frequently is. It almost allows the reader to take it as a ghost story. "The German Student" is essentially an invitation, a lure; it teases the reader with glimpses of mysterious depths to be probed but does not let him plunge gratuitously into sensationalism. It is narrated by a character with an appropriately ambiguous physiognomy, not the "nervous gentleman," who is initially only the frame narrator of Part I, but an old man, "one side of whose face" is "no match for the other." One of his eyelids hangs "like an unhinged window-shutter," giving the face the "dilapidated" look of "the wing of a house shut up and haunted." This is the half that is "well stuffed with ghost stories" (p. 22). Juxtaposed to the regular features of the other side of the face, however, the haunted half seems on occasion an extended wink. This narrator symbolizes an important relationship suggested in the sequence of stories in Part I, the proximity of the matter-of-fact and the ludicrous to the mysterious and the frightening. Irving deliberately starts by inviting and laughing at stock responses and moves gradually toward showing what it is like to be truly possessed.

The ending of "The German Student" reduces the tale to the level of one of the oldest jokes in the world—the thoroughly incredible happening, the authenticity of which the narrator facetiously establishes by the appeal, "I had it from the best authority. The student told it me himself. I saw him in a mad-house in Paris" (p. 64). And before the ending something in the style fights the force the story would have if it were

---

is told with a straight face to mystify the slow-witted listener. It is also one of Irving's rare dialect stories. Though the narrator's brogue is basically a literary stereotype, on the whole Irving uses it adroitly and manages to make the tale reflective of an Irish love of good humor.

altogether in earnest. The language is essentially the rhetoric of the standard gothic tale, but Irving uses it a little too obviously, makes it move too fast, so that explanations come too directly and abruptly, and character is almost flaunted as stereotype: "Her face was pale, but of a dazzling fairness, set off by a profusion of raven hair that hung clustering about it. Her eyes were large and brilliant, with a singular expression approaching to wildness" (p. 61). This is a language that Poe was to use effectively by supercharging it. Irving, however, is so deft and casual that when he glibly tosses off sentences such as "He was, in a manner, a literary ghoul, feeding in the charnel-house of decayed literature" (p. 58) one suspects parody.

Yet if one gives "The German Student" half a chance and reads it as the fantasy of a psychopath, it makes a fearful sense. The protagonist is an extreme instance of a characteristic Irving hero, the overly passive and imaginative, alienated observer. The "ghost" here, a revitalized female corpse, owes her existence to the German student's desires and frustrations, both of which she personifies. Disillusioned and disgusted by the excesses of the French Revolution, he lives a recluse, his withdrawal from action being a distinct reminder of Rip Van Winkle's long sleep through the American Revolution. Because of his shyness his ardor for the opposite sex leads only to fantasy. Creating his mistress in a dream, he realizes her one night at the foot of the guillotine in the shape of a forsaken lady who wears a black band around her neck. In the morning, after she passes the night in his room, he discovers that she is dead. Symbolically, he has been making love to Death herself: the lady has been guillotined the day before. The nightmarish discovery exposes the guilt-ridden evasiveness of the hero's creation of a totally abstract ideal.

Implicit in "The German Student"—indeed in the *Tales* as a whole—is the recognition that Poe was to make fully explicit in his famous letter on "Berenice," that the writing of romantic fiction is often a sustained struggle with material

that is potentially, if not inherently, ridiculous.[19] Necrophilia
may lie further within the purview of Poe's fiction than of
Irving's, but the ending of "Berenice" comes almost as close
as "The German Student" to reducing psychopathic compulsion
to Bedlam comedy. After all, Berenice's thirty-two teeth
rattling on the floor merely modulate the dull thud—at once
ludicrous and horrible—that one hears in the chamber of the
German student as a policeman loosens the black band at the
lady's throat and the guillotined head rolls to the floor.[20]

Burlesque, parody, hoax and mystification are important
components of the literature of the 1820's, perhaps because
both readers and writers needed some antidote to the extravagance of the sensationalist fiction which was currently popular.[21] Poe claimed that "Berenice" was a not entirely successful
experiment in heightening "the ludicrous . . . into the grotesque,"[22] but one wonders whether he would not have been
content to have it accepted as parody. The prose of the first
paragraph, for instance, so breathless with elevated platitude
and labored paradox, is hard to take seriously in the light
of Poe's burlesque of exaggerated styles and verbal sleight-of-
hand in "How to Write a Blackwood Article." Or, if "Berenice"
is not Poe's "German Student," perhaps "Ms. Found in a

[19] Poe to White, *Letters of Poe*, I, 57–58.

[20] Poe gives a sustained madhouse joke in "The System of Doctor Tarr and
Professor Fether." Headlessness, it is worth observing, is an important image in
two of Irving's stories. Leslie Fiedler is probably correct in suggesting that the
headless horseman of "Sleepy Hollow" is something more than a hoax. *Love and
Death* (New York, 1960), p. xxi. It cannot be too strongly emphasized that sterility
or impotence, projected in symbols of decay and drying up, is one of Irving's
perennial concerns, and that in this context images of maiming and cutting down
("Rip," "The Angler," "Dolph," "Buckthorne," "Tom Walker") seem to carry
an unconscious implication of fear of castration.

[21] See in *Blackwood's*, for instance, "Specimens of the Italian Art of Hoaxing,"
XII, 589–600; "The Unicorn and the Mermaid," XII, 660–62; "The Suicide," XVI,
158–61; "Wonderful Passage in the Life of Mansie Wauch, Tailor," XVI, 456–59;
"Confessions of an English Glutton," XIII, 86–93; "Letter from a Washerwoman,"
XIII, 232–38. There are further installments of "Specimens of the Italian Art of
Hoaxing" in Vols. XIII and XIV.

[22] Poe to White, *Letters of Poe*, I, 57. The letter is somewhat ambiguous, but
of the four varieties of heightening which Poe lists, this, from the ludicrous to the
grotesque, seems most closely to correspond with what he says elsewhere in the
letter about "Berenice."

Bottle" is. Here the narrator, in a tight fix worthy of the
Blackwood's tradition, retains all the equanimity he needs to
prepare a careful record of his impressions and pass them on
via the bottle for posterity; meanwhile the flying Dutchman of
a ghost ship which speeds him on to the Pole is freighted with
an uncommonly large cargo of gothic props. The element of
contrivance suggests parody; one even detects a wink or two at
Irving himself.[23] Yet the style of "Ms. Found in a Bottle,"
if frequently exaggerated to the verge of burlesque, still keeps
teasing the reader to surrender to the fantasy.

Had Poe ever managed to get his "Tales of the Folio Club"
published as a book, his intentions might now seem clearer.
We do know, however, that the stories in the series were, as in
Tales of a Traveller, to be told by individual narrators—at a
club-meeting—that there was a good deal of humor in the
characterizations of the narrators, and that the discussions by
the members after each tale were to be burlesques of literary
criticism. Not all the Folio Club tales can be identified with
certainty, but it is clear that they ranged from outright burlesques to pieces as apparently typical of the more exalted Poe
as "Silence" and "The Assignation." And it is possible that,
particularly with the example of Irving in the *Tales* before him,
he planned to give at least one of the tales a tone that would
place it in a twilight zone between the ludicrous and the
serious.[24]

[23] The ship suggests Irving's "Storm-Ship" (*B*). And the little old men personifying "the spirit of Eld" could hardly have been conceived as anything but
parody. On one level also the story can be taken as a spoof on German philosophy.
The narrator is a variation of the stock comic figure of the German student or the
student of German thought (see note 24). Though he has, he thinks, always studied
the German moralists in order to reject them, the fantastic events he experiences
finally make him in effect a convert.

[24] For attempts to ascertain the contents of "Tales of the Folio Club," see T. O.
Mabbott, "On Poe's 'Tales of the Folio Club,'" *Sewanee Review,* XXXVI (April,
1928), 171–76; James S. Wilson, "The Devil Was in It," *American Mercury,* XXIV
(October, 1931), 215–20. In "Poe's 'Ligeia' and the English Romantics" (*University of Toronto Quarterly,* XXIV [October, 1954], 8–25), Clark Griffith argues
that "Ligeia," not of course one of the Folio Club tales, is *both* the tale of
terror it has always been taken to be *and* a satirical allegory of the dependence
of English romanticism on German sources. I am inclined also to see at least
some degree of satire or parody in "Ligeia." The style seems to me, as to Griffith,

In their theoretical statements Irving and Poe both put great stress on style as the instrument for redeeming the sensationalistic material of popular fiction.[25] In actual practice this often meant strengthening the authority of the narrative voice in the story. It is no accident that both writers were interested in the storyteller, in the relation between the tale and the telling. Both saw that an audience will accept almost any plot or story, no matter how fantastic, if it is made convincing by being put in the mouth of someone with a reason or need for telling it. Poe made fun of the stylistic excesses of current fiction—"the tone laconic," "the tone elevated, diffusive, and interjectional," "the tone metaphysical," "the tone transcendental," and "the tone heterogeneous." He pretended to have no use for the writer who goes out of his way to discover "piquant" phrases, allusions, and figures of speech.[26] But in his own stories he out-Blackwooded *Blackwood's,* using styles dazzling, mystifying, and overpowering enough to call special attention to the narrators using them.

Style always creates at least one character in a Poe story—the narrator—even though the other personae, existing only through him, may remain obscure. Out of the narrator's desire and need to hold an audience spellbound (even, if necessary, by publicly incriminating himself) emerges Poe's celebrated unity of effect. The narrator of "The Imp of the Perverse," who

---

at times too heightened to be taken seriously—the first sentence, for instance. I tend to see "Ligeia" as a much more subtle version of the basic experience in Irving's "German Student." In both stories the disordered mind of the psychotic protagonist brings to life the phantom that controls it and then loses the woman who is the embodiment. Both protagonists are students, and in each case the phantom is associated with German philosophy. Griffith sees Ligeia as a personification of German Transcendentalism. In Irving it is made much more obvious that German idealism—"fanciful speculations on spiritual essences"—has driven Wolfgang, a student from Göttingen, to create "an ideal world of his own around him." *TT,* p. 57.

[25] In the important letter to Brevoort, Irving says that "in these shorter writings, every page must have its merit. The author must be continually piquant; woe to him if he makes an awkward sentence or writes a stupid page; the critics are sure to pounce upon it." *WIHB,* II, 186. And Poe, speaking of pieces like "Berenice," says, "To be sure of originality is an essential in these things—great attention must be paid to style, and much labour spent in their composition, or they will degenerate into the turgid or the absurd." Letter to White, *Letters,* I, 58.

[26] Poe, "How to Write a Blackwood Article."

wants to tear out his tongue but cannot stop its wagging, is the archetype. He says that when finally driven to confess his crime he "spoke with a distinct enunciation, but with marked emphasis and passionate hurry"—like a tale-telling heart. And now, on the verge of execution, he cannot stop writing about himself and analyzing himself, using himself as the chief example of a theory of impulse which he has devised. Tonal unity in Poe, given his use of the first person, insures unity of effect by turning everything in the story into a reflection of (because literally an expression of) the narrator, even when, as in "The Fall of the House of Usher," he seems only a relatively passive observer. This is one way in which Poe far surpasses a writer like Charles Brockden Brown, who, for all his brooding sense of terror as a psychological and moral reality, is apt to petrify his characters, particularly his narrators, by the false rhetoric that he foists upon them.

Irving seldom managed to achieve a structural unity or compactness comparable to Poe's, but he understood the importance of tonal unity or consistency.[27] By experimenting with pseudonyms and narratives-within-narratives he largely avoided those disconcerting shifts back and forth between high seriousness and comic relief that mar so much nineteenth-century fiction presented under the aspect of omniscience. The shifts are disconcerting because they presuppose as narrator a being who may laugh when he should be moved to tears, or vice versa. But Irving is apt to modulate by changing narrators: the new voice justifies the change in tone. Or, by utilizing his most characteristic narrative voice, the friendly, sympathetic yet slightly whimsical voice of Crayon or one of his variants (the nervous gentleman or the later Diedrich Knickerbocker), he achieves con-

---

[27] And what he was able to contribute to short fiction in the way of tightening structure (even in falling short of Poe) and tying symbolic significance to character and locale can be easily appreciated by comparing the *Tales* with a typical contemporary collection of romantic pieces such as *Popular Tales and Romances of the Northern Nations* (3 vols.; London, 1823). This largely German collection, including stories by Tieck, Musäus, and Fouqué, is impressive in its wealth of imagery and incident and its symbolic suggestiveness but is often crude stylistically and structurally, and on the whole pays little attention to rendering character and setting in detail.

siderable flexibility in mood and attitude within an individual story without sacrificing tonal unity. The humor in that voice, without seeming irreverent, grounds fantasy in the familiar. Furthermore Irving's efforts to establish a relationship between story and narrator edge, toward a conception of fiction as the revelation of character. By emphasizing the telling as much as the novelty or surprise which the popular audience demanded, he, like Poe, was able to bring out connections between action and character, gesture and motive, spectacle and response.

Not all of his ghost stories turn out to be jokes. In Part I of the *Tales* the involvement of the nervous narrator in a situation calculated, even more than the one in "The Stout Gentleman," to unnerve him finally signals the beginning of disclosures which are less easy to laugh off than the bogus sensations we have previously been given. Upon retiring for the night, he becomes himself the victim of a "haunted chamber" in the old mansion in which the hunting-dinner has been held. A combination of the room's gloomy appointments—"lampblack portraits" and "massive pieces of old-fashioned furniture"—recollections of "haunted" rooms in the stories told earlier, and a stomach overtaxed with "wine and wassail" give the narrator "a violent fit of the nightmare." Waking up is no real release, for he now discovers a candle, melted into a fantastic shape, throwing an unpleasantly bright light on a portrait which he is compelled to examine. It represents a man in the throes of "intense bodily pain"; a menacing scowl and "a few sprinklings of blood" contribute to a total impression of "ghastliness" (pp. 66–68).

The "Adventure of the Mysterious Picture" temporarily transforms the Crayonesque observer into the eyewitness recorder of fantastic events ultimately immortalized by Poe. The nervous narrator is forced to resort to gothic rhetoric. In this particular lonely chamber his experience moves beyond mere anxiety toward terror. The combination of objective fact and subjective suggestion, the union of what the narrator observes and his way of observing it, operates to multiply fears. The very "idea of being hagridden . . . all night, and then bantered on . . . haggard looks the next day" proves "sufficient to produce

the effect" (p. 69), as in the theory of impulse as self-fulfilling
prophecy that Poe was to work out in "The Imp of the Perverse."[28]

The next morning the host gives the story behind the picture,
and this time, unlike the similar occasion in "The Adventure of
My Uncle," there is no holding back. Instead of French jests,
we ultimately get Italian passion. In the "Adventure of the
Mysterious Stranger" the host describes his encounter years
ago in Italy with the painter of the gruesome portrait, a sensitive,
appealing, yet strangely guilt-ridden young man. The face in
the picture represents a fantasm that haunted the painter. "The
Mysterious Stranger" is not an independent tale. It serves,
with "The Mysterious Picture," to introduce "The Story of
the Young Italian," a manuscript in the possession of the host,
who proceeds to read it to the gathering. Together, the two
introductory pieces help arouse interest in the character of the
painter Ottavio, the "Young Italian."

Far more than with an external intrigue, the concern of this
story is with the question: what compulsion drives the intelligent, gifted man whom we see in "The Mysterious Stranger"
to a crime which plants the bloody image of the "Mysterious
Picture" on his conscience? Pledged, in effect, to an investigation of terror, Irving does not try to buy his way out of the commitment with a melodramatic tease like "The Student of Salamanca" or the sensational pathos of a "Broken Heart" or an
"Annette Delarbre." He offers a murderer with whom the
reader is expected in large part to sympathize. Indeed "The
Young Italian," like its companion piece in Part III, "The
Story of the Young Robber," is a startling work when held
against the stereotype of the genial Washington Irving.

"The Young Italian" is a flawed story because it attempts
to cover too much of Ottavio's lifetime in too short a space and
fails, on the whole, to linger over individual scenes long

---

[28] One reviewer, in praising "The Mysterious Picture," said that it was "so
graphical, that we fear our unfortunate friend Geoffrey is himself an occasional
sufferer from the nocturnal visit of Ephialtes." Anonymous review, *Edinburgh
Magazine*, XV (September, 1824), 330.

enough for the reader to become thoroughly involved. There is material enough here for a novella or novel. Irving must have partly realized this himself, since he went to the trouble of breaking up the long narrative line and putting parts of the story into the two introductory pieces, each of which, being more concentrated, is artistically more satisfying. A casual reading may make it seem that Ottavio is too often a victim of circumstances, that what happens to him and what he does have too little relation to the kind of person he is. In both "The Young Italian" and "The Young Robber," though Irving can sympathize with his impassioned protagonists in the extremity of their ordeals, he has trouble fully identifying with them. The terror in these stories—Irving's only attempts to deal with emotions of an intensity comparable to those in Poe, Monk Lewis, or Brockden Brown—avoids being "of Germany" only by being, according to another gothic convention, "of Italy" and not entirely, as Poe claimed his to be, "of the soul."[29]

Of course he does not plunge directly into terror with the zest of a high gothic novelist. The whole complicated process of arranging stories in a sequence building to a violent climax shows an effort at something more subtle—and this is a necessity, since Irving obviously remains self-conscious about his gothic appropriations. Yet his embarrassment is in one sense a good sign, for, like Brockden Brown, he understands that in fiction violent action is virtually meaningless except as a reflection of character in deep conflict with itself. Both writers see the need for getting inside the soul in torment, though in comparison with Poe and Hawthorne, both fail to do so convincingly—Brown, because of the pretentious jargon with which he overlays introspection and character analysis; Irving, because on the whole, in spite of his inability in the Italian stories to get away completely from gothic rhetoric, he underplays his material.

Where Hawthorne, perhaps following Brown's lead, in a few years would begin to probe directly into hidden sources of the

[29] Preface to *Tales of the Grotesque and Arabesque* (1840).

difficulties of his characters and Poe would exhibit their distractions more fully, Irving still tended to stay on the surface. His method is more appropriate to the seriocomic vein in which he worked best. He uses symbols almost exclusively as his means of hinting at Ottavio's real trouble—which is not so much his trying to win the heroine Bianca as his desiring her to begin with. And the symbols do not call so much attention to themselves that a reader looking only for action would stop to ponder them. Yet settings, events, and secondary characters are consistently set up in "The Young Italian" so that they mirror aspects of Ottavio's inner difficulty. And this difficulty is referred back to his childhood situation in his family in a way that, if initially somewhat stereotyped, gradually becomes compelling. One wishes "The Young Italian" could have been done as pure fantasy or dream. There is a discrepancy between the story's failure to convince as literal narrative and its fullness as imagery. But the force it gathers at the second level indicates that Irving knows something, consciously or unconsciously, about violent impulse, guilt, and remorse.[30]

Like the protagonist of "The Young Robber" and Buckthorne, the central character in the longest and most important narrative in Part II of the *Tales*, Ottavio is a highly emotional and imaginative young man trying to free himself of parental domination and establish himself as an adult husband or lover. His mother dies early, leaving him spoiled, subject to tumultuous emotional upheavals, and at the mercy of a harsh father, who shows his favoritism for an older brother. The monastery where Ottavio is later sent becomes a metaphor of the motherless, femaleless family to which the boy now belongs. He is given in charge of his uncle, a rigidly puritanical monk and an obvious surrogate for the father. He acquires, in other words, a father "superior" *in loco parentis*. His confinement in the monastery connects his father, whom he fears and hates, with the more for-

[30] One American reviewer, who was extremely critical of the *Tales* and complained of "triteness in the thoughts and barrenness of incident" in "The Mysterious Stranger" and "The Young Italian," still curiously acknowledged that matters "have been arranged and presented in a manner tending to the strongest effect on the reader." *Minerva* (New York), New Series, I (4 September 1824), 348.

bidding aspects of religion. The superstition of the monks, who are shut off from the world in an isolated mountainous region not far from Mt. Vesuvius, turns the volcanic terrain under the monastery into the beginning of the infernal regions, about which the monks frighten the boy with stories. Fatherhood, the authority of religion, punishment, hellfire, and death thus come close to standing for one another in Ottavio's experience.

As his life develops, further symbolic extensions or duplications of his relations with the members of his immediate family give substance to Ottavio's capacity for hate and love, violence and remorse. His growing-up becomes a constant re-enactment, usually with surrogates in the roles opposite him, of the original drama of his childhood—his effort to regain his mother's love, his jealousy of father and brother, his revolt against them or flight from them. After several years he escapes the monastery and his father and goes to Genoa, only to be confronted at every turn, in effect haunted, by replicas of an overidealized mother. Emblems of death and decay give way to those of birth and life. Amid the splendors of palaces and gardens in Genoa, Ottavio is overcome by a painting of the Madonna in the "church of the Annunciata" (p. 95). Again, however, as elsewhere in Irving, the roles of mother, sweetheart, and sister are to become blurred. Ottavio finds a temporary foster father in the painter to whom he is apprenticed, the painter of the Madonna—the apotheosized mother-wife. At the same time he falls in love, and the very name of his beloved, Bianca, emphasizes her purity, which the imagery makes fully religious. While she is immured in a convent for her education, Ottavio nurtures his love and reproduces her face in numerous paintings. "I have stood, with delight, in one of the chapels of the Annunciata, and heard the crowd extol the seraphic beauty of a saint which I had painted. I have seen them bow down in adoration before the painting; they were bowing before the loveliness of Bianca" (pp. 96–98).

Before long, however, the painter dies, bequeathing to Ottavio "his little property," and commending him to the protection of a Genoese nobleman, another "foster-father" (p. 98). By coincidence Bianca loses her father too and is taken into the same house under the same protection. That overtones of incest should develop, suggesting a fear of, or longing for, the forbidden as an essential emotion, is almost to be expected of gothic fiction, but the intrafamilial relationships in "The Young Italian" seem even more hectic than the convention demanded. Bianca, whose purity and saintliness already seem to reflect Ottavio's unconscious devotion to his dead mother, inevitably becomes something of a sister to him at this juncture, and the situation is further complicated by the presence of a foster brother, the nobleman's son Filippo, a young man close to Ottavio's age.

Thus, to lose Bianca to Filippo just when he does—after his real father and brother, by a striking coincidence, have died, setting him free and bequeathing him an inheritance—is, in one sense, to be deprived again of maternal love, to be rejected once more in favor of a brother. His frenzied murder of Filippo, who steals Bianca from him, becomes explicitly a kind of fratricide: "I fled from the garden like another Cain—a hell within my bosom and a curse upon my head" (p. 117).[31]

The Hawthornesque overtone here is consistent with other aspects of Irving's treatment of Ottavio's experience. He accepts, for the sake of his fiction, the Italy of romance, the Italy of Ann Radcliffe. But his Italy to a degree also anticipates that of Hawthorne and James. He manages in the introductory piece, "The Mysterious Stranger," to suggest that there is a second story, just as important as that of the murder, the story of the Englishman's reaction to the gradual unfolding of Ottavio's history. What intrigues Irving as much as the cloak-and-dagger aspect of Italy, the Latin passion and sublime vistas, is a contrast or interplay between the spectacle of Italy and the more staid responses of the Anglo-Saxon spectator. We see this, for instance, in the fact that the host at the hunting dinner was compelled years earlier, because he was basically a sympa-

---

[31] Heiman has noted Irving's personal dependence on his brother William as a substitute father after the death of Deacon Irving. "Rip Van Winkle: A Psychoanalytic Note," *American Imago*, XVI, 12–13.

thetic human being, even though encumbered with "an Englishman's habitual diffidence and awkwardness" (p. 80), to minister to Ottavio's appeal for friendship and instinctive understanding. On that occasion the agony of Ottavio's unutterable
guilt transformed the Englishman into a kind of priest, who
granted absolution before hearing the confession.

The English host is to Ottavio as Kenyon is to Donatello in
The Marble Faun. After he kills Filippo, Ottavio, like Donatello a "creature of passion before reason was developed"
(p. 86),[32] suffers an almost Hawthornesque remorse: "Oh could
I but have cast off this crime that festered in my heat—could
I but have regained the innocence that reigned in my heart
as I entered the garden at Sestri . . ." (pp. 117–18). He too
surrenders to justice after the moral firmness and sympathy
of his older friend (a last substitute for father or brother?)
have helped him achieve a full realization of the significance
of his crime. And Ottavio anticipates Donatello in his reliance
on the church. As the narrator says of Ottavio in "The
Mysterious Stranger," "His had always been agony rather than
sorrow" (p. 84).

It is, however, the music in an Easter Week service rather
than clerical exhortation that is chiefly responsible for the
final contrition—one recalls the passage in *Travel in Europe*
which describes Irving's being deeply moved by Easter music
in Rome.[33] In both Hawthorne and Irving it is the aesthetic side
of Catholicism that carries the primary moral force. Hawthorne, of course, the greater Puritan as well as the greater

---

[32] Ottavio also has affinities with the narrator of Poe's "William Wilson," another "self-willed" child, "addicted to the wildest caprices, and a prey to the most
ungovernable passions," who is immured in a gloomy gothic boarding school
affiliated with the church and presided over by a paradoxical pastor, all "demurely
benign" and fatherly in appearance but stern and "sour" in administering "the
Draconian Laws of the academy." And the narrator's other self, his conscience,
which seems both to stimulate and reproach his rebellion, is embodied in another
student, who is for a while mistaken for the narrator's own brother. Irving, who
thought highly of "William Wilson," was intrigued by the idea of the double, a
man haunted by his alter ego, and he may actually have been partly responsible
for Poe's inspiration for "William Wilson." See STW, II, 358; Edward Wagenknecht, *Washington Irving* (New York, 1962), p. 202.
[33] *TIE*, III, 68.

writer, felt much more keenly the impact of a religion that
utilized music, painting, sculpture, and elaborate ceremony.
What Irving merely sketches in, Hawthorne later worked out
with elaborate care. Several weeks before his crucial Easter
experience, for instance, we see Ottavio, "haggard and agi-
tated," going to "operas, masquerades, balls" (p. 83), mingling
with the crowds in the pre-Lenten carnival celebration. Effective
as it is to conceive of the fugitive from justice trying to mask
his despair in Mardi gras festivities, Irving gives little more
than the bare idea, whereas Hawthorne fully develops a scene
in which Kenyon catches a glimpse of the guilty couple, Miriam
and Donatello, in a carnival procession; the suggestiveness of
costume, *décor*, and gesture almost turn the episode into a
ballet.

The geographical distinction in Part I supports a contrast
between the commonplace and the romantic. Underlying everything in the "Strange Stories" is the ordinariness of the fox-
hunting dinner, the heavy eating, the resulting dullness, the
humor without great imagination. In the general torpor powerful disrupting emotions seem only a remote possibility, something foreign or alien. It is proper to have a certain amused
curiosity about a crime of passion provided one doesn't become
really concerned about it. Yet the interest in ghost stories itself
comes to seem a sign of a latent capacity for being emotionally
aroused; at bottom there turns out to be a connection between
England and Italy.

Stereotyped as Irving's conceptions of national character are
in the *Tales*, he manages to use them suggestively as emblems of
varying attitudes toward fiction, art, and imagination. And
through the contrasts the investigation of possibilities and
limitations in various modes of fiction becomes more explicit.
Part III repeats the basic pattern of Part I, exposing English
reserve to Italian openness and emotion. Meanwhile, Part II,
located entirely in England, maintains a consistently humorous
tone but manages to present humor itself as an accommodation
to a world in which imagination and emotion are constantly up-

setting balance and self-control. Finally, in Part IV, Irving shifts again to America, a setting in which for him the comic and the gothic, the humdrum and the grotesque, the real and the illusory, the natural and the supernatural seem almost to become aspects of one another.

Part II of *Tales of a Traveller*—"Buckthorne and His Friends"—offers a variation on the theme of storytelling by using authorship or the lives of authors as subject matter. It reminds the reader that authors are fundamentally all-too-human beings. What Crayon discovers to be an essential element of the artistic temperament is a thoroughly normal, if usually self-defeating, impulse to see the world as magical, mysterious, romantic. The literary frame of reference for Part II is no longer the gothic tale or the sensational anecdote but the periodical essay, as Irving sets the subject of authorship in the context of a world very much concerned with fashions. The first two pieces, "A Literary Dinner" and "The Club of Queer Fellows," show us authors both in and out of popular favor, poor devils, authors trying to keep up with the latest literary fads, grubstreet hacks elbowing their way toward success, and successful writers trying to live up to their roles. A later piece, "Notoriety," discusses the "oddity fanciers among our ladies of rank," whose "routs are like fancy balls, where every one comes 'in character,' . . . playing a part, and acting out of his natural line. . . . The fine gentleman is always anxious to be thought a wit, and the wit a fine gentleman" (pp. 165–66).

The narratives in Part II accordingly stage re-enactments of the standard neoclassical drama which turns on the conflict between provincialism and urbanity. Buckthorne and most of his friends have at one time or another left the country, where they were brought up, to go to London to be writers or to get ahead in the theater. Their stories superficially have the appearance of those eighteenth-century *récits* in which a young person in difficulty through his ignorance of the ways of the world implores an editor for advice, or in which the deviator from the norm confesses the error of his ways and resolves to mend them.

But there are important differences. As in Irving's earlier works, the assumption is that eccentricities are an inevitable part of being human and, if not to be admired or cultivated, perhaps not to be censured either. For, after all, while his writers and actors sometimes behave like country bumpkins, their rebuffs from the town are viewed by an author who has himself been through the mill of literary fashion. Sympathetic as he was with the plight of the artist, Irving could not help feeling, at least on occasion, that he, like Buckthorne, had been "beguiled away by the imagination . . . from the safe *beaten* path of life" and had lost himself "in the mazes of literature."[34] Like one of the other characters, he had been a literary success in his home town before going out in the world to try to make good in the literary capital. In Part II his purpose is to show a constantly recurring relationship between aspiring imagination and cold hard facts. Irving gives us the comic view, but there is poignancy in the comedy. The attitude of the "practical philosopher," who is Buckthorne himself, is to accept one's limitations, to be a small frog in the big pond. But the wear and tear still show on those who have reached this sensible solution.

In the frame narrative Crayon gets to know Buckthorne in London, is taken by him to literary gathering-places, is introduced to writers and grubstreet hangers-on, and listens to shop-talk and stories of various careers. These narratives develop a single basic impression, and their cumulative effect is to make it possible for Irving sometimes to cut a story short without giving us the protagonist's whole life history because its general outlines can be inferred through analogy to what has already happened to him or to other characters in other narratives. This is particularly true of the main story of Part II, which Crayon finally teases out of Buckthorne himself. Except for a brief epilogue, it stops when Buckthorne gets to Grub Street. It is concerned only with an earlier period of his life, which is viewed from the perspective of a mature man looking back ironically on the callowness of his youth.

[34] Irving to Pierre Paris Irving, 29 March 1825, PMI, II, 233.

In general outline "Buckthorne, or The Young Man of Great Expectations" follows a pattern familiar in eighteenth-century letters to editors: a youth, who takes the fortune he expects to inherit too much for granted, reaches an advanced state of waywardness, alienates family and friends, is disinherited, repents of his folly, changes his ways, and proves himself worthy of the position for which he was originally intended. But Buckthorne's weakness is not vice or luxury. His story focuses on the anxiety and delight, as well as the imaginative self-deception, that a literary bent can engender. He does not so much fall from the good graces of his rich uncle as fail ever to get into them. Nor does this seem very much his fault; it stems from his imaginative temperament; he and his uncle were not made to love each other.

Buckthorne starts out in high hope and almost makes a great success of himself, only to miscalculate his talents, fail, and find himself once more back home where he began. The pattern is repeated several times; he partly learns from, and is partly confirmed in, his tendency to mistake dream for reality. In the process Irving suggests mysterious affinities between the events in a hero's life and an intention in natural forces. By providing a world at large shaped to a central character and reflecting his problems, he begins to produce an effect of fantasy even though he is not consciously adapting legends. Buckthorne's prevarication turns into a kind of dance in which the powers of life or nature seem constantly to lead him on.

"Buckthorne" ought to be considered in relation to the *Tales* as a whole, and specifically in contrast to "The Young Italian." Both stories go to extremes: Ottavio's embodies imagination in a virulently self-destructive form, virtually indistinguishable from psychosis, while Buckthorne's miraculously rides, or is ridden by, the vagrant inclination through a series of clashes with reality to eventual good fortune and a state as close to liberation from whimsy as Irving can envision or tolerate. The usual truth is obviously somewhere in between, and Irving stalks it throughout the *Tales*. All around Crayon, Grub Street is littered with poor devils, most of whom will neither stop chasing phantoms altogether nor find the security of accepting their third-rateness.

Though less passionate than Ottavio because he was subject to milder repressions as a child, Buckthorne has been conditioned by an analogous set of circumstances, spoiled by "the most excellent, the most indulgent of mothers" (p. 171) and governed by a father who is a stern believer in the educative value of flogging. The rich and miserly uncle, again a surrogate for the father, is "a veteran spider, in the citadel of his web." Buckthorne, when he visits him, occupies the room that had been his mother's before her marriage, sees little of the old uncle, and is denied entrance to his "stronghold," which is located "in a remote corner of the building, strongly secured, and generally locked." On Sunday "this withered anatomy" issues from his private quarters to compel the household to listen while he reads at length from the Bible or *Pilgrim's Progress* (a caricature, incidentally, of Irving's own father's Sunday ritual).[35] Taking a page from his uncle's favorite book, Buckthorne makes an early mistake in writing a poem in which he describes the old man's estate "under the name of Doubting Castle" and transforms its owner into the "Giant Despair." When he loses the poem about the house, the uncle finds it (pp. 175–79).

Most of the men he encounters—fox-hunting friends of his father, his uncle and his uncle's servant Iron John, schoolmasters, parsons, and the fathers of the girls he pursues—function to thwart his desires or frustrate his expectations. These men, who are largely unimaginative, ridicule the poetry he writes or see his interests as worthless. Meanwhile, mothers and sentimental girls lavish affection on him and wax ecstatic over his poetry. He generally responds in kind, penning verses to girls in which he addresses them with names like "Sacharissa."

On one occasion, a soft, sensuous form of religion, combined with the attractions of a girl in a provincial city who swoons over his poetical advances, brings him to the verge of his total undoing. Small-town piety works on him to produce an agony of

[35] PMI, I, 23.

apparent remorse and contrition: "Sinner that I was!" he says, "the very dignity and decorum of the little community was rebuking to me. I feared my past idleness and folly would rise in judgment against me. I stood in awe of the dignitaries of the cathedral . . ." (p. 228). But Buckthorne has not turned into Ottavio. His early life has not been nearly so wasted as he, in his desire to find ideal meaning in it, now pretends. His self-humiliation is a function of his sentimental need to believe that the girl he is wooing is too good for him. The psychology of the gesture is quite clear: "This routine of solemn ceremony continually going on, independent, as it were, of the world; this daily offering of melody and praise, ascending like incense from the altar, had a powerful effect upon my imagination" (p. 227). One is reminded of Irving's delight in the music and ritual in the Italian churches[36] and suspects him here of self-mockery. He seemed sometimes to doubt the genuineness of the very experiences that moved him most.

Thus the imagery in the story functions systematically to illuminate the conflicts of the artistic temperament confronting the practical world. On his uncle's gothicized estate stagnant ponds and fallen statues, suggestive of sterility or impotence, reflect the fears which at times render Buckthorne ineffectual as a human being. Similarly a temporary connection which he forms with the theater makes him a clown, the dupe of his illusions. As Pierrot in the traditional *commedia dell'arte* pantomime, he plays a role that mirrors the failure of his off-stage attempts to make life conform to his vision of the way things ought to be. "I had merely," he says, "to pursue the fugitive fair one; to have a door now and then slammed in my face; to run my head occasionally against a post; . . . to endure the hearty thwacks of Harlequin's wooden sword" (p. 194). He falls in love with the girl who plays Columbine, and on the day on which a girl who has previously spurned him shows up in the audience, he is stung into returning Harlequin's thwacks. The effort to give dramatic proof of his manliness breaks up the pantomime and costs him his job.

[36] *TIE*, III, 68.

Yet, ironically, by this particular bit of clowning he does win Columbine, at least temporarily. Buckthorne makes much of the incongruity in his situation at the fair grounds after his expulsion from the theater, "my mountebank dress fluttering in rags about me; the weeping Columbine hanging upon my arm, in splendid but tattered finery," the tears ruining her make-up. "Having wandered through the fair," he says, going on to a Miltonic allusion that ought to have delighted Hawthorne, "we emerged, like another Adam and Eve, into unknown regions, and 'had the world before us where to choose' " (p. 199). Being a clown thus becomes curiously synonymous with being human, with being thrust out into the world to make one's way, as is emphasized when in the course of their wanderings Buckthorne and Columbine come to the spot overlooking London where Dick Whittington first heard Bow bells.[37]

The story should probably end here, or on a similar note of romantic irony, for this represents Irving's deepest insight into the nature of the artistic temperament. But he goes on to have the rich uncle die and leave his fortune to a suddenly revealed illegitimate son, so that Buckthorne is forced to become a grub-street hack in order to support himself. Once he proves that he can put imagination to work for him instead of throwing it away on silly females, he earns an inheritance: his bastard cousin conveniently dies and leaves him the estate.

Rude awakenings, unfortunately, have at last brought Buckthorne too much to his senses, for in the process of reforming and becoming respectable he not only gives up girls like Columbine for a commonsensical squire's daughter; when he goes to live on his estate, he also retires from literature.[38] The

[37] Another time Buckthorne takes up boxing and is thrashed; lying on his bed, he moralizes "on this sorry ambition, which levels the gentleman with the clown" (p. 223).

[38] "Buckthorne and His Friends" reflects Irving's conception that at best a career as a professional writer is a precarious one. The failure of the Tales would not brighten his view of authorship. Writing to his young nephew, Pierre Paris Irving, who was already dabbling in letters, Irving, in the midst of his disappointment at the reception of the Tales, warned him against a writer's career, saying, "I hope none of those whose interests and happiness are dear to me will be induced to follow my footsteps, and wander into the seductive but treacherous paths

formula of the periodical *récit* may have seemed promising to Irving as a way of handling his subject without running the risk of romantic excesses, but it finally pushed him into creating a world of pat reasonableness where imagination is denied a legitimate place. One knows, however, from the excitement of Buckthorne's own narrative, which is produced by the protagonist's response to a world charged with illusion, that the problem was not as easy as the neat ending makes it seem.

The inn at Terracina, the locus of storytelling in "The Italian Banditti" (Part III), stands much closer to the scene of action than the bachelors' hall in Part I. The persons telling and listening to the stories are themselves travelers on the bandit-infested road between Rome and Naples. When the stories are finished, the travelers resume their journeys. In the end, the frame narrative itself emerges from the inn and pursues a group of travelers along the road until they run into trouble. In the meanwhile the stories, as in Part I, have begun in burlesque and worked up to a violent climax, an arrangement which invites the reader to ponder the implications of the vogue for gothic sensation.[39]

In "The Story of the Young Robber" a girl is first raped by a gang of outlaws and then handed over to the protagonist, her sweetheart, to be executed. But for all the terror of this tale, the prevailing tone of "The Italian Banditti" remains comic or satiric, the frame narrative being rendered in a deliberately

of literature." Letter of 7 December 1824, PMI, II, 219–20. What he began to envision instead for the person with literary interests was the possibility of an American lawyer or businessman who would also be a scholar or man of letters and who would thus perform a double social function. He rhapsodized on this theme in two long letters to his nephew (PMI, II, 218–22, 233–38). His exaggeration shows how easily his own imagination could still deceive him. Yet as he grew older he was to cling more and more to this cultural ideal.

[39] Irving knew the road between Naples and Rome (see *TIE*, II, 26–34; III, 19–30; and Nathalia Wright, "Irving's Use of His Italian Experience in *Tales of a Traveller*: The Beginning of an American Tradition," *American Literature*, XXXI [May, 1959], 191–96). But his memories do not make for straight realism. His attitude toward "banditti" was shaped in part by his early familiarity with romantic treatments of the subject such as Schiller's *Die Räuber*, and by the popular glorification of the outlaw Joseph Musso, whose execution he had witnessed at Genoa in 1804. See Reichart, p. 151; STW, I, 58; II, 292.

exaggerated, melodramatic style, which the irony of studied remarks or the ludicrousness of situation pulls against. The
dominant tone is set at the beginning when a government courier
gallops up to the inn in his underdrawers. Bandits have stripped
him of his "leather breeches," which " were bran new, and
shone like gold" (p. 274). While this indication of the way
bandits behave is blunt and prosaic enough, most of the travelers
depicted in Part III prefer to wrap the possibility of an encounter with them in some sort of illusion. They see "banditti"
instead of bandits, the Italian word carrying delicious romantic
connotations. The sentimental view is that bandits are noblemen
in disguise, noble at least in spirit if not by title. In "The Adventure of the Popkins Family" two daughters of a London
alderman, who are "very romantic" and eager to sketch the
"savage scenery" that reminds them of Mrs. Radcliffe (p. 322),
go through an attack, watch bandits plunder their parvenu
papa's rich equipage, and emerge "quite delighted with the adventure," which they can't wait to write into their diaries. They
find the chief of the band "most romantic-looking" and the
whole group "quite picturesque" (p. 325).

Still another attitude is embodied in a young Venetian woman,
who exudes passion and sentiment at the slightest provocation
and enjoys giving herself chills of fear by listening to accounts
of the atrocities the bandits are supposed to inflict upon their
captives, especially women. It is the Italian characters who are
generally the most emotional about the bandits (excluding the
silly Popkins females, whose romanticism is a naïve, virginal
sentiment, derived solely from books). The Roman poet and
improvisatore who tells "The Belated Travellers" is so charmed
by his own capacity for romantic exaggeration that he seems
almost to believe his story, though it is a stock tale of coincidence
and hairbreadth escape from bandits, which is largely, for
Irving, a parody.

Irving's satire, working up to the horror of "The Young
Robber," exposes the dishonesty of fiction that gives the reader
the vicarious thrill of experiencing what is evil or forbidden
without having to suffer any consequences. He brushes aside

the pious pretensions of the sentimental romance, in which the reader is teased by the glamor of sin only to have the heroine finally resist it or to have a blond secondary heroine brought in to save the day for chastity after the dark heroine has been debauched. He reminds his readers throughout Part III that the appeal of much sentimental and gothic fiction is the allure of illicit sex. The bandits, who are, to begin with, symbolic of the forbidden, the outlawed, come before long to stand in the eyes of the travelers for the ultimate in sexual dexterity.

The opening impression of the frame narrative, the "Crack! crack! crack! crack! crack!" of the estafette's whip as he rides trouserless toward the inn, turns into a refrain conveying the suggestion of male sexual prowess. When asked by the "fair Venetian" if the bandits are cruel, the estafette exults in asserting his own masculinity, swearing by the body of Bacchus and, in one quick thrust of activity, glancing at the lady while simultaneously giving his fresh horse the spur and returning the sharp answer, " 'They stiletto all the men; and, as to the women-----' Crack! crack! crack! crack! crack!" (pp. 273–83). The whiplash of the courier as he rides off functions as a comic leer, but the sadistic overtone foreshadows the climax of Part III.[40]

Against the main force of bandit virility stands the chaste virgin of sentimental fiction, facing exposure to, or initiation into, the mystery of sex or love. Innocence is constantly tempted or threatened in the bandit tales, except in the case of the Misses Popkins, where it has already been galvanized to desex them. The heroine of "The Belated Travellers" has the conventional narrow escape from bandit molestation, and the contrast between her miraculous reunion with her true love at the end and the fate of Rosetta, the victim of the assault in "The Young Robber," epitomizes the effect Irving continually strives for in Part III.

[40] The *U.S. Literary Gazette* (I, 229) complained of "indecency drowned in the crack! crack! of the postillion's whip."

A persistently risqué innuendo suggestive of illicit or suppressed sexuality threads its way through the repeated encounters of innocence and experience. The "delicate and droop-
ing" (p. 301) naïveté of the heroine of "The Belated Travellers," for instance, is offset by the worldly sophistication of an
old Spanish princess, who, with the girl, is beseiged by bandits
at an isolated carriage stop. The princess, we are told, "mingled
the woman of dissipation with the devotee. She was actually on
her way to Loretto to expiate a long life of gallantries and
peccadilloes by a rich offering . . ." (p. 308). And the bawdy
comedy of "The Adventure of the Little Antiquary" substitutes
for the innocence of a young girl that of another of Irving's
"rusty, musty" old bachelor-scholars, "always groping among
ruins." Instead of robbing him of his prize possession—the
Venus in his antique intaglio ring, which he worships with the
"zeal of a voluptuary"—the bandits simply show him that the
ring is a counterfeit and "his Venus a sham" (pp. 289–94).

But it is in the comic relationship between the Venetian lady
and an English gentleman in the frame narrative that the sexual
suggestion becomes clearest as commentary on the basic allure
of sensational fiction. Irving is refreshingly frank in his treatment of this woman, making her, significantly, not a virgin
but a young wife on her honeymoon, and hinting that initiation
has not so much deepened her love for her husband as heightened
her general sexual curiosity. The stories she hears about the
bandits are an outlet for this curiosity, though to herself she
disguises it as fear, and her exaggerated display of fear serves
as a device for attracting male attention. The plot of the frame
narrative turns on her attempts to provoke an amorous response
in a skeptical English *Milor,* a stock character who absolutely
refuses to believe in the threat of attack by bandits and dismisses all the stories as nonsense. The "fair Venetian's" sexual
interest in the man is allowed to become all but overt: " 'I have
no patience with these Englishmen,' said she, as she got into bed—
'they are so cold and insensible!' " (p. 368). In the end, after
they have left the inn, he *is* aroused, though he remains as un-
demonstrative and inarticulate as ever; and in what in the

context is another parody of the conventional thriller, she comes as close to getting what she seems unconsciously to want as Irving's comedy can allow. Bandits attack her party and are on the point of ravishing her when the Englishman, coming along the road behind, rescues her, noiselessly and singlehandedly. Freed from the gang that has overpowered her husband, she throws herself into the arms of her deliverer: he has finally proven himself, in that ambiguous phrase earlier invoked in Part III, *un gallant uomo*.

A good deal of the time, it must be admitted, sex is introduced furtively in *Tales of a Traveller* through innuendo that is not expected to register on the pure of mind.[41] And when Irving deals with the subject overtly in "The Young Robber," one sees, as in the violence in Part I, both compulsion and constraint. Something in him apparently has to be expressed, but when it finally bursts out, the abruptness suggests compunctions. Unable to transform himself fully into the young robber, he uses as narrator an intelligent and educated Frenchman, who gives the story in the youth's own words "as near as I can recollect" (p. 353). The Frenchman's memory is imperfect and his own style too elevated for the savage disclosures it conveys. Irving thus softens the blow for his readers and himself. Nonetheless, the situation carries considerable force.[42]

The gruesome appropriateness of "The Young Robber" to Part III is that it actually gives the sentimental heroine the savage love that, one is inclined to argue, the reader always unconsciously hopes she will get, a love that, destroying what she is— the embodiment of purity and innocence—means her death. During one of the robbers' forays the young protagonist secretly visits Rosetta but is detected by the others, who are constantly on the lookout for kidnap victims. They carry her off, and when her

---

[41] And what the *U.S. Literary Gazette* remarked about "the description of Dolph Heyliger's mistress" applies in parts of the *Tales* as well—that which "might have been said openly without any breach of propriety" is "slyly smothered" and thus becomes an "indelicacy" (I, 229).

[42] The *U.S. Literary Gazette* called "The Young Robber" a "shocking story," in which "a scene the most revolting to humanity is twice unnecessarily forced on the reader's imagination" (I, 229).

father refuses to pay ransom for the girl on the ground that she is already dishonored, bandit law dictates that she must die.

Rosetta's chastity is emphasized by her fairness in contrast to the "sunburnt females" (p. 354) of her town. On the day that she is carried off for ransom by the robbers, she is appropriately arrayed in white, for it is to her death-marriage that she is bound. The hero cannot—perhaps will not—rescue her. Although he does not participate in the mass ravishing, he realizes that he has been an accomplice, having been solely responsible for her capture, and he has hoped, once she was taken captive, to keep her for himself. Even before her death sentence is pronounced, he plans to demand to be her executioner. And when he finally has her to himself in the blackness of the forest at night, he has no thought of suicide or of sacrificing himself in an attempt to free her. Rather, he flatly accepts the bandit law and performs his joint act of love and execution with a deliberateness that suggests ritual. Rosetta lies locked in his arms the better part of the night, and—the most convincing touch in the whole story—he takes a lover's pride in describing his agility with the dagger. In contrast to the raping, her death comes with "a painful and concentrated murmur, but without any convulsive movement" (p. 363).

It is a demonstration of Irving's antididacticism that he withholds judgment or indictment. Terror and revulsion do not cut off sympathy, even though the young robber transforms himself, without quite realizing that it is *he* who has undergone initiation, into a full-fledged outlaw. There is a sense in which her father's refusal to ransom Rosetta has had compelling appropriateness: she was *already* dishonored in the young robber's intention. One interprets motives here, without pretending certainty. The narrative is not explicit, but one begins by observing the combination of horror and satisfaction in the final killing, implying who is to say precisely what permutations of love, reverence, fear, hate and profanation, directed toward what objects. Irving's own conscious awareness of the ambiguities was no doubt less than complete. But this rather heightens than discourages interest. The image of female innocence had inspired enough devotion in him, as both his life and work attest, that the savagery of the assault on the sentimental heroine in "The Young Robber" implicates him in his own fiction.

Rosetta, it should be noted, like Bianca in Part I, is an example of the dominant figure of what Leslie Fiedler calls the "Sentimental Love Religion," that is, the virtual deification of the sentimental heroine in fiction in the wake of Richardson. Fiedler sees this as part of a general reaction against the austerity of Protestantism, particularly Calvinism.[43] The imagery of "The Young Italian," as we have seen, virtually transforms Bianca into Virgin and Mother. Ottavio's love for her is part of a revolt against the paternal aspect of religion. The murder and remorse suggest the intensity of hatred and guilt attached to the reaction. One can't be sure whether fear of his father or antipathy to puritanical religion moved Irving most, but there is no doubt of his aptitude for using the two emotions as metaphors for each other.

In "The Young Robber" we find another protagonist in conflict with paternal authority. He defies his father's wish that he go into the church—which would mean celibacy as well as submission to rigid discipline—and finds "easy success" among the "sunburnt" girls of the town (pp. 354–55). But his promiscuity, which never fully satisfies him, seems a function of a capacity for idolizing women, probably in part a compensation for failure to reach the inaccessible. As the story goes on, it is Rosetta's father who becomes the chief embodiment of the paternalism which the suitor is driven to oppose. He keeps Rosetta secure at home, so that the young man can get near her only in church, or by stealing into the vineyard where she occasionally walks. When the father picks out a potential husband for her—*another* older man to block the young man's way—the two suitors fight, and the older is killed. Eventually taking refuge in a gang of robbers, the hero soon discovers himself under the domination of an outlaw as rigidly authoritarian as any in the community he has fled: his new "father," the robber chief, though originally himself a rebel against tyranny, has become an absolute sovereign.

[43] *Love and Death*, chap. i.

Again in "The Young Robber" the church has two sets of connotations, male and female. Its severity and discipline relate it to paternal authority, which the protagonist rejects in refusing to become an ecclesiastic. Yet he establishes his own "Sentimental Love Religion" by going to church to worship Rosetta, his private virgin, whose white raiment mirrors his immaculate conception of her. And while mothers, on the literal level, are omitted from this story, the church becomes a virtual mother to the young robber after he kills Rosetta's suitor, since it offers him temporary sanctuary from law, judgment, and punishment.

The yearning for a maternal manifestation of divinity thus makes itself felt through Irving's young Italians. For all his apparent casualness about religion, he shared in certain attitudes that had much to do with the shaping of American literature's concern with the puritan tradition. Part of him joins the quest for a god of love as refuge from the terrible vengeance of a god of power, a quest that was to become fully explicit in the corposants scene in *Moby-Dick,* where Captain Ahab defiantly orders God the father to appear in His "lowest form of love," as "holy mother," if He wants to be worshiped.

Yet something in Irving seems also to revolt. One wonders whether the outrage he commits against the sentimental heroine through the agency of the chief, the band, and the young robber is an act of vengeance or an attempt at exorcism that he feels compelled to make. Defining the personal significance of any detail is impossibly risky. Yet one can hardly overlook the fact that only recently, as he was trying to write *Tales of a Traveller,* he had been paying court to another young woman who seemed a perfect embodiment of purity and innocence. Indeed, if anything, Emily Foster seems to have carried the pursuit of goodness and virtue even farther than Matilda Hoffman had. An ardent evangelical, Emily took an active interest in Irving's religious attitudes. He did not respond, however, to the low-church side of her.[44] Just how much he did care for her, whether he actually proposed to her and was rejected, is not clear. Once more, the situation was complicated by his interest in a mother,

[44] See Wagenknecht, pp. 143, 155–56, 202.

in this case Emily's own mother, and the theory has been advanced that again Irving, though he couldn't admit it to himself, was actually in love with the mother rather than the daughter.[45]

In any case, this was a period when memories of Matilda, her stepmother, his engagement fifteen years earlier, and Matilda's death were, we know, revived and intensified. Of Irving's unhappiness on leaving the Fosters after the Dresden interlude there is no doubt.[46] He was thrust back into a loneliness to which he had never fully accommodated himself. His emotional life was destined to incompleteness, to a division between casual flirtations or, possibly, sexual encounters and an almost quixotic worship of the ideal from afar.

Tales of a Traveller seems surely in part a product of the turmoil of this period. One must at least observe the conflicting emotions: the lure of forbidden sex and the consequent sense of guilt in "The German Student," the murderous frenzy of Ottavio and the young robber over the loss of Bianca and Rosetta, and the final violence of the deflowering of innocence. More seems to lie behind these stories than simple, unadulterated grief or frustration. One senses a confusion in Irving's motives, and some shame at the confusion. Something in him, perhaps resentment at having, in one way or another, been forbidden full emotional satisfaction, perhaps resentment at having almost desexed himself out of loyalty to Matilda's memory, seems to seek vengeance on the sentimental heroine. Given free rein with conventional gothic material, he half-consciously exposes the suppressed and possibly distorted feelings implicit in the appeal of the sentimental or romantic ordeal of innocence. The more exaggerated the ideal of purity, the greater the likelihood that the basic desire which creates and enshrines the ideal is tainted. This was to be the great discovery of Melville in *Pierre*.

For the end (Part IV) of *Tales of a Traveller*, Irving goes back to his American scenes and subjects and to the type of story that he was especially suited to write. His legends, largely com-

---

[45] Heiman, *American Imago*, XVI, 26–27.
[46] Reichart, pp. 104–5.

pounded from scraps of folk tales and popular fiction that he was apt, like the traveler and reader he was, to have picked up almost anywhere, are a good compromise between gothic urgency and the looseness of eighteenth-century narrative (whether in picaresque or periodical *récits*), between focusing on the matter of fact and on the extraordinary or supernatural. They enable Irving to utilize his eye for image and to characterize by reflection and suggestion, since in the folk stereotypes he uses he has no particularly complicated personalities to contend with. He does not, of course, work very well inside character unless the persona is someone more or less like himself—Crayon, for instance, or one of the other nervous narrators. Legends also bring his sense of place and sense of time or timing into greater play, for with characters who are neither significant enough to stand by themselves as universals nor sufficiently introverted to ignore the external world, he needs at least an immediacy of impression. He achieves this in part by establishing harmonies between character and terrain, by producing the picturesqueness of local color.

Furthermore, without resorting to parody or burlesque of the form he is using, he is able in the American section to continue reminding his readers of the fictitiousness of fiction and to tie *Tales of a Traveller* together by his most convincing demonstration of the fact that the effect of the story depends primarily not on what it is but how it is told. His narrators have a way of telling pretty much the same story in different forms, and Irving does not seem to mind our seeing the similarity. In Part IV the story becomes the vanity, the mutability, of what the subtitle of "Wolfert Webber" calls "Golden Dreams." In "Buckthorne" they were called "Great Expectations," a phrase which, while specifically anticipating Dickens, serves also as a reminder of the extent to which the didacticism of the eighteenth century and the romanticism of the nineteenth made coming of age the substance of fiction, using youth as an archetype to represent the frustrations of being human.

Parts I and III tell with passion the basic story of the unfulfilled promise, the exploded illusion, and Part II tells it philosophically, "without vexation of spirit," though Buckthorne and Crayon both "perceive the truth of the saying, that 'all is vanity' " (p. 168). After the hopes and despairings of youth— the German student, Ottavio, the "poor-devil author," Buckthorne's "strolling manager," the bandit chief, and the young robber—Irving turns youthful desire, longing, or lust into middle-aged avarice in Tom Walker and Wolfert Webber and presents much the same story—as an old story, as a legend.

It was essentially the story that the alienated observer had been fond of telling on himself and his world all along, the nervous narrator's story ("The Stout Gentleman") of the final satisfaction that gets away. Before long, the burden of this lament was to become an impediment to Irving's development as a writer. For the time being, within the framework of *Tales of a Traveller*, it did not hurt to have situations and characters repeating themselves in the same way that Webbers from one generation to the next continue to resemble one another, to have the "inquisitive" gentleman's literal-mindedness in Part I evolve not only into the skepticism of the *Milor* in Part III but into the indifference of a "one-eyed" captain in Part IV, who has little to say in response to tales of buried treasure but "Fudge!" And there is a general appropriateness in reminding the reader that the devil is ubiquitous, that is, in one sense a commonplace: "in all the stories which once abounded of these enterprises, the devil played a conspicuous part" (p. 387). These "enterprises" are the treasure hunts of Part IV, "The Money Diggers." The devil presides "at the hiding of the money," taking it "under his guardianship; . . . this, it is well known, he always does with buried treasure, particularly when it has been ill-gotten" (p. 391). He changes only his name from one context to another:

"I am the wild huntsman in some countries; the black miner in others. In this neighborhood I am known by the name of the black woodsman. I am he to whom the red men consecrated this spot, and in honor of whom they now and then roasted a white man, by way of sweet-smelling sacrifice. Since the red men have been exterminated by you white savages, I amuse myself by presiding at the persecutions of Quakers and Anabaptists; I am the great patron and prompter of slave-dealers, and the grand-master of the Salem witches."

"The upshot of all which is, that . . . you are he commonly called Old Scratch." (p. 396)

Almost everyone attends to the tale of golden dreams and great expectations. People who have any imagination at all are busy listening to it or re-enacting it. Most, like the "fair Venetian," Tom Walker, and Wolfert Webber, do both. No one ever learns enough from this story to get what he most desires, and this is the story. It is always, in a larger sense, a *folk* tale. Man spends his life verifying it. Buckthorne's adventures lead to the resignation of laughing at, as one of his friends says, "the humbug of the great and little world; which I take it, is the essence of practical philosophy" (p. 268). Even so, there can hardly be a happy ending unless it is imposed by an author from without. Only a few, like Wolfert Webber, are granted this reward.

Part IV again leaves plot up in the air: "In fact, the secret of all this story has never to this day been discovered; whether any treasure were ever actually buried at that place" (p. 471).[47] Irving gives rumors instead of truth and even treats character cavalierly. Wolfert Webber, almost dead of being unable to find buried treasure, hears that he has become rich through an unexpected increase in the value of his modest property and cries, "Say you so?" Whereupon, "half thrusting one leg out of bed," he announces, "why, then I think I'll not make my will yet!" (p. 475). He gets up to finish out a long life.

For all the gothic machinery of rumors of treasure, dreams, and mysterious figures rising out of the sea and returning to it, there is no ghost in "Wolfert Webber" but "the ghost of a money-bag" (p. 458). What occasionally makes the story intense is Irving's sense of humor (or ruling passion), which threatens to transform caricature into monstrosity. He begins to speak of the Webbers quite whimsically: "The whole family genius, during several generations, was devoted to the study and

---

[47] The quotation is from "Wolfert Webber." The same device is used in "The Devil and Tom Walker." *TT*, p. 400.

development of . . . one noble vegetable," the cabbage. And he goes on mock-heroically, "The Webber dynasty continued in uninterrupted succession; and never did a line give more unquestionable proofs of legitimacy. The eldest son succeeded to the looks as well as the territory of his sire . . ." (pp. 410–11). Naturally enough, the Webbers look like cabbages. This is normality. But after three seemingly prophetic dreams Wolfert stops raising cabbages by day and begins to work his land for gold at night. Now the harder he works the poorer he becomes. He digs away the rich soil and turns up "sandy barrenness." Fruit ripens on the trees, birds fly from their nests, and caterpillars turn into moths fluttering "with the last sunshine of summer." But with the falling leaves whispering of winter, Wolfert Webber has no harvest.

> Haggard care gathered about his brow; he went about with a money-seeking air, his eyes bent downwards into the dust, and carrying his hands in his pockets, as men are apt to do when they have nothing else to put into them. He could not even pass the city almshouse without giving it a rueful glance, as if destined to be his future abode. (pp. 426–27)

Remembering now the beginning of *Moby-Dick*, with Ishmael, the "hypos" getting the better of him, discovering that he is "involuntarily pausing before coffin warehouses, and bringing up the rear of every funeral," one comes to appreciate the persistence of comic compulsiveness or "gothic risibility" as an approach to character in nineteenth-century American fiction.[48] Wolfert Webber, frantically bent on unearthing buried gold, is a not-too-distant relative of General Von Poffenburgh, who madly decapitates cabbages in *Knickerbocker*, and he is the next of kin to Hawthorne's Peter Goldthwaite, who, as a treasure-hunter, goes him one better, tearing apart the inside of his house instead of digging up his garden.

Irving's best work starts with the ludicrous and pushes to the verge of the fearful. "The Devil and Tom Walker," sparing

---

[48] In a lecture for a course on the novel at Harvard in 1951, Thornton Wilder attributed what he believed was a false style in the early pages of *Moby-Dick* to Melville's efforts to emulate the Knickerbocker school.

the reader an obvious moral, is able, in its somewhat harum-
scarum, folktalish way, to bring certain aspects of Puritanism
into dramatic focus by connecting Yankee shrewdness and Puritan respectability. Irving starts with the comic Yankee stereotype, like the lean, litigious New England lawyers of *Knickerbocker*, but develops, in advance of Hawthorne, an imagery of
darkness, rottenness, and emptiness to contrast with the seemingly shining solidity of proper and pious professions; he sees
the traditional encounter with the devil in forest and swamp as a
function of attitudes visible in pulpit and counting house.[49] For
Irving gothic props ultimately help make a legend out of something ordinary in American experience. The commonplace becomes slightly fantastic or grotesque. It is in this transformation
that he relies most on those elements in fiction which he told
Brevoort he most valued: the "play of thought, sentiment, and
language; the weaving in of characters, . . . the half-concealed
vein of humour."

The comic clash of mundane and erudite connotations in
Irving's prose style often enhances this sense of oddity in the
narrative. Tom Walker's horse, for instance,

> whose ribs were as articulate as the bars of a gridiron, stalked about
> a field, where a thin carpet of moss, scarcely covering the ragged
> beds of puddingstone, tantalized and balked his hunger; and some-
> times he would lean his head over the fence, look piteously at the
> passer-by, and seem to petition deliverance from this land of famine.
> (p. 392)

Playing off the commonplace against the elegant and the refined sustains the seriocomic tone which is so essential to the
voice of Crayon, the nervous gentleman, or to the later Knicker-

---

[49] In both "Tom Walker" and "Philip of Pokanoket" Irving begins to depict
the Puritan's sense of being in close contact with the "invisible world." In part
at least he derived his knowledge of the Puritan conception of the supernatural
directly from reading the Mathers. In "Philip of Pokanoket" (*SB*, p. 364) he
refers specifically to Increase Mather. Osborne's "Irving's Development" suggests
that Cotton Mather's *Magnalia* is the source of some of the ideas and images in
"Tom Walker." Unpublished Ph.D. dissertation, University of North Carolina,
1947, p. 369. The impression that Cotton Mather made on Irving can be further
gauged in Ichabod Crane's superstitiousness (tied directly to his reading of
Mather—see *SB*, pp. 423–24) and in the treatment of the witchcraft delusion in
Knickerbocker. K, pp. 281–84.

bocker, who is again the narrator in Part IV of the *Tales*.[50] Much
of the time the voice is at least mildly ironic, perhaps almost
unconsciously whimsical, as when it brings studied witticism
and wordplay, alliteration, balanced antithesis, hyperbole,
literary allusion, and extensive metaphor to bear on the homely
subject of Tom Walker's hypocrisy:

> Having secured the good things of this world, he began to feel
> anxious about those of the next. He thought with regret on the
> bargain he had made with his black friend, and set his wits to work
> to cheat him out of the conditions. He became, therefore, all of a
> sudden, a violent church-goer. He prayed loudly and strenuously, as
> if heaven were to be taken by force of lungs. Indeed, one might
> always tell when he had sinned most during the week, by the clamor
> of his Sunday devotion. The quiet Christians who had been modestly
> and steadfastly travelling Zionward, were struck with self-reproach
> at seeing themselves so suddenly outstripped in their career by this
> new-made convert. Tom was as rigid in religious as in money
> matters; he was a stern supervisor and censurer of his neighbors,
> and seemed to think every sin entered up to their account became
> a credit on his own side of the page. (p. 404)

But in the end Tom Walker's pretensions are undercut by the
bluntness of the language used to describe the sudden deterioration of his estate. "On searching his coffers all his bonds and
mortgages were found reduced to cinders." Here was an image
of which both Irving and Hawthorne were fond: "In place of
gold and silver his iron chest was filled with chips and shavings.
. . ." And Irving finishes Tom off with, "two skeletons lay in his
stable instead of his half-starved horses, and the very next day
his great house took fire and was burnt to the ground" (pp.
406–7).

Irving's American legend develops out of a few basic themes
or images. Around Tom Walker's "forlorn-looking house" stand
several "straggling savin-trees, emblems of sterility" (p. 392).
What sends him to the devil is a wife like the one from whom
Rip Van Winkle was unconsciously running. Yet at the same

[50] I have made a more extensive comment on Irving's style in my introduction
to the Irving section in *Major Writers of America*, ed. Perry Miller (New York,
1962), I, 189–90. See also Stanley T. Williams' Introduction to Irving's *Selected
Prose* (New York, 1950), pp. xi–xv.

Junior

time Tom is just the husband calculated to drive a wife into the forest with the household valuables as an offering to the Black Man. Who is to say which comes first in the Yankee (American), acquisitiveness or emotional or sexual barrenness? The important thing is that, as so often in Irving, the qualities are implicit in each other. It is the stark imagery of the lovelessness of Tom Walker's marriage that momentarily gives a routine tale of New England miserliness a nearly numbing intensity like that which, for all the underplaying, occasionally takes the reader unawares in "Rip Van Winkle." Dame Walker rushing off with her "silver teapot and spoons" in her apron (pp. 398–99) is a woman either completely desexed by miserliness and hatred or so starved for love that she is willing to set up housekeeping in the forest with the devil. And perhaps in her these are the same thing. In any event, the encounter with the devil consumes her much more quickly than it does her husband, who subsequently discovers her apron in the forest, "hanging in the branches of [a cypress] tree, with a great vulture perched hard by." Symbolism can hardly convey more than we sense at this point. Tom Walker, looking at the actual remains of his wife, sees also in the vulture the symbol of the thing that gnawed on her in her life, the thing that in the form of the Black Man destroyed her and that still presumably preys upon her in hell. But he is also contemplating the emblem of what will happen to himself: "As he scrambled up the tree, the vulture spread its wide wings, and sailed off screaming into the deep shadows of the forest. Tom seized the checked apron, but woeful sight! found nothing but a heart and liver tied up in it" (pp. 399–400).

Yet Irving's America, when it is de-puritanized, is still, if not the land of milk and honey, at least the land of the fat cabbages and pumpkins renowned in native humor and folklore. In "Wolfert Webber" moneygrubbing temporarily transforms a rotund Dutchman into a lean Yankee, but cabbages and not savin trees are the dominant image of this story. Initially, as the city expands and encroaches upon the suburbs, Wolfert's small farm is "hemmed in by streets and houses," intercepting "air and sunshine." City riffraff molest his property. "The expenses of living doubled and trebled; but he could not double and treble the magnitude of his cabbages; and the number of competitors prevented the increase of price; . . . while every one around him grew richer, Wolfert grew poorer . . ." (pp. 412–13). But if he becomes before long a dreary autumnal figure, his daughter belongs to spring and summer. She "ripened and ripened, and rounded and rounded." At seventeen we find her "ready to burst out of her bodice, like a half blown rose-bud" (p. 414). And it is the practical daring of his daughter's suitor which pulls Wolfert out of his middle-aged slump. The love that redeems greed here is a very mundane affair, not idealized or pedestalized but made deliberately profane, if not indeed sacrilegious. Locating a "soft valley of happiness" between her breasts, like a landmark toward which pilgrims progress, Irving decorates the "entrance" with a "little cross," suspended from a "chain of yellow virgin gold" as though to "sanctify the place" (p. 414). As one might expect, Amy becomes explicitly an antisentimental heroine. Wolfert, in his anxiety about his finances, forbids the house to Dirk Waldron, her suitor, who, though a "lively, stirring lad," has "neither money nor land." On the surface Amy proves

a pattern of filial piety and obedience. She never pouted and sulked; she never flew in the face of parental authority; she never flew into a passion, nor fell into hysterics, as many romantic novel-read young ladies would do. Not she, indeed! She was none such heroical rebellious trumpery, I'll warrant ye. On the contrary, she acquiesced like an obedient daughter, shut the street door in her lover's face, and if ever she did grant him an interview, it was either out of the kitchen window, or over the garden fence. (pp. 416–17)

Here, for better or worse, was the spirit that was to conquer the continent. And when Wolfert stops looking for Eldorado in his cabbage patch, abandons the hope of pirate loot in favor of a more modest form of profiteering "over the garden fence" in real estate, he steps out of the grave he has been digging for himself and returns to life again.

IX

The Unreal World
of Washington Irving

INTIMIDATED by the hostile reviews of *Tales of a Traveller*, Irving began to feel "extremely anxious to secure a little income from my literary property, that shall put me beyond the danger of recurring penury; and shall render me independent of the necessity of laboring for the press . . . publishing is detestable."[1] He was haunted by an "evil genius" in Paris who made a special point of telling him how roughly the critics were handling him in England and by an anonymous "friend" who sent him unfavorable notices from the United States.[2] For several months he did little writing. Meanwhile, financial setbacks dimmed his prospect of gaining freedom from authorship. Though he had no dearth of relatives and friends in business to suggest seemingly safe speculative schemes, too often he lost money on them. He had invested in a Rouen steamboat line[3] and had had hopes for a "very pretty little sum annually" from "the Bolivar copper mine."[4] But profits did not materialize. The failure of a London bank wiped out a fund he had set aside for his brother Peter, now an invalid.[5] And early in 1826 two British publishers failed—"severe shocks in the trading world of literature."[6]

[1] Letter to Brevoort, 11 December 1824, *WIHB*, II, 184.
[2] See PMI, II, 218, 228, 253.
[3] STW, I, 288.
[4] See PMI, II, 240–41.
[5] STW, I, 291.
[6] Irving to A. H. Everett, 31 January 1826, PMI, II, 249. Murray, Irving's own publisher, did not succumb. Irving worried, however; one of the failures, Constable and Co., had recently proposed that he write a life of Washington for it. PMI, II, 238.

In the midst of the bad news, in the latter part of 1825, he had begun working on a collection of essays treating aspects of American life. Apparently they were to be in part an answer to a growing tendency in the United States to criticize him as an expatriate who had been neglecting his own country.[7] He had substantially written several of the essays by January of 1826, when he put them aside in favor of a literary endeavor that seemed to offer larger and more immediate financial returns. Alexander H. Everett, the American Minister to Spain, whom Irving had met previously in Paris and the Hague, urged him to come to Madrid in order to make an English translation of a book on Christopher Columbus which was about to be published by the Spanish historian Martín Fernández de Navarrete. Irving, who wanted to go to Spain anyway, took the word of Everett, one of the esteemed *North American Review* essayists, as to the significance of the book.[8] When he arrived at Madrid, he discovered that it was a collection of source materials relevant to Columbus rather than a coherently developed narrative. But, shrewdly perceiving the need for a biography based on Navarrete's researches, he set to work at once to write the *Life and Voyages of Christopher Columbus.*[9]

Thus began his transformation into a biographer, historian, and antiquarian purveyor of legends. From now on, circumstances would combine to pull him largely away from fiction. He would never make enough money to free himself from writ-

[7] Irving's "Note book containing extracts of poetry & prose, hints of a tale or farce . . ." ("bound as Memoranda in hand of Irving," unpublished manuscript in the New York Public Library) contains quotations from Horace, Voltaire, Byron, and Irving's friend Egerton Brydges, all offering consolation to authors beset by carping and laborious critics. Other passages, from Voltaire and Milton, have a bearing on the question of an author's responsibility to his country. Williams believed that the essays would have contained strong criticism of America. STW, I, 292. Unfortunately, the manuscript has not survived.

[8] Four days after hearing from Everett, Irving wrote his friend C. R. Leslie in London, asking him to offer the translation to Murray for a thousand guineas if the publisher was interested. Murray preferred to wait and see the manuscript first. PMI, II, 250–51.

[9] The best account of Columbus available in English at the time was the very brief section on him in William Robertson's *The History of America.* Irving designed his biography for "those who learn the history of Columbus . . . for the first time." Letter to Everett, 23 April 1828, PMI, II, 312.

ing, but it would be easier to find historical subjects with popular appeal and to handle them in a way that was professionally
acceptable than to write tales and sketches that would satisfy both
the public and himself. The strain on the inventive faculty was
not so great. And if antiquarianism finally proved a kind of
trap, it was not in turning him into a grubbing little sublibrarian. There was a social side to scholarship that the little man in
black had never suspected, the companionship of book-collec-
tors, gentleman historians and bibliographers, academics, and
government officials like Everett, all with a stake in high culture.

One sometimes regrets the change. *Tales of a Traveller*
shows an insight into the nature and function of short fiction
that might have taken him farther, even in spite of his reluctance
or inability to look to the magazines as a vehicle for publication
and to concentrate on the single story standing by itself. But
doubts hover above such a surmise. Anxiety about keeping up
his reputation would hardly have been diminished by his inability to vary significantly the one tale to which he tended to
reduce all experience. His difficulty was both temperamental
and intellectual. His literary vitality had always depended on
his somehow fighting his own judgments and conclusions—
fighting them in the very process of accepting them. If he
found the world nonsensical, he had at least been able to laugh
at it, often in the beginning in indignation. But now he was
beginning to be resigned to the great world's littleness. The
joke was growing tiresome, almost ceasing to be a joke. And
where laughter did not altogether subside in nostalgia, it
threatened to become merely automatic.

Not that there was anything approaching a sudden collapse.
Indeed, to the casual observer the transition from the middle
to the final phase in Irving's career, his evolution into the elder
statesman of American literature, may seem to be contingent
on little more than his return to America in 1832 and the shift
of his interest from fiction to history. His six years in Spain
were highly productive, and at least two of the four books that
came out of that sojourn represent Irving at close to top form.
It is only when the Spanish works are taken together that one

sees the gradual stifling of imagination in one single stock response.

Before that happened, the theme of mutability metamorphosed Columbus from a renaissance and neoclassical, into a romantic, hero. Emerging in 1828, almost midway between the *Columbiad* and *Moby-Dick*, Irving's most important non-comic character has more in common with the morbid voyager Ahab than with Barlow's enlightened discoverer. Here the "enchafèd flood" begins to flow into American literature, and the original voyage of discovery, which had once seemed a fit subject for an epic celebration of America, comes instead to look like the beginning of American tragedy.

> For three days there was a continuance of light summer airs from the southward and westward, and the sea was as smooth as a mirror. A whale was seen heaving up its huge form at a distance, which Columbus immediately pointed out as a favorable indication, affirming that these fish were generally in the neighborhood of land. The crews, however, became uneasy at the calmness of the weather. They observed that the contrary winds which they experienced were transient and unsteady, and so light as not to ruffle the surface of the sea, which maintained a sluggish calm like a lake of dead water. Every thing differed, they said, in these strange regions from the world to which they had been accustomed. The only winds which prevailed with any constancy and force, were from the east, and they had not power to disturb the torpid stillness of the ocean; there was a risk, therefore, either of perishing amidst stagnant and shoreless waters, or of being prevented, by contrary winds, from ever returning to their native country. (*C*, I, 149–50)

Beyond this ominous stillness, Columbus is to encounter difficulties which will in time make his years of controversy with those who doubted the possibility of finding the East by sailing west seem trifling. Endless storms and ships wrecked, warfare, cannibalism, rebellion, treachery, imprisonment await him. Arching over all, the rich illusion, the golden dream that it is the Indies that he has found or has to find is gradually to turn his life into an insane quest for the unattainable. And when the illusion subsides, he will be left exposed, in moments of doubt, to guilt and remorse for the suffering in which he has involved others.

Irving's *Columbus* is a diorama of shifting images, analogues, and archetypes. If the admiral is on occasion almost Ahab, he becomes, by the time misery has been piled upon malice in a "perfect jubilee of triumphant villainy" (II, 287–88), a scapegoat in irons, like Billy Budd in the darbies, ready, though innocent, to endure any sacrifice in the name of their Catholic majesties, Ferdinand and Isabella. Religious allusion—including his penchant for donning a monk's habit and going on penitential journeys—makes Columbus a perpetual pilgrim, though what he seeks most of the time is not the Celestial City but a terrestrial paradise. Allegorizing the geography of discovery, he leaves Bunyanesque names behind him on the map— "Cape Thanks to God," the "River of Disaster," the "Coast of Contradictions." Elysium is as far as to the New World, and there it is everywhere and nowhere. Each new island seems more beautiful than the last; exploration leads from one "Valle de Paraiso" to another. The "perfect nakedness" of the natives of Hispaniola seems like the "state of primeval innocence of our first parents" (I, 229). But that state does not endure. Technically, discovering Edens makes Columbus the first American Adam, and, though a comparative innocent, he is implicated in the fall, indeed in many falls. It is not only his original settlement at Hispaniola, La Navidad ("The Nativity"), which proves abortive. He brings the *meum* and *teum* of the Old World with him into every garden and valley.

Irving's shift from fiction to history was in a sense only nominal. While at work on *Columbus*, he wrote Brevoort that people suspected him, on account of his "having dealt so much in fiction," of being unable to "tell truth with plausibility."[10] And if this was not actually his own suspicion, one at least wonders whether he was not aiming for the opposite effect—to tell truth implausibly. His open reversion to a pseudonym in his next "historical" work, *A Chronicle of the Conquest of Granada*, supports such an inference. He put *Columbus* together too hurriedly for it to be as accurate and original as historians

[10] 23 February 1828, *WIHB*, II, 204.

would like it to be.[11] He was even inclined on occasion (perhaps to compensate for the impossibility of doing exhaustive research) to "let his imagination go completely,"[12] reconstructing colorful scenes not only from what existing records clearly indicated had happened, but from what a knowledge of the era of discovery led him to believe *might* have happened. And he heightened diction, tone, and characterization to the point of inviting criticism.[13]

Not that nineteenth-century historians dismissed *Columbus* as unimportant. Stanley Williams' verdict seems sound, that instances where Irving consciously invents facts or distorts what in his time was considered to be the evidence are "relatively rare."[14] In spite of its faults, the book proved to be usable until more detailed studies of the subject appeared.[15] But, although literary historians agree that the book is well written, almost no one reads it today. Nor is the fact that it has been superseded historically the only reason. Gibbon, Prescott, and Parkman, for instance, continue to find readers in spite of the water that has flowed over or seeped through the dams they put up. In addition to style, their works all have bulk and solidity, which give a sense of authoritativeness, and they contain opinions which, because of the strength of the personalities behind them, need to be reckoned with even when they are wrong. The trouble with *Columbus* as history is that there is not enough factual weight to hold it down. It has been praised occasionally, even in the twentieth cenutry, but for the most part only after having been eased into virtually another category from that of history

---

[11] "How incredible," remarks Williams, "to imagine this American more than the interpreter, during his twenty-one months in Madrid," of materials Navarrete had spent 35 years gathering. STW, II, 300. Most of the remainder of my discussion of *Columbus* is taken, with slight changes, from my article "Irving's *Columbus:* The Problem of Romantic Biography," *The Americas*, XIII (October, 1956), 127–40.

[12] Samuel Eliot Morison, *Admiral of the Ocean Sea* (Boston, 1942), I, 117.
[13] STW, I, 322–23.
[14] *Ibid.*, II, 310.
[15] See *The Literature of American History*, ed. J. N. Larned (Boston, 1902), p. 62; Edward G. Bourne, *The Northmen, Columbus, and Cabot, 985–1503* (New York, 1906), pp. 360, 377, 403; Morison, II, 125.

or biography.[16] Williams goes so far as to say it is really a romance.[17]

One can hardly believe that, even as rapidly as he was working, Irving could not, had he desired to, have packed the book with more information than it actually contains. The unassimilated information that he says in his Preface was at his disposal in Madrid in 1826–27 would have been an Eldorado for most scholars. He had access not only to Navarrete's partially published *Colección de los Viages y Descubrimientos* but also to the manuscripts themselves, which it had taken Navarrete a lifetime to collect. Furthermore, he was allowed in Madrid to work in the personal library of the American collector Obadiah Rich, which contained several important unpublished histories of the period of colonization.[18] Yet Irving considered such materials for the most part "minor."[19] What then was major?

Quite simply, what was already generally known about Columbus. For Irving, the story of Columbus did not need to be unearthed in Spanish archives. It simply needed retelling. Irving was to fill it out in certain places and in the end, by shifting emphases, develop an original interpretation. But he did not feel obligated to dig for new facts or question the basic soundness of the story as it had been told and retold countless times. Although he did rely heavily on certain unpublished manuscripts, by and large they were not primary documents, such as letters or state papers, but narratives of the career of Columbus by early writers like Bartolomé de las Casas.[20]

---

[16] See Barrett Wendell, *A Literary History of America* (New York, 1928), p. 179; George H. Putnam, "Irving," in *The Cambridge History of American Literature*, ed. William P. Trent *et al.* (New York, 1917), I, 259; H. S. Canby, *Classic Americans* (New York, 1931), p. 71; Van Wyck Brooks, *The World of Washington Irving*, (New York, 1944), p. 319.

[17] "Washington Irving," in *Literary History of the United States*, ed. Robert E. Spiller *et al.* (New York, 1948), I, 249.

[18] See *Manuscripts and Printed Books in Possession of Obadiah Rich, Esq.* ("Printed by Order of the House of Representatives," 27 December 1827).

[19] Letter to Everett, 23 April 1828, PMI, II, 312–13.

[20] This attitude of Irving toward his materials and the approach to historical composition which it produced led Williams to the conclusion that he deserved

Versions of the story had appeared in long and studious histories of the Indies or of America, in collected and uncollected narratives of remarkable voyages and discoveries, and in anthologies of famous lives. Yet it had been told in a noticeably conventionalized way. The form had sprung in part, apparently, from the records Columbus had made of his own life in journals and letters, many of which had been available to both his son Ferdinand and to Las Casas, the original historians of the discovery of America. These two had composed in rather similar fashions, often quoting or paraphrasing Columbus himself. Antonio de Herrera in his turn had relied almost exclusively on Las Casas and Ferdinand; in form he was closer to Ferdinand. And since Las Casas' *Historia de las Indias* remained unpublished, Herrera and Ferdinand had become the chief sources for most of the later accounts. After the early eighteenth-century translations of Ferdinand and Herrera, the words themselves, from one version to another (in English at least), begin to have a familiar ring.[21]

Time and again, whether they elaborated or condensed, writers arranged parts of the whole story in approximately the same relation to each other. The opinions of the ancients about geography and the New World usually came near the beginning, closely tied to the reasons that induced Columbus to infer the existence of lands to the west. During the second voyage there was apt to be a description of the customs of the natives of Hispaniola based largely on Fray Ramón Pane's account left among the papers of Columbus. And Columbus' reunion with his brother Bartholomew some time later was the occasion for the full story of the latter's mission to England, begun many years previously. After (and not before or during) the narrative of the third voyage to the Gulf of Paria and

---

censure for his "plagiarism, if such it may be called." I have elaborated on Irving's procedure at greater length, attempting to show that "plagiarism" is not the word for it, in "Irving's *Columbus*," pp. 130–31.

[21] Herrera, *The General History of America*, trans. John Stevens (London, 1725), Vol. I; *"The Life of" Christopher Columbus . . . "Written by His Own Son,"* D. Ferdinand Columbus, in *A Collection of Voyages and Travels*, ed. Awnsham and John Churchill (London, 1704), Vol. II.

northward to Hispaniola, the theory that Columbus elaborated that the earth is pear-shaped and crowned at the stem by the terrestrial paradise was usually revealed. The end of the third voyage introduced news of the discoveries of other navigators. And the end of Columbus' life brought the reader to his character.[22]

In spite of formal variations, the character of Columbus had remained substantially the same. A wise man, in spite of kings and administrators, he had led a life so little blameworthy that it served to atone for the lusts and avarice of others. It is true that Oviedo had accused him of being a cruel governor[23] and that Las Casas had blamed Indian slavery on Columbus.[24] But these charges had been largely ignored until they were revived by Muñoz[25] and Navarrete;[26] it could be argued that as Spaniards trying to exculpate their countrymen of the supposedly unwarranted slaughter and exploitation of the Indians in the early years of the colonization of Latin America, they were overeager to shift responsibility to the Italian admiral. Otherwise, Columbus was an unlucky viceroy in a wilderness, who bestowed fatherly affection upon the natives until rebellion was provoked by the refusal of his subordinates to obey his prudent directions. He did not need Irving to make him a great man.

With all the heroism, however, there remained in the center of the life of Columbus a common core of suffering. The meaning lurks in a brief summing up such as the following: "Thus died the great and glorious *Columbus* whose Fame will always encrease, but whose Life was a remarkable Instance on what a sandy Foundation they build their Happiness who depend upon the Gratitude of Princes."[27] And it is most explicit

---

[22] All of these arrangements are followed by Irving. For a list of works in which their incidence is very high, see my "Irving's *Columbus*," p. 132, n. 21.

[23] Gonzalo Fernández de Oviedo y Valdés, *Historia General y Natural de las Indias*, ed. José Amador de los Rios (Asunción, n.d.), Bk. II, chap. xiii.

[24] *Historia de las Indias* (Mexico City, Buenos Aires, 1951), Bk. I, chaps. c, cii, civ–cv.

[25] Juan B. Muñoz, *Historia del Nuevo-Mundo* (Madrid, 1793), pp. 241–44.

[26] *Colección de los Viages y Descubrimientos* (Madrid, 1825–37), Vol. I, par. 62.

[27] *The "American" Traveller* (London, 1741), p. 366.

in Pierre François Xavier de Charlevoix, who says that the life
of Columbus was

plus qu'aucune autre mêlée de bonheur & d'adversités, d'opprobres
& d'applaudissemens; de ce que la fortune peut procurer de
Grandeurs à un Particulier, & de ce qu'elle peut lui faire essuyer de
revers. Il jouit peu de sa gloire, & des dignités, dont il fut revêtu;
au contraire, il ne fut presque pas un jour sans avoir à souffrir,
ou les douleurs les plus aiguës, ou les contretems les plus fâcheux,
ou les chagrins les plus cuisans.[28]

The historiography of Columbus, then, had been largely an
accumulation of testimony in acceptance of a set of primitive
beliefs. A lover of folklore, Irving had in Columbus a full-
fledged legendary hero. And his aim in retelling the story,
although he introduced some new material and tried to be accurate, was apparently to make sure that his hero was not forced
to descend out of the realm of myth. Thus he preserved the
general framework or conventions within which Columbus' life
was usually exhibited.

In his *Life and Voyages*, however, he did uncover an internal
source of failure in his hero, a flaw of potentially tragic proportions. He is careful, as we have seen, to emphasize the names
Columbus gave to landmarks in his travels. The name reflects
the idea of a thing, which, for Columbus, is apt to become the
thing in itself. When he is forced to turn back from his quest
for the passage to India on the last voyage, it is more important
to this biography that he believes he is stopped just short of
the Ganges than that the world subsequently knows he is only
coasting along Central America. By fully documenting the piety
of Columbus, which earlier published writers had only mentioned, Irving makes more inevitable the ultimate failure of his
hero. His hopes go far beyond the exploration of a few paltry
islands to the liberation of Jerusalem and the christianizing of
the Grand Khan.

Columbus loses himself in a sort of quixotism, through which,
even though Irving adheres rather closely to most of the conventions of the story, his hero is transformed into something

[28] *Histoire de l'Isle Espagnole ou de S. Domingue* (Amsterdam, 1733), II, 43–44.

other than what he had been for preceding centuries—renaissance theory put into practice. In the end his life becomes what,
though it had largely been forgotten, Las Casas originally
christened it, "un luengo martirio."[29] History here does not
outgrow myth, but the myth becomes richer. Irving was almost
the first writer to have Columbus embark not so much to discover lands unknown to the west as to find a convenient way of
converting spices to gold and the Grand Khan to Christianity
(I, 131–32). More than his predecessors, he helped his hero
build illusions of the Orient out of misconstrued allusions to
the Caribees.[30] And the details of vows and castings of lots,
which earlier historians, impressed by the modernity of Columbus, had had to pass over quickly so that he might not seem over-
superstitious, in this account make his plans for a crusade more
plausible.[31] It had been traditional, for instance, to emphasize
the craftiness of Columbus in sealing an account of his discovery in a barrel against the possibility of the ship's going
down during the storms which accompanied the first voyage
home. But to Irving it is important that when the weather became severe lotteries were held, each man promising that if the
lot fell to him he would, if he got home safely, make a pilgrim-
age to a shrine. More than once Columbus, as though singled
out by Heaven, himself drew the bean marked with a cross and
subsequently fulfilled the vow.

The third voyage, to the verge of what Columbus thought
was literally the earthly paradise, though it might have seemed
somewhat out of the line of the renaissance hero as seen by the
neoclassical historian, comes now as no great surprise.[32] And
when finally we see his visions and hear a voice urging Colum-

---

[29] I, 393.

[30] This is a good example of how Irving selected material. Where Columbus in
his "Journal" seems more often than not preoccupied with recording geographical
data, Irving's summary of the first cruise among the islands serves chiefly to swell
Columbus' hopes that he had actually reached Asia. Cf. *C*, Bk. IV; Navarrete, I,
19–123. For the crusading spirit, Irving relies on a letter from Columbus to the
Pope. Navarrete, I, 280–82.

[31] *C*, I, 252–59, 285–86.

[32] *C*, II, 139–47. Sources here are Las Casas (II, 40–61) and a letter from Columbus to the King and Queen in Navarrete, I, 242–64.

bus to persevere, promising his mission's ultimate fulfillment, we are fully prepared for the obstacles which intervene between him and the completion of the last voyage.[33]

In François Antoine Prévost's *Histoire générale des voïages*,[34] it is true, Columbus and his few real followers, representing righteousness, had begun to seem dwarfed by the forces of evil. And later in Muñoz, Columbus became slightly quixotic in his search for Japan and India and his exacting from his followers an oath that defined Cuba as the beginning of a continent. It was like the Don's asking someone who hadn't seen her to swear that his Dulcinea was the most beautiful woman in the world— Irving was to make this scene even more dramatic (I, 442). In Muñoz also the islands of the New World seemed heavenly until mortalized by avarice.[35] But Prévost's account was only the beginning of a biography. And Muñoz, whose first volume stopped at 1500 and who never completed the rest of his work, was writing not a biography but an entire history of the New World.

It was by utilizing more fully than any of his predecessors the unpublished history of Las Casas and the writings, especially the journal, of Columbus himself that Irving was able to complete the reinterpretation of Columbus.[36] These works were the most important of the "minor" materials in Rich's library and Navarrete's *Colección*. Irving may carefully prepare nineteenth-century readers with such statements as this:

Days of constant perturbation, and nights of sleepless anxiety, preyed upon a constitution broken by age, by maladies and hardships, and produced a fever of the mind, in which he was visited by one of those mental hallucinations deemed by him mysterious and supernatural. (II, 394–95)

[33] *C*, II, 256–57, 410–12. Irving is indebted here to two letters in Navarrete, I, 265–76, 296–312.

[34] Paris, 1754, Vol. XII.

[35] *Historia*, Bk. V, pars. 15–16; Bk. III, pars. 15–25; Bk. V, par. 9; Bk. VI, the very beginning and the very end.

[36] In fiction up to Irving's time Columbus seems to have been little different from the character implied in previous history.

But there have been too many voices and visions explaining
Columbus to himself and to us, too many storms and afflictions
at crossed moments as apparent punishments for sins and pre-
sumptions, too many predictions come true, and altogether too
many points of similarity between this hero and other god-
ridden figures in literature for us to believe any longer that the
motivation is altogether accidental or human. Irving has
adapted from romance the device of symbolic coincidence to
set this story back on a providential basis.

The stereotype suggested by Williams for Irving's Columbus,
"man of sensibility,"[37] is probably illuminating enough if it is
broadly interpreted. Perhaps the one quality he never loses is
his quixotism, the quixotism of the nineteenth century, which
involves the pathos (as opposed to the bathos) of mistaking illusions for reality. It must be observed, however, that though
Columbus, according to Irving's interpretation, is a man of
moods, he has not the diseased will of a Werther or of a nineteenth-century Hamlet. Some of his moods elevate him to an
altogether different role: "As the evening darkened, Columbus
took his station on top of the castle or cabin on the high poop of
his vessel, ranging his eye along the dusky horizon, and maintaining an intense and unremitting watch."[38] And to his crew,
the heroism of the admiral was apt to appear less super- than
inhuman.

> In their secret conferences they exclaimed against him as a
> desperado, bent, in a mad fantasy, upon doing something extravagant
> to render himself notorious. What were their sufferings and dangers
> to one evidently content to sacrifice his own life for the chance of
> distinction? . . . How much further were they to go in quest of a
> merely conjectured land? Were they to sail on until they perished,
> or until all return became impossible? In such case they would be
> the authors of their own destruction. (I, 153)

[37] STW, I, 324.
[38] C, I, 161. To Columbus himself, a swelling of the sea which unexpectedly
interrupts a prolonged calm "seemed providentially ordered to allay the rising
clamors of his crew; [like] that which so miraculously aided Moses when con-
ducting the children of Israel out of the captivity of Egypt." I, 150–51.

Irving allows for as much variation in the temperament of Columbus and in opinions about him as there is change in fortune and the weather. His gentleness, patience, and intelligence in pointing out to his crew that what they read as bad omens are signs of the nearness of land—these qualities in Columbus inspire confidence that he, like Odysseus, has the sort of perseverance necessary for getting safely home. But what seems right and righteousness one moment becomes "obstinacy" the next, "in tempting fate by continuing on into a boundless sea" (I, 150, 158). It did not take much to metamorphose Homer's Odysseus into the Dantesque Ulysses, who passed beyond the Pillars of Hercules to his sorrow. And the boundless ambition of Columbus is occasionally almost Faustian. Indeed it is his intractable resolution to take the crew on with him against their will, though it is from his point of view of divine rather than diabolic inspiration, that most strongly suggests the later, seagoing Faust, Ahab. When his men are boisterous, Columbus "assumed a decided tone. He told them it was useless to murmur; . . . he was determined to persevere, until by the blessing of God, he should accomplish the enterprise" (I, 158–59). His offering (and finally claiming for himself) the reward (a doublet rather than a doubloon) for the man who first sights land (I, 160–61) also suggests Ahab.

In the process of calling new experiences and new-found lands by old names, Irving expatiates to the point of sustaining a Columbus who is not only partially but almost exclusively mythical.[39] For the biography is inescapably general. The events that it describes always resemble or represent one another, and in it a man is always typical of a class, a society, an age, an idea, or of humanity at large. Because the exploration of similitude and dissimilarity is the essence of Irving's method, he, to a much greater extent than most historians, refuses to treat par-

[39] Old and New Testament figures are probably the most numerous type of analogue to Columbus in Irving, a fact which points up the reliance on Las Casas and Columbus himself. Some of the passages in their writings which help to transform the voyages of discovery into a religious quest are: Las Casas, I, 27–28, 160; II, 8, 9, 26, 63; Navarrete, I, 102–3, 113, 265–66 (see notes by Bourne, p. 371), 275 (Bourne, p. 369), 297.

ticular events in isolation. He is general to the point of destroying the significance of particulars. The details of this life are
actually unimportant: what we are concerned with is its "character," its meaning as a whole. History here is completely external or superficial because we view the subject at a distance,
where only a total significance appears. Irving makes little attempt to get inside the subject, to deal with intricate matters of
fact or motive. Economic, social, political, and intellectual considerations are not investigated. It suffices to assume that at this
time, Spain and Portugal were jealous of each other, without
explanation. As far as Irving is concerned, Columbus is de-
tained by the Portuguese on his return from his first voyage because it is his role to meet and overcome opposition until finally
overcome himself. This is the rationale behind the secondary
figures in the story, Roldán, Bobadilla, and Porras. They are
all representatives of the same force, the principle of evil, which
ruins paradises and stains the careers of the best of men.

For Irving, history remained fiction, even though his tone
shifted from the comic to the romantic. *Columbus* is—as much
as any American novel—a romance. It makes the career of
the discoverer of America a fabulous quasi-allegorical quest.
It sees the New World as a land of wonder and enchantment,
where nature contrives effects with bewildering lavishness. In
one sense the newness turns out to be an illusion, part of the
enchantment. Irving, however, remains unsure of the values of
the ordeal of innocence to which he subjects his early American
hero. Thus despite the tragic implications that Irving begins
to bring out in Columbus, his biography gives us a pathetic
world but not quite a tragic hero. The sense of inevitable ruin
still closes down his horizon. Could one ask anything more of
the author of *Knickerbocker*?

Without what is called a tragic vision, Irving's one tale, as
the sound and the fury of his early work had suggested, ran the
risk of signifying nothing, at least if retold once too often.
Small wonder, then, that his next book was a partial parody of
history developed around the character of a sort of Spanish

Knickerbocker, the bigoted Christian chronicler Fray Antonio
Agapida. Irving called this book "a kind of experiment in literature."[40] He could not contemplate it as "a grave historical production, or a work of authority."[41] Neither did he mean it to be
of "a mere light amusing kind"; instead he tried to aim at
"something . . . *between* a history and a romance."[42] He claimed
to have "introduced nothing . . . not founded on historical authority": "every fact is drawn from historical sources."[43] But when
we stumble over his Bolingbroke-like assertion that the book is
a digest of early chronicles and contains "the striking facts and
achievements, *true or false*, of them all,"[44] we begin to wonder
what a "fact" is.

The *Conquest of Granada* begins as a joke. Irving pretends
to be presenting parts of an old chronicle compiled by Fray
Agapida. Many of the early readers thought it was a bad joke:
they took Agapida for a real person and read on expecting accuracy in small details. When some readers tried, and failed, to
find an original manuscript by Agapida, the cry went up that
Irving had taken the name of history (or at least of *Chronicle*)
in vain.[45] But such readers seem to have been overly inclined to
be fooled, for the first function of the joke is to make it obvious
that the criterion of literal fidelity to the sources does not apply
in this context. Agapida is fictitious. The editor's (Irving's)
equivocation on the first page of the Introduction ought to leave
no doubt.

But to go from the book to the sources is to be surprised by its
substantial reliability—that is, if one has assumed that when an
author bothers to invent a chronicler he may as well invent the
chronicle to go with him. As a contemporary study of Prescott
wisely observes, however, "Historians of a later day too easily

[40] Letter to Prince Dmitry Dolgorouki, 10 January 1829, PMI, II, 366.
[41] Letter to A. H. Everett, 21 October 1828, PMI, II, 348.
[42] Letter to Thomas Aspinwall, 4 April 1829, quoted in STW, I, 344–45 (my
italics).
[43] Letter to Dolgorouki, 13 December 1828, PMI, II, 349; letter to T. W. Storrow,
22 October 1828, *Washington Irving and the Storrows*, ed. Stanley T. Williams
(Cambridge, Mass., 1933), p. 134.
[44] Letter to Everett, PMI, II, 348 (my italics).
[45] STW, II, 308–14.

assumed that the romantic school was seduced away from the truth" by glamorous materials.[46] Prescott himself asked readers to compare Irving's account of the wars of Granada with his own in *Ferdinand and Isabella*, to prove, not the soundness of the latter, but the usefulness of the former—as history.[47] The two writers relied on essentially the same sources.[48] Like Irving, Prescott was fond of "a good, gossiping chronicle or memoir"; he actually defended such materials as major and generally reliable historical sources and justified the technique, used in both *Columbus* and *Granada*, of building a history on a foundation of earlier narratives.[49]

Through Agapida, Irving simply excuses himself from having to take infinite pains. The pen name of an historian frees him

[46] William Charvat and Michael Kraus (eds.), *William Hickling Prescott* (New York, 1943), p. liv.

[47] Prescott, *History of the Reign of Ferdinand and Isabella the Catholic*, ed. J. F. Kirk (Philadelphia, n.d.), II, 108.

[48] So did Miguel Lafuente Alcantara in Vols. III and IV of *Historia de Granada* (Granada, 1845–46). The following are the chief sources of the *Conquest of Granada* (the editions in which I have examined them are not necessarily those used by Irving): Andrés Bernáldez, *Historia de los Reyes Católicos Dn. Fernando y Da. Isabel* (Seville, 1870), Vol. I (Irving consulted this in manuscript at Rich's); Geronymo Çurita, *Los Cinco Libros Portreros de la Segunda Parte de los Anales de la Corona de Aragon* (Zaragoza, 1610), Vol. IV; Estevan de Garibay y Çamalloa, *Compendio Historial de las Chrónicas* (Barcelona, 1628), Vol. II; Juan de Mariana, *Historia General de España* (Madrid, 1734), Vol. II; Hernando del Pulgar, *Crónica de los Señores Reyes Católicos* (Valencia, 1780); José Antonio Conde, *Historia de la Dominacion de los Arabes en España* (Madrid, 1821), III, 211–65; [Denis Dominique] Cardonne, *Histoire de l'Afrique et de l'Espagne, sous la domination des Arabes* (Paris, 1765), III, 250–320. For detailed discussion of Irving's use of sources, see Louise M. Hoffman, "Irving's Use of Spanish Sources in *The Conquest of Granada*," *Hispania*, XXVIII (November, 1945), 483–98; STW, II, 309–10.

[49] Charvat and Kraus, p. liii. The connection between Samuel Rogers' "The Voyage of Columbus" (*Poems* [London, 1814]) and Irving's work in both *Columbus* and *Granada* may be fairly close, especially since the two writers were friends as early as 1820. The "Columbus" of Rogers is only a "fragment," and in its machinery it is dependent primarily on the epic tradition. But he defended its extravagance on the ground that the conception of Columbus in his poem was true to the "spirit in the old Spanish Chroniclers of the sixteenth century." *Poems* (London, 1820), p. 175. "Columbus was a person of extraordinary virtue and piety, acting under the sense of a divine impulse" (p. 171). Rogers had read much of the historical literature on Columbus, as his notes show. He pretended that his poem was a translation of a manuscript found in the convent at La Rabida. One is intrigued by the similarity in sound between "La Rabida" and "Fray Antonio Agapida." The *Analectic* had discussed Rogers' "Columbus" in a review of his *Poems* published during Irving's editorship. *AN*, II, 472–83.

from the pretense of being an impartial scientific scrutinizer and enables him to tell the story in whichever way it sounds best, without having to worry about refined criteria for testing the reliability of evidence.[50] The story becomes not so much what actually happened—the truth—as what Agapida reports, as Irving is apt to remind us, for instance, by placing next to Agapida's explanation of certain occurrences a quite incompatible explanation by Arab chroniclers (*G*, pp. 35, 433–34). The book, however, is not a mock-history like *Knickerbocker*. Agapida is mildly amusing, but although Irving is still poking fun at historians, he is trying to take fiction fairly seriously.

In the long run one regrets the lack of historical detail. The recurrence of disaster tends to wear the book down. Irving opens before us a panorama of Andalusia as a constant reiteration of high, sterile sierras intersected by green valleys, each one of which is like paradise. Each is controlled by one town strongly fortified, usually built from the top of a hill to the gardens and orchards surrounding it. Each town is attacked or besieged successively by an army; in every garden there are desperate battles, in which the Christians tangle themselves up in Moorish irrigation ditches. Almost all of the war can be comprehended through any one of these encounters, for this history amounts to little more than many repetitions of the fall of Alhama, the first city taken. From our distant position the knights all look alike, and we recognize the whereabouts of the leaders only by their larger tents or longer trains of attendants.

The short chapters of the book are well adapted to the landscape. Often one of them is just long enough to cover a raid through a valley, the capture of a fortress, a battle in a garden, or some other sally or adventure. Their shortness and regularity emphasize the resemblance of the actions to one another, and it is this resemblance, this repetition, which Irving exploits to unify

[50] In a note (*G*, p. 85) Irving says he prefers to Pulgar, Bernáldez, "that most veracious and contemporary chronicler," whom he had, nevertheless, rejected in the matter of Ali Atar's age, without any explanation (*G*, p. 72). Mariana (II, 485) and Çurita (IV, 321) differ with Bernáldez (I, 172) on this point. Elsewhere (*G*, p. 31, note) Irving claims to be following "the most reliable authorities" but doesn't even say who they are, let alone why they are reliable.

WASHINGTON IRVING

his story, since it lacks the cohesiveness of constantly present and steadily developing characters or plot.

The prediction inspired by the birth of the last King of Granada, Boabdil el Chico, in the very beginning puts the *Conquest* into the same category of literature as any story whose ending is predestined or presupposed; all are like the "book of fate," wherein it is written "that this child will one day sit upon the throne, but that the downfall of the kingdom will be accomplished during his reign" (p. 29). Arabian fatalism gives history a meaning with a familiar ring. The end of the story will be a fall, and what leads up to the end will be a falling.

As long as it is a question of mortality, truth is the same for orthodox Christian, Mohammedan, and skeptic. Thus Irving, while smiling at the excesses of bigotry in the old chroniclers, nonetheless can rely to a large extent on their formulations of events, their style, tone, and imagery, to convey his own feelings about the story. The effort to universalize, to capitalize on a wealth of suggestive language and detail in order to turn the fall of Granada into an emblem of mutability, is the chief significance of the book. "In a word, so beautiful was the earth, so pure the air, and so serene the sky, of this delicious region, that the Moors imagined the paradise of their Prophet to be situated in that part of the heaven which overhung the kingdom of Granada" (pp. 19–20). Granada is, quite simply, Eden, no longer Granada. The unqualified epithets of fable, proverb, and Oriental tale almost reduce it to a pure symbol. Its entire existence is in the implication of something beyond it. Its loss will be exile from paradise.

Other events in the story get their primary meaning only in relation to this crowning loss. Thus Zahara "is but a type of Granada" (p. 36). And Alhama is "the key of Granada" (p. 48). When the Christians take it in retaliation for Zahara, and a Moorish horseman rides to Granada with the news, " 'Woe is me, Alhama!' was in every mouth; and this ejaculation of deep sorrow and doleful foreboding, came to be the burthen of a plaintive ballad, which remains until the present day" (p. 48). When Irving repeats something like this burthen after almost every loss, chapters of his book begin to seem like the stanzas of the ballad.[51]

For a time, Moorish and Christian forays balance one another, sometimes chapter by chapter. And Agapida's manner of speaking transforms a series of defeats on both sides into examples of the unprofitableness of certain vices—haste, avarice, pride, unwillingness to learn from the mistakes of others. Yet, because it is Agapida rather than Irving speaking directly, one doesn't feel a heavy-handed didacticism; it is in character for an old chronicler to moralize.

The history of the war thus reduces to little more than a series of fables, if not simply the repetition of one parable. Granada seems doomed because the Moors are weak internally; they fight among themselves; the possession of paradise means luxury, effeminacy, jealousy, and eventual betrayal. Just as Boabdil is the personification, not of cowardice and cruelty, but of indetermination and weakness of will,[52] so in the whole kingdom the same frailties are nationalized. This means that specific fluctuations of public opinion are not remarkable; we learn to expect them periodically; the fact of instability alone is important. Individuals tend to lose personality and substance. The usurper El Zagal, Boabdil's uncle and one of the three alternating monarchs of Granada, becomes little more than "a new idol to look up to, and a new name to shout forth" (p. 183).

Subsequently the war means the multiplication of Moorish losses. The tone of the tale becomes more sorrowful as the "right wing of the Moorish vulture" is torn off, the "right eye of Granada is extinguished" and its "shield . . . broken" (pp.

---

[51] The Alhama ballad (of which there is a famous translation or adaptation by Byron) contains a prediction of the fall of Granada. See Eugenio de Ochoa, *Tesoro de los Romanceros y Cancioneros Españoles* (Paris, 1838), pp. 369–90. Ballads may well be a source of inspiration for the form or structure of *Granada*. Irving undoubtedly knew numerous ballads about the wars of Granada. There are many in the famous sixteenth-century romance by Ginés Pérez de Hita, *Historia de las Guerras Civiles de Granada*, which Irving had read several years earlier and which may first have stimulated his interest in the subject. STW, I, 488.

[52] In his anonymous article on the book in the *Quarterly Review* (XLIII [May, 1830], p. 69), Irving points out that this is a new interpretation of Boabdil.

255, 260). Happiness cannot last, lessons cannot be learned, or if learned, not remembered long enough. With the Moors unable to unite in their own defense, the Christians have only to mutilate the kingdom by wrenching away single fortified towns until the city itself, the heart of Granada, is exposed unprotected.

At Ronda, defeat of the Moors is made even more certain by the conversion of gunpowder to the Christian cause. By the end, the loss (or attainment) of what is most cherished becomes a ritual. The strongest wall can always be demolished, undermined, or scaled, which makes the denouement a lengthy lamentation. Every character has set gestures to make or speeches to give. The war becomes a spectacle seen from the outside. The inner emotions are taken for granted. Or they are left to the reader's imagination, where they can be occasionally evoked by a formal word or movement, as when we, the public, witness the long procession of Isabella's arrival at Ferdinand's camp before Moclin, symbolizing the union and unity of the Catholic monarchs in a crusade: they bow three times to one another out of respect for their respective sovereignties and then embrace symbolically as man and wife (p. 252).

In much the same way, El Zagal, after being an idol and a name, finally becomes an *exemplum* for the benefit of anyone who can read: a sign he bears outside explains his life inside. Having surrendered his territories to Ferdinand, he is given the small kingdom of Andarax so that he may remain a monarch at least in name. But he finds "his little territory . . . and his two thousand subjects, as difficult to govern as . . . the distracted kingdom of Granada." Thus he loses Andarax as well: "His short and turbulent reign, and disastrous end, would afford a wholesome lesson to unprincipled ambition, were not all ambition of the kind fated to be blind to precept and example." Appropriately he is punished by being blinded. And in Africa, near death, he stumbles about carrying "a parchment" bearing the legend, "This is the unfortunate king of Andalusia" (pp. 478–80).

Boabdil also plays out his part as he should. In the final ceremony he initiates the surrender of Granada with these words:

"Go, Senor, and take possession of those fortresses in the name of the powerful sovereigns, to whom God has been pleased to deliver them in reward of their great merits, and in punishment of the sins of the Moors" (p. 522). Yet for Boabdil now there is nothing to look forward to, and Irving is careful to describe the last act, which severs king and kingdom forever. Leaving the fabulous palace of the Alhambra, Boabdil orders the gate through which he passes to be walled up behind him. Turning toward Africa, he begins his exile. Then from a hill beyond the city he faces around for one more look at what has been lost. As Irving reminds us, the site of this token of homage still bears the name of "The last sigh of the Moor" (p. 526).

For Irving a consciousness of human experience eternally repeating itself both makes and unmakes history. At his best (in *Columbus*) his work heightens, through his predilection for analogy and symbolic connection, an impression that Chateaubriand regarded as inevitable in a confrontation with the past: "Celui qui lit l'histoire ressemble à un homme voyageant dans le désert, à travers ces bois fabubuleux [sic] de l'antiquité, qui prédisaient l'avenir."[53] This was typical of the attitude of many romantic scholars. Searching for patterns of similarities and reading historical remains in the same way a modern critic reads a poem or a novel, some historians, for instance, were ready to convert every fragment of the past into an indication, a symbol, or an expression of the nature of the forces that had produced it. Thus a later scholar was intrigued by Barthold Georg Niebuhr's "wonderful ingenuity in combining scattered facts, his piercing eye for the detection of latent analogies, . . . his power of recomposing the ancient world by just deduction from small fragments of history, like the inferences of Cuvier from the bones of fossil animals. . . ."[54] But, although the "science" of historical criticism, the foundation of modern historiography, may have developed through this sort of analogical process, "the

[53] *Essai historique, politique, et moral, sur les révolutions anciennes et modernes, considérées dans leurs rapports avec la Révolution Française* (London, 1814), p. 42.
[54] George Grote, "Grecian Legends and Early History," *The Minor Works*, ed. Alexander Bain (London, 1873), p. 75.

history of Niebuhr," according to one authority "opened more
questions than it closed"[55]—a statement that, if liberally interpreted, is applicable to the whole period.

Questions as to the meaning or worth of documents were apt
to become, by implication, questions as to the nature of things in
general. Beyond suggesting, for instance, what primitive societies
had thought, believed, and lived for, ancient myth, poetry, or
law might ultimately be looked at as clues to the intention or
the purpose of whatever was responsible for history or existence
itself, of whatever underlay everything, was inmost, most significant, most real. This was the direction in which much romantic scholarship pointed. In looking for the interconnections
among bits of historical evidence, it was apt to discover a virtual
identity among art, science, and philosophy.[56]

For an example that will bring us back closer to Irving, we
may take the brothers Grimm, who found the fairy tales they
collected from different regions especially meaningful in groups,
where they seemed to enlighten or reflect one another. Fairy
tales, legends, and folklore in general, the spontaneous expression, according to the Grimms, of a people who belonged together
and to the same place, gradually appeared to them to reduce to
a very few ideas or to one fundamental myth. The signs led
Jacob Grimm, through his studies of German etymology and
mythology, to a glimpse of popular (or human) expression as
hardly more than the continual opposition and combination of
two primary observations or points of view (or ideas) mirrored
in the concept of gender in nouns or names. What were male and
female symbolized in turn, or were symbolized by, sky and
earth, life and death, soul and body, heaven and hell, or good
and evil. History, then, or human experience in general, seemed
but the constant repetition of these two antithetical notions or
motions in slightly varied forms.[57]

[55] Lucy M. Salmon, *Why Is History Rewritten?* (New York, 1929), p. 62.

[56] At times Eduard Fueter's judgment seems sound, that romantic historiography
was too hastily built on Burke and philology. *Histoire de l'historiographie moderne*,
trans. Émile Jeanmaire (Paris, 1914), pp. 524–25.

[57] A good discussion of the implications of the Grimms' work and its relation
to its intellectual environment is Ernest Tonnelat, *Les Frères Grimm, leur oeuvre
de jeunesse* (Paris, 1912).

That Irving had at least a casual familiarity with some of
the higher metaphysics of folklore-collecting there can be no
doubt. If his conversations with Scott had steered clear of abstract speculation, he surely knew, if only through the *Analectic,*
about the ideas on comparative mythology underlying Chateaubriand's defense of Christianity. He had also gone to Germany
with the avowed purpose of gathering legendary material and
may well have encountered there romantic doctrine as far-
reaching as that advanced in *Phantasus,* where Tieck, whom he
met in Dresden, insists on the basic allegoricalness of fiction and
history, and, indeed, of all experience.[58] Most revealing, however, is an article by Francis Cohen (later Sir Francis Palgrave)
that Irving appears to have read in the *Quarterly Review* in
1820.[59] In reviewing several books on medieval legends and
myths, including the Grimms' *Deutsche Sagen,* Cohen expressed
amazement at the "degree of uniformity . . . in the ideal world,"
that is, in the realm of imagination, where "the fables of popular
superstition" are created. He found an "affinity" in all folklore,
if not in all nature. In going on to describe it he made explicit
a conception of experience that is implicit in much of Irving's
work from *Tales of a Traveller* through *The Alhambra,* and gives
it a considerable cumulative force, for all that he ultimately over-
works it. The conception is of a constantly recurring fable,
whose moral can never be realized:

> . . . all mythology has been governed by a uniform principle. . . .
> Divested of its mythic or poetic garb, it will be found that the creative
> power is the doctrine of fatality. Oppressed by the wretchedness of
> its nature, without some infallible guide, the human mind shrinks
> from contemplation, and cowers in its own imbecility; it reposes in
> the belief of predestination, which enables us to bear up against
> every misery, and solves those awful doubts which are scarcely
> less tolerable than misery.—The Gordian knot is cut, and the web is
> unravelled, when all things are seen subordinate to Fate, to that stern
> power, which restrains the active intelligences of good and evil,

[58] Tieck makes such assertions in speaking through his character Ernst at the
end of the introductory dialogue of *Phantasus.* The extent of Irving's familiarity
with Tieck's works is uncertain. See Walter Reichart, *Irving and Germany* (Ann
Arbor, 1957), p. 145.

[59] Writing to Brevoort, Irving reports meeting Cohen, whose articles in the
Quarterly he has read. Letter of 15 August 1820, *WIHB,* II, 131–32.

dooming the universe of spirit and of matter to be the battle-field of endless strife between the light and the darkness.—Whether the rites of the "false religions full of pomp and gold" have been solemnized in the sculptured cavern or in the resplendent temple, in the shade of the forest or on the summit of the mountain, still the same lesson has been taught. Men and Gods vainly struggle to free themselves from the adamantine bonds of destiny. The oracle or the omen which declares the impending evil, affords no method of averting it. All insight into futurity proves a curse to those on whom the power descends. We hear the warning which we cannot obey.[60]

It did not, of course, take Francis Cohen or German historiography to bring Irving to reduce history to a series of ups and downs. Such a reduction had always been implicit in the vogue for ruins and mutability. Romantic historiography, whether, as with Michaud, Barante, Thierry, and Turner, it simply stressed narrative and pageantry, or, as especially in Germany, it became more deeply speculative, undoubtedly helped make Irving less self-conscious about his interest in the past than he had been in *Knickerbocker*. Since the romantics granted considerable license in the use of the past, the pretense to objectivity and dispassionateness now had less relevance. The didactic drive had diminished: to expect the lessons of the past to be put to use directly was coming to seem naïve. The romantic historian now stood ready frequently to exploit the subjectivity which had made virtual nonsense of Knickerbocker's "history."

But the full transcendental leap or plunge was something that Irving could not make. The higher (or inner) reality, if it existed, was beyond him. He might read the past symbolically, but he would not have believed with Jules Michelet that the idea "qu'enferme toute symbole, brule d'en sortir, de s'épancher, de redevenir infinie."[61] Chateaubriand might argue for the development in historiography of "cette philosophie qui tient à l'essence des êtres, qui, pénétrant l'enveloppe du monde sensible, cherche s'il n'y a point sous cette enveloppe quelque chose de

[60] Cohen, "Popular Mythology of the Middle Ages," *Quarterly Review*, XXII (January, 1820), 350–53.

[61] *Origines du droit français cherchées dans les symboles et formules du droit universel* (Paris, 1837), p. lxv.

plus réel, de plus vivant; cause des phénomènes sociaux."[62] But Irving did not see through the physiognomy or phenomenology of experience to a permanent reality. The symbols in the enchanted forest of the past kept mirroring his own insecurity. The sublime was too close to the ridiculous for his comfort.

Inadvertently his history finally comes close to seeming a parody of the speculative impulse behind the work of many of his contemporaries. For the search for higher meaning in history carried the risk of oversimplification. And reductivism threatened to redefine history as stasis. Chateaubriand offered a system of history as the function of only three basic truths or concepts or forms.[63] And his friend Pierre-Simon Ballanche went further:

> En effet, sous un certain rapport, le genre humain pourrait être considéré comme le même individu passant par une suite de palingénésies.
>
> Mais en remontant à l'origine, il fallait bien rencontrer le dogme un et identique de la déchéance et de la réhabilitation, ce dogme sévère et unanime qui explique la suite des destinées humaines, leur développment sous forme d'initiations successives, chaque initiation précédée d'une épreuve, et toute épreuve infligée comme expiation.[64]

One is puzzled whether to see in Ballanche's sense of ordeal and initiation, death and rebirth, an archetypism potentially as profound as Jung's, or a view of history just the reverse of Agapida's and virtually as naïve. It took romanticism a long time to shake off altogether the dust of "ruins." Ballanche boasted that "il est impossible de pousser plus loin la synthèse historique."[65] But, as Chateaubriand himself said, with an accent faintly suggestive of Agapida, "L'Histoire dans tous les siècles, a fait de pareils rapprochements qui ne prouvent rien, sinon la ressemblance des adversités parmi les hommes."[66]

[62] *Études historiques*, in *Oeuvres complètes* (Paris, 1826–31), IV, xlix.
[63] *Ibid.*, IV, cxj.
[64] *Oeuvres*, III (Paris, 1830), 16.
[65] *Ibid.*, p. 20.
[66] *Oeuvres complètes*, III, 185. One of Chateaubriand's slighter works is closer to Irving's *Columbus* and *Granada* than anything else I have been able to find. By this I do not imply an "influence" but a common body of impulses in the time pushing writers in similar directions. Only in Chateaubriand's *Mémoires, sur S. A. R. Monseigneur le Duc de Berry* (*Oeuvres complètes*, Vol. III) do I find the sense of representativeness and the need to analogize pushed to a point comparable to

According to Gertrude Stein, "Romanticism is then when everything being alike everything is naturally simply different, and romanticism." She was not talking about an historical period but about "composition." For her, romanticism is a state of liberation which the writer reaches if he is fortunate: "In the beginning there was confusion there was a continuous present and later there was romanticism which was not a confusion but an extrication. . . ."[67] A good many allegedly "romantic" writers of the nineteenth century might find it hard to qualify under such a conception. If romanticism is extrication, is anyone, except in rare moments, a full-blown romantic? But while the search for the true romantic (according to Gertrude Stein's definition) may be endless, it is not futile. For it compels a recognition of the extent to which romanticism historically was an epistemological ordeal, an effort of accommodation to a self-reflecting world. Out of "everything being alike" comes not only the pathetic fallacy but romantic organicism, the macrocosm in the microcosm, and nineteenth-century "metaphysical" and symbolist styles—whether Gertrude Stein would see extrication here or not.

Washington Irving, in any case, did not cross over into "and romanticism." *Salmagundi* and *Knickerbocker* had developed a comedy of confusion in which the ordinary distinctions of common sense seemed to disappear before one's eyes. And pre-romantic impulses made him something of a symbolist, a wayfaring spectator in a world not of facts but of signs, in part a pilgrim, in part a picaro (in his whimsy), in part an exile. But while he had continual trouble distinguishing between "self" and "not-me" because of the way they kept reflecting each other, he never got close enough to Concord to bring them fully together, either by absorbing all nature into the Self or by surrendering the self completely to a merger with Nature. A largely

---

that found in Irving, where the subject or substance threatens to dissolve in pure formality and symbolism. As in Irving, the controlling idea is the inevitability of loss and defeat, though Chateaubriand has a much stronger sense of a social institution's outliving individuals and gaining authority and even beauty through the sacrifices of devoted public servants.

[67] *What Are Masterpieces* (Los Angeles, 1940), pp. 35, 37.

passive observer, he saw signs, but without sufficiently varied meanings. He never allowed imagination to create its own world. His sense of sameness never became acute enough to make a real difference.

Shortly after completing the *Conquest,* he was on the road through the mountains to Granada, a sort of Quixote, as he pictures himself in *The Alhambra,* looking for adventures (attacks by bandits), with a muleteer who was a ringer for Sancho Panza. In Irving's mind the trip became a kind of flight from time, his personal quest for a terrestrial paradise, doomed, however (as he knew in advance), to failure. For the Alhambra proved to be only one more inn, even if it was by far the most beautiful one in which he was ever to sojourn, the one in which he was treated with greatest deference—because it was all one royal suite, and he had it to himself. The doors seemed to open magically to admit him, but a few weeks later they reopened routinely for his expulsion.

> My serene and happy reign in the Alhambra, was suddenly brought to a close by letters which reached me, while indulging in oriental luxury in the cool hall of the baths, summoning me away from my Moslem elysium to mingle once more in the bustle and business of the dusty world. How was I to encounter its toils and turmoils, after such a life of repose and reverie! How was I to endure its commonplace, after the poetry of the Alhambra! (*AL,* p. 422)

By adding and rearranging material, Irving managed in the revised edition of *The Alhambra* to intensify the suggestion, already apparent in parts of the original, that his temporary withdrawal from the "dusty world" was a kind of enchantment.[68] His imagination seems to transform landscapes and interiors into settings for romances and Arabian tales. Transports of joy lift him out of the present and carry him back into a timeless fictitious past, although he likes to think that he is only playing with illusions, temporarily keeping the everyday world at a safe distance. He still has one eye on a present which

---

[68] The passage just quoted, for example, is not contained in the original editions (Philadelphia, London, and Paris, 1832). My references are all to the revised text (*AL*). Where I cite passages that do not occur in the original, I so indicate in my discussion.

lives in the shadow of the past he now inhabits; he amuses himself by observing the petty retainers and vagabonds who swarm
about the premises. Thus he says, typically,

> It is a whimsical caprice of fortune to present, in the grotesque
> person of this tatterdemalion, a namesake and descendant of the
> proud Alonzo de Aguilar, the mirror of Andalusian chivalry, leading
> an almost mendicant existence about this once haughty fortress,
> which his ancestor aided to reduce; yet such might have been the lot
> of the descendants of Agamemnon and Achilles, had they lingered
> about the ruins of Troy! (pp. 71–72)

This is, after all, part of the charm of the place—the contrast, the sense of loss, paradise seen through the dilapidations
of time. Irving likes to look down from his lofty balcony at
what is going on in the real world of Granada; he is still a
"spectator," who wants to watch "the drama of life without
becoming an actor in the scene." He forms "conjectural histories" for himself to explain what he sees, and takes a Crayonesque pleasure in seeing himself, as always, somewhat mistaken
—the nervous narrator once more passing time in a rural inn
(pp. 118–20). As only a would-be, not an actual, Quixote, however, he is not about to deny the existence of the outside world.
Thoreau in his retreat at Walden might fish for stars. Irving
at the Alhambra, though a long-time friend to anglers, only
thinks about it (p. 74).

Actually his enchantment was only beginning. His return
to the United States in 1832, the same year in which *The
Alhambra* was initially published, was to accelerate the process.
Then, under the spell of being "earnestly, devotedly, and affec-
tionately caressed" by the public, he would begin to turn into
that "man of quiet pursuits"[69] of whom we have heard so much,
the old bachelor of the mellow years at Sunnyside, as charmed
by the bevy of nieces who surrounded him as he had been by
the cool seclusion of a Moorish courtyard. Gradually he would
cease to be the anxious Geoffrey Crayon and become Wash-

---

[69] Dickens thus describes him at a reception at the White House in 1841, shortly
after Irving's appointment as American Minister to Spain. *American Notes for
General Circulation*, chap. viii.

ington Irving as he has been preserved for us, a serenely un-
complicated self, resting in semiretirement on a good many
laurels, regretful at having had to abandon the Alhambra
physically but quite comfortable in his memory of it. Having
accepted his celebrated name,[70] he would now be dedicated as a
writer to perpetuating charm, grace and wistfulness, elevating
these qualities into genteel elegance when the occasion demanded, as in his biography of Washington (1855–59). In the
offing was the drowsiness of Sleepy Hollow, where he already
planned to sleep out the centuries.

In the end, Irving, to use Philip Young's words, seems to
have "fallen from time," like a figure from the Moorish-
Spanish tales that, obviously charmed by their resemblance to the
German legends of enchanted sleep underlying "Rip Van
Winkle," he had stuffed into *The Alhambra*. The mountain on
which the Moorish palace is situated, like the famous Kyff-
häuser mountain, was the legendary repository of numerous
heroes who waited "motionless as statues, maintaining a sleepless watch for ages" (p. 164). Many of them had overly treas-
ured the possibility of a permanent possession of worldly goods
and thus in a sense had sought to cheat the voracity of time.
Now they waited, sealed in a living tomb, where time both
passed and stood still, since nothing ever happened.

For Irving there was no rebirth of creative power in the withdrawal to the Alhambra, no imaginative rejuvenation. He
left the Moorish paradise, at best a man with much of his youth
and vigor behind him, a man to whom time now seemed to make
less difference, who was becoming more content or resigned to
seeing it pass, a man satisfied, like Van Winkle, to tell charming but inconsequential stories. The final version of *The
Alhambra* suggests that there had been a kind of death; the

[70] Although initially published as the work of Crayon or the author of *The
Sketch Book*, or as the "new sketch book," *The Alhambra* was much more loosely
associated with Crayon than were the earlier works. It very soon began appearing
in Irving's own name. The revised edition of his works eventually confirmed this
difference between the later and the earlier Crayonesque books: Irving now listed
The Alhambra in his own name, while retaining the pseudonym for *The Sketch
Book*, *Bracebridge*, and the *Tales*. See under individual titles in Williams and
Edge, *A Bibliography of the Writings of Washington Irving* (New York, 1936).

procession that escorts Irving from the palace, past his own
last sigh and into an exile like Boabdil's, is almost a funeral:
"Humble was the cortege and melancholy the departure of
El Rey Chico the second" (p. 425). In the final analysis, occu-
pying the Alhambra in memory and living out the magic spell
in the mountain underneath amounted to virtually the same
thing.

The Alhambra of 1850 is a better book than the original
because it is unified around the author's often poignant identification with Boabdil. "The Author's Farewell to Granada,"
for instance, was not a part of the original book; instead Irving
had ended with two historical sketches. A melancholy sense of
loss, it is true, does dominate the first third of the 1832 text,
but thereafter an unevenness of tone becomes a distraction. A
breezy comic element figures more prominently in the style than
it is allowed to in the final version, where changes of phrasing
have been made and additional material has tipped the balance
in another direction. It is in the 1850 version, especially as a
result of two new stories, the "Grand Master of Alcantara" and
the "Legend of the Enchanted Soldier," that one gets the
stronger sense of Irving repeating his one basic story of loss
and disillusionment. In 1832 there was still something in him
which resisted complete surrender to sentimental melancholy.
Nevertheless, even in the original text there is a thinness of
material and a casualness of tone which tend to give the impression that he is only going through the motions of storytelling. In
the end, in the final version, he seems too preoccupied with en-
shrining a memory, coating it over with a glossy prose, to attend
to commonplace details. Imaginative escape from the mundane
was the religion he had been flirting with all his life, the
religion now fully tolerated in an increasingly sentimental age
by an emotionally indulgent public, which, for all its surface
convictions, had its own deep uneasinesses.

The sense of time had helped make his fiction. He had prized
time enough to pay careful attention to recording its passage.
His ability in the better stories and sketches to get the illusion of
time right was part of an important development in the history

of fiction. But in *The Alhambra,* even in the original version, the sense of inevitability tends to inundate time. The stories, one knows, are all going to be pretty much the same. Irving was no longer interested in lingering over them.

The irony on which both history and art depend does not exist where there is insufficient dissimulation or dissimilation—that is, at least the pretense or appearance of dissimilarity in sameness. Irving eventually lost his sense of how eccentric and *un*-common common things can appear—at least at first sight. In "The Stout Gentleman" a traveling salesman had become a latter-day knight-errant only after every visible mannerism and accoutrement on or about him had found its ironical counterpart in the world of chivalry—"changing the lance for a driving-whip, the buckler for a pattern-card, and the coat of mail for an upper Benjamin" (*B*, p. 76). But even by 1832 one could become for Irving a "son" of the Alhambra (p. 51) without seeming to do much more than eat and sleep there.

Index

Adam. *See* Eden, exile from
Adams, Henry, 59, 62, 63
Adams, John, 90
Adams, Raymond, 156*n*
Addison, Joseph: and the *Spectator*, 17; writings on Italy, 37–38; on the writing of history, 70; mentioned, 46, 147. *See also Spectator*
"Adventure of My Aunt, The," 198
"Adventure of My Uncle, The," 197–98, 206
"Adventure of the German Student," 199–200, 201, 227
"Adventure of the Little Antiquary, The," 222
"Adventure of the Mysterious Picture," 205–6
"Adventure of the Mysterious Stranger," 206, 210, 211
"Adventure of the Popkins Family, The," 220
Adventures of Captain Bonneville, The, 79*n*
Agapida, Fray Antonio. *See Chronicle of the Conquest of Granada, A*
Ahab, Captain: in corposants scene, 226; compared with W. I.'s Columbus, 239, 240, 248–49; mentioned, 157
Alhambra, The, 1, 149, 259, 263–67
Alison, Archibald, 41
Allston, Washington, 2, 39
Alsop, Richard, 63*n*
Analectic Magazine: under W. I.'s editorship, 107–15; mentioned, 12, 252*n*, 259
"Angler, The": compared with Goldsmith's "The Distresses of a Common Soldier," 144–45
"Annette Delarbre," 171
"Art of Book-Making, The," 132, 151
"Art of Fiction, The," 163
Associationism, 107, 108*n*, 118–19. *See also* Picturesque
Astor, John Jacob, 13
Austen, Jane, 70
"Author's Account of Himself, The," 130–31
Aylmer (in "The Birthmark"), 162

"Balcony, The," 149
Ballanche, Pierre-Simon, 261

"Balloon Hoax, The," 100
Ballston Springs, N.Y., 24, 56
Barante, de, Amable Guillaume Prosper, Baron, 111, 260
Barlow, Joel, 82, 87
"Bartleby the Scrivener," 133, 158, 162
"Belated Travellers, The," 220, 221, 222
"Benito Cereno," 158
"Berenice," 99, 159, 200–1
Bewley, Marius, 158
Blackstone, William, 10, 39, 120
Blackwood's Edinburgh Magazine, 197*n*, 201*n*, 203. *See also* "How to Write a Blackwood Article"
Blair, Walter, 97
Blithedale Romance, The, 153. *See also* Coverdale, Miles
Boabdil el Chico (last king of Granada), 254, 255, 256, 257, 266
"Boar's Head Tavern, Eastcheap, The," 132, 144
Boethius, Anicius Manlius Severinus, 43, 68
"Bold Dragoon, The," 198–99
Bolingbroke, Henry St. John, First Viscount: pragmatic theory of history, 71–72, 251; W. I.'s notes on, 71, 75; contrasted with W. I. and Emerson, 75–76; mentioned, 111
Bonaparte, Marie, 160
Bones, Brom, 142, 143, 154, 161
Boorstin, Daniel, 120
Bostonians, The, 88
Bracebridge, Squire, 143, 166–82 *passim*
Bracebridge Hall: folklore in, 119; and W. I.'s romanticism, 126; composition of, 164–65; Geoffrey Crayon's role in, 164–66; detailed discussion of, 169–74, 180–89; mentioned, 98, 129, 195. *See also Pioneers, The*
Brackenridge, Hugh Henry, 49, 58, 62, 73, 95
Brevoort, Henry, 13*n*, 29, 44, 107*n*, 193, 195, 232, 240
Brooks, Van Wyck, 40*n*
Brown, Charles Brockden, 72, 159, 204, 207
Brown, Goodman, 151–52, 162
Bryant, William Cullen, 91
Brydone, Patrick, 36, 37, 40, 41–42, 55, 108

DATE DUE